GAY'D IN DAGENHAM

A memoir of growing up gay in blue-collar suburban Essex and beyond

DYLAN COSTELLO

Copyright © 2015 Dylan Costello

All rights reserved.

ISBN-10: 1517597870
ISBN-13: 978-1517597870

This book is dedicated to all those that have stood by me and loved and supported me for who I am. You know who you are.

CHAPTERS

Prologue	– 8
1 – The Boy in the Green Parka	- 10
2 – The Six Year Old Beard	- 17
3 – The Woo-Woo and the Opal Fruits	- 26
4 – Shoulderpads, TV Hunks and Raffle Tickets	- 35
5 – Please Don't Flush My Head!	– 46
6 – The Teenage Gigolo	– 57
7 – Viva Espana!	– 68
8 – The Double Handjob in the Yellow Skoda	– 75
9 – We're Not in Kansas Anymore	– 83
10 – The Home and Away Star and the Milk Tray Man	– 93
11 – A 'Lavender Marriage'	– 100
12 – The Fijian Nymphomaniac and the Ping Pong Ball	– 109
13 – The Catalyst of the Australian Vagina	– 116
14 – The First Time	– 127

15 – Coming Out	– 137
16 – The Evil First Boyfriend	– 148
17 – Coming Out (Again)	– 158
18 – Never Fall in Love with a Dallas Cowboy	– 164
19 – Pink Vomit in the USA	– 172
20 – The LA Gay Man's Bible of Excuses to Make When You Are Afraid to Commit	– 179
21 – Too Many Dates Make You Incontinent	– 189
22 – Goodbye Mum	– 195
23 – A Happy Ending	– 201
Epilogue	– 205

PROLOGUE

Warning. This book is gay. Very gay. Uber gay. Gayer than Dorothy Gale's blatantly drug-fuelled trip into a glitzy, glittery land where she hangs out with three men, one furry, one stiff and one who needs a damn good stuffing, as together they go around killing misunderstood unattractive women who only need a decent nose job and a bit of foundation to hide a worrying skin complexion. This book is only mildly less gay than Dorothy's shenanigans but still gay enough.

So turn back now if the idea of reading about gay love, homosexual leanings and man-on-man action offends you. Life should never be defined by one's sexuality but this book is. It has to be. This memoir is to serve a purpose, to show that all the crazy stuff experienced by one gay man, the highs and the lows - is the stuff of life. *Anyone's* life.

And I remember *everything*. I have a photographic memory, able to recall every tiny detail. It can be a blessing and in the case of some encounters with certain men, it can be a curse.

And so this is the true story of me, myself and I, a boy from the suburban blue-collar Essex town of Dagenham who was born gay. Yes *born* gay. In the same way as someone is born straight, born rich, born poor, born black or born white. Some things are just in the genes. Nature wins over nurture; it's as simple as that. Each and every one of us enters this world as a blank canvas with it impossible to predict the events, the journeys, the experiences, the love, the heartbreak, the joy and the sorrow that will colour it and define one's life - a life that is a series of cause and effect machinations of fate. My destiny from the moment I was born was to eventually realise that I was a boy's boy who would grow into being a man's man, my life propelled forwards as an adventure in evolving as a young boy in Dagenham, having those first strange feelings in infancy towards another boy, on through childhood crushes and awkward teenage unrequited love, then accepting my true sexuality into adult life, dealing not only with attitudes to my homosexuality from family, friends and strangers, but also homophobia, my own fear, the rise, fall and rise again of my self-confidence

- and unyielding support and love, realising that whilst others might not deem me 'normal', my experiences of wanting to find love were the same as anyone else's.

This memoir will show what it was like for this young boy who was born gay, how the growing realisation of his sexuality shaped his life. And yet all the time he just wanted to find love, love with another man, a romanticised view of how gay love should be. Did it forever elude him as the years went by? Or did he one day find it? And if so, with whom?

1 - THE BOY IN THE GREEN PARKA

1980 (aged 5)

He had found the love of his life. Despite all the ups and downs and the constant threats from the Dark Side, true love had blossomed for this dashing young hero. And now, here he was, stood side-by-side with the one he would spend the rest of his life with, about to be joined forever in holy galactic matrimony. Toy Han Solo looked at toy Princess Leia, radiant in her wedding dress intricately and lovingly cobbled together from a few perforated sheets of peach *Andrex* toilet roll. Leia wasn't fussed that it wasn't the luxury version that was extra comfy on the bum. *"I love you Han"* she purred lovingly, imaginary tears of joy invisibly streaming down her pretty little unblinking plastic face. Then *Bang! Bang! Bang!* The wedding halted mid-vows.

I was scared. What was that noise? Was it my Dad's rusty Ford Capri packing up outside to great fanfare yet again? Or was it what it sounded like... a gun? If so, my parents had failed to tell me when we moved to our council flat that we would endure gun warfare.

But whatever the din of matrimonial intervention was, I was more upset at the interruption of Princess Leia and Han Solo's toy wedding, taking place in the comfort of my bedroom with Darth Vader, a myriad of stormtroopers and three different versions of Luke Skywalker in attendance. Chewbacca hadn't been able to make it due to getting lost in the school playground a week before - or he had possibly been stolen by my on/off best friend Martin Schofield. I had yet to gather enough proof that Chewie was probably residing with most of my stickle bricks which also mysteriously went missing every time I played with Martin.

I ignored the gunshots. But then there was a gasp. *The* gasp. I recognised it immediately as my Mum's. It was the kind of oral noise she expelled to signal her utter shock at something, possibly the witnessing of something so terrible and untoward, maybe the hearing of something so awful it would make your ears bleed. Like hearing that Fat Pam from across the way had gone shopping to the Co-Op in just her nightdress again. Or more than likely, it was just Mum's horror at realising yet again that she couldn't wipe her arse because of her five year old son's desire to give toy Princess Leia the wedding dress he felt she truly deserved.

I ran into the living room to see what was going on. Mum was staring at the telly, her hand over her mouth.

"Someone just shot J.R!" she exclaimed. I didn't know who this J.R man was but I couldn't help but wonder what he could possibly have done to make someone want to shoot him. Regardless, it had been enough to make my Mum unleash her signature gasp and I would not see her gasp like that again until many years later when I would be somewhat in J.R's shoes, telling Mum something so shocking about her first born son that it might warrant some people in the world to want to shoot *me*.

But that was still years away and right now I was just an innocent five year old. An innocent *gay* five year old. Although of course, I was yet to know it...

*

I had never heard of the word gay - let alone understand what it meant. Over the years of course, the definition of it and the experience of *being* it would propel me on many adventures but not now, not in 1980 as a five year old boy in suburbia. Home was Dagenham after all, a blue-collar working class town on the borders of East London and Essex. Here, boys were boys and girls were girls and eventually boy gets with girl, gets girl pregnant at fourteen, fifteen if they're a late starter, and they live not-so-happily ever after in a council flat in Dagenham East.

The thing is I was already living in a council flat in Dagenham East, so I guess you could say I had that box prematurely ticked. My maternal Nan Shirley - a fearsome but with a heart of gold cockney, never seen without a *Benson and Hedges* cigarette perennially dangling from her mouth or her massive immaculate strawberry blonde perm in full bloom (or a head full of curlers about to unveil it. She literally had a whole cupboard full of *Silvikrin* hairspray) - had moved out to Dagenham from Poplar as a child in the 1930s when Dagenham was supposedly 'the place to be', a burgeoning suburban town swallowing up refugees from London's East End in search of better housing and more space. And Nan was *proper* East End, a mix between Peggy Mitchell and the Nan from the Catherine Tate show. She was a true matriarch, running a black-market trade in cigarettes from the comfort of her reclining armchair and always saying exactly what was on her mind in her "effing and blinding" way with words. Married on Christmas Day 1945 to my Grandad Bert, a sailor in the Navy, they went on to have four kids, the eldest being my Mum Valerie, born in 1948. My Mum then met my Nan's half-sister Reenie's husband Alan's brother Larry (keep up!), they were married in February 1974 and then in October that same year, I came into existence in Rush Green Hospital in Romford.

Mum - a florist and Dad - a ceiling fixer - were still living at my Nan and Grandad's house when I was born, which must have had Tardis-like space considering it was a three bedroom semi occupied by Nan, Grandad, Mum, Dad, Mum's two sisters Janet and Carol, brother Roger and now, me. Sleeping quarters for newborn me was in a dorm style set-up sharing with my two Aunties whilst Mum and Dad had a sofa bed in the living room. Needless to say it wasn't long before Mum, Dad and I left this Brady Bunch style set-up and moved to our first council flat on the other side of Dagenham, where Mum soon popped out my younger brother in 1976 and where I lived my first formative years before starting school at Leys Infants in autumn 1979.

*

It was this first day at Leys Infants which to this day remains my earliest memory. Me, crying my eyes out at the gates, not wanting my Mum to abandon me in this strange new environment. Then reluctantly going inside to meet my new peers - cocky Terence with the perpetual bogie birthing from his nostrils, Doton, the only 'coloured' boy (as people in Dagenham referred to black people) - and macho heart-throb identical twins Perry and Gavin Cooper. I didn't want to be *here*. I just wanted my Mum! But of course, come home-time that same day, I didn't want to leave. For a whole new world had been opened up to me - namely that I had spent the entire day happily playing in the wendy house with the girls in my class. Looking back, it was clearly obvious that I was gay from the get go. Legend has it that I was nice shade of purple when I was born - thanks to getting stuck in the birth canal and being wrenched out with forceps like a stubborn wobbly tooth. And purple really is just a slightly darker shade of pink so the proof is in the pudding really. Yes, even at the moment of my entrance into this world, I was already subconsciously edging closer to opening that closet door.

*

And so, as my first day at Leys Infants became my first week, then my first month and the 1970s became the 1980s, it was here that I would first experience The Love That Dare Not Speak Its Name. The love for another boy. My love for The Boy in the Green Parka.

I can't exactly remember how these feelings suddenly developed, but back then, in the early Summer of 1980, in-between organising lavish *Andrex*-sponsored *Star Wars* weddings, all I knew was that I was in love for the very first time. Now of course, being only five years old, I had no concept of what being in love was, let alone with another boy. I knew I loved my parents and grandparents but this was *different*. I just had this inexplicable weird feeling when, day after day, I found myself staring wistfully at James. (I remember being quite proud of myself for finding out that his name was James. Clearly, I was quite the detective at five years old). James was always wearing his green parka coat with the furry hood, the de-rigueur fashion for any infant schoolboy in Dagenham at the dawn of the 1980s - a somewhat innocent era some could say. Though despite the perceived innocence, underneath it all, the idea of anyone's child being gay was well and truly abhorrent to the point where having your spawn become a serial killer would be far more preferable. Homosexuality may have been decriminalised thirteen years before but Section 28 was just a few years away from being introduced by Margaret Thatcher and her own government, which, like me, was also in its infancy. I guess, like any homophobe, dear old Maggie would have also taken pleasure in the fact that sadly, as is the case in most epic love stories; James and I were doomed from the start.

*

James was one year younger than me and was ensconced in the adjoining pre-school and so tragically off-limits. We were separated by a fence that despite its flimsiness, might as well have been made of electrified barbed wire. The Boy in the Green Parka could thus only be worshipped from afar. Well, technically about twenty feet or so, but in infant terms it was a distance akin to the width of the Atlantic Ocean. Whilst my on/off best friend Martin and I were hanging out at playtimes near this Berlin Wall-esque fence, I would be feigning interest in Martin pulling apart a collection of various insects, for I was too busy gazing through the diamond shaped holes in the fencing at the object of my affections playing only several yards away, happily unaware of my devotion. Martin never seemed to question why we always had to hang out in this exact same spot in the playground every day, or indeed why his best friend would rather spend these times staring at some random kid in a green parka rather than engaging in experimental insect dissection with him. Unrequited love was making me a crap best friend.

Maybe it was the realisation of this that led me one day to make the mistake of confiding in Martin about my weird feelings towards James. I should have kept my mouth firmly shut. Martin was obviously more clued up to the existence of all things gay - as he demonstrated with great glee by promptly sharing my confession very publicly in the playground with Doton, Perry, Gavin and Terence - whose forever-present bogie practically burst Big Bang-like with the shock revelation. I was then subjected to a test - a kiddy version of electro-shock gay-to-straight conversion therapy - by being dared to touch tongues with another boy in the playground. Martin quickly volunteered. It didn't even care to occur to me that Martin might have been more like me than he cared to admit. Nevertheless, the boys were suspicious of *my* self-confessed admiring glances towards James and via the tongue-touching test, were probably trying to out me, a pre-pubescent witch hunt orchestrated by their tabloid-reading parents. If only I really was that paranoid at five years old. Or was it that everyone except me was aware of this *thing* that a boy could apparently feel for another boy? Was it a fact that my parents were shielding me from some horrible truth of the existence of something far worse than the bogey man? And if they were, then *why*? Could it be that they already suspected their son was born *that way*?

*

But all was not lost in this infant world of forbidden love, for every day provided one chance - and one chance only - to get close to James, to actually *be* in his presence, to be able to physically *feel* the polyester fabric of the hallowed green parka, to experience the sensation of the butterflies that would swarm inside my belly should I be able to look *that* closely at his dark hair and big brown eyes. One solo window of opportunity. Lunch time. AKA the daily mission to sprint to the lunch hall just fast enough to try to be able to secure a seat at his table, or even more prized, The Seat Next To Him, propelled by the adrenaline of the giddy anticipation I felt at the approach of this golden hour. This magical time of day was my golden ticket to Green Parka Heaven. It involved meticulous planning, unashamed bolshiness, expert queue jumping tactics and the ability to be fast on one's feet. It was a military exercise that future war-mongering Maggie would be proud of. But of course, this daily event in attempting to snatch some precious time with James came with some concerns and worries. What would I do or say if I ever *did* get the chance to sit next to him? Talk about the weather? The latest price of Lego in Woolworths? Whether he approved of toy Princess Leia's homemade honeymoon outfit? I wasn't even six years old yet; intelligent conversation over a meal and drinks had not yet formed in my manners. It could end up something of an awkward first date.

But none of those fears mattered, because for what seemed like an eternity in kiddy years, I had repeatedly tried - and failed every time - to secure The Seat Next To James - to be able to be one of his many admirers as he royally held court at his table, flirting with his subjects in-between each soggy over-fried chip and mouthful of lumpy custard - and I wasn't about to give up now. I was *that* determined to be James' lunch time companion. I would do anything - *anything* - to be the one to secure that coveted Seat Next To Him.

But then one day, *it* happened. The embarrassing knack for public humiliation that would be a defining theme throughout my childhood - kicked off on style on this day - and quickly and permanently - put paid to my attempts to sit next to James. Until the day I die, I shall always refer to this cataclysmic disaster that occurred as The Incident with the Chocolate Sponge Pudding.

*

Lunch time had started off as it usually did, with me unleashing myself into the lunch hall like an underage athlete in *Chariots of Fire II - The Race to the Green Parka*, bribing my way nearer to the front of the queue, legs shaking in impatience as I moved ever so slowly towards the trio of dinner ladies serving up the daily dose of pure unhealthiness. Why was the queue moving so slowly today? Why was Donna Baker taking so long to choose between chips or mash?! It's all made of the same thing! You'll be eating potatoes either way! Just choose! I guess you could say my patience now was wearing a bit thin. I could see James already leaving the line and making his way to his seat, as usual followed by a couple of admiring girls.

"*Next!*"

I snapped back into life as I could see one of the dinner ladies beckoning me over. I eyed her, and then eyed James and The Seat Next To Him - empty thus far! I was tempted to just bolt towards James - but a boy needed his food - something to be able to play with as I gazed at my idol and batted my big blue eyes at him. I grabbed my egg and chips and chocolate sponge pudding for dessert - never forget dessert! The Seat Next to James was *still* empty! James glanced around, probably wondering who would take it. I swear he caught my eye and winked at me. Of course he didn't, but hey, I was blinded by love! The memory of what happened next will forever be etched into my mind in slow motion. I saw someone else make their way to The Seat Next to James. A pretty young girl obviously starting early in securing her future husband and father of her children, the type of girl who in adult life would smugly reminisce about how she and *"her Jamesy"* had been sweethearts since primary school. Upon seeing her making her own purposeful beeline for James, I can't quite remember if I actually did scream *"NOOOOOOOOO!!!"* or whether it was a voice in my head but before you knew it, a rush of adrenaline and panic had surged inside me - and I was leaping over the adjoining table, lunch and dessert deftly balancing on my arm. I was nearly there. The Seat Next to James had suddenly taken on an ethereal glow. My throne! My throne! Sadly, in my blind haste and panic, I hadn't taken into account the selfish shortcut taken by the mini bride-in-waiting aiming for her own slice of Green Parka Goodness. Then I slipped. Then skidded. The next moments were a blur. A confusing explosion of crashing chairs, an upturned table, kids screaming, teachers yelling and several chocolate sponge puddings simultaneously launched into the air all at once like a display of cheap, disappointing fireworks. The debris settled to reveal everyone in the lunch hall staring at me. I was covered in the splattered collateral damage of chocolate sauce and the shrapnel of pieces of sponge pudding in my hair. I was a terrorist. I didn't know what a terrorist was. Al Qaeda was just a jumble of seven letters you picked out of the green bag whilst playing *Scrabble*. Too many vowels but hey, you got the Q! But I was one. A suicide-chocolate-spongebomb wielding mini-terrorist, causing sheer carnage in Leys Infants lunch hall all because of my bewildering love for the Boy in the Green Parka. I looked at James, hoping for a smile of sympathy that might kick start our love. James just laughed at me. He *laughed*. Our relationship was over before it had even begun. That was the last time I ever tried to get close to him. We were done. Like a spurned lover, I would soon come to seek solace in someone else. A girl.

2 - THE SIX YEAR OLD BEARD

1980 – 1982 (aged 5 – 7)

Deep down I was probably grateful to now be able to spend my playtimes hanging out with my peers rather than have my face perpetually glued up against a fence like a sad little stalker. My little face was no doubt also thankful to finally be able to get rid of the diamond-shaped indentations. The disaster with James - aka He of the Disparaging Laugh - was a sign. Maybe The Incident with the Chocolate Sponge Pudding had been a cosmic warning of the chaos that would ensue should I pursue these inexplicable feelings towards other boys. Thankfully, the goldfish memories us wee kids possessed at the time enabled my friends to forget the incident - and my feelings for James - had ever happened - and the drama was never discussed again. In the proceeding weeks at lunch time, I had mastered the art of avoiding any semblance of eye contact with James, trying to act my nonchalant best as I chose to sit as far away from his table as physically possible. If there was a lunch table available on the moon, I would have sat at it. I wanted to believe that The Incident with the Chocolate Sponge Pudding had just been some kind of random dream sequence not dissimilar to those found in the American TV shows that my Mum loved to watch, the moment when the screen goes wobbly and misty and the soundtrack warps before the narrative snaps back to reality.

Luckily, the awkward lunch times would not last too much longer as one day James vanished and was never seen again. I never knew where he suddenly went. If my life was indeed like one of Mum's soap operas then James had just been unceremoniously written out of it. Maybe he and his family had fled Dagenham, put into witness protection so that James could be safe from the weird little boy in the purple polyester trousers and the oversized knitted jumper from his Nan and who probably still had minute shrapnel-like traces of chocolate sponge pudding in his hair. Or maybe they had just moved. I never enquired as to the nature of James' sudden disappearing act nor did I ever see him again. The universe had course corrected and put me back onto the path that I was supposed to take. That of being a *normal* boy.

*

Subconsciously I must have known what being 'normal' truly meant, for as the six weeks summer holidays of 1980 came around, I took my life in a somewhat more butch direction, finding proper 'boys time' by hanging out regularly with on/off best friend Martin and the Cooper twins as we spent our idle Summer days at the twins' house, building *Meccano* and playing with toy soldiers, *Action Men* and *Star Wars* figures that didn't sport toilet roll wedding dresses, in-between being served *Tizer* and ice cream floats by the twins' elder sister and her friends. Yes, according to the Dagenham way of life, this was apparently the correct way things were meant to be, the boys playing with their toys whilst the girls waited on us hand and foot. The twins were clearly misogynist and sexist even at this young age but I was their protégé and I had to learn how things were meant to be and what made us boys, boys. For us boys were boys and girls were girls. Society, especially in Dagenham, told us that there was no room for a deviation from that simple fact. And a boy I was.

*

As my second year at Leys Infants commenced in September 1980, my desire to be a 'normal' boy meant that the inordinately inappropriate amount of time I spent playing in the wendy house had to be curtailed. Well, actually I was banned from there, barred by a trio of female bouncers, a unholy trinity of pig-tailed mini divas who had declared it their domain, ruthlessly conquering the safe confines of the wendy house's frilly four walls like a slightly less dramatic and much smaller scale World War Three with glitter and *Copydex* glue instead of grenades. Needless to say I didn't dare question their authority let alone try to explain why a boy like me had only wanted to hold innocent tea parties with the dolls and teddy bears who resided in there. Nevertheless, I wasn't that bothered, as I was now 'one of the boys'. However, confusion as to what being a boy actually meant would soon upset the applecart of my clearly hetero infant life. For the irony being that whilst the little gay boy in the making was being banned from the wendy house for suspicious eyebrow-raising tea parties, his parents were spending their evenings glued to gay people on their television screens.

My whole family were television addicts, evenings being when my Mum had control of the TV, scheduling her viewing around her favourite soaps whilst on the weekend, my Dad would spend the entire day watching an ostensibly endless tedious show called *World of Sport* that seemed to be on for hours and hours and hours on a Saturday and hosted by a moustached individual with the sniggering-inducing name of Dickie. And yet, sport aside; in the times that the whole family would come together and watch television in unison, it was to enjoy the kind of shows populated by gay people, although of course, the sexuality of the majority of them was never known at the time. Larry Grayson, Russell Harty, Kenny Everett, John Inman in *Are You Being Served*, Liberace playing his piano in televised concerts, our television screens were filled with gay men, albeit most of them hiding their sexuality, even as adults. Of course, I was still too young to have any idea whatsoever what gay was and, like my parents; these male celebrities were just over-the-top entertainers to be laughed at, with their true sexual proclivities never acknowledged and certainly never up for discussion.

It was the comedy duo *Hinge and Bracket* that changed everything. A pair of funny old women that appeared on our TV on a Sunday evening, they were doppelgangers of both my Nans and how hilarious I found their brand of bawdy comedy. But that hilarity gave way to sheer confusion when I soon found out that they weren't women at all. They were men.

*

It was Terence with the perma-snot appendage to his left nostril that delivered the shock revelation to my innocent, naive self about the true nature of *Hinge and Bracket*. You could say that Terence was the token smug know-it-all in our class. His inability to wipe his nose was seemingly counter-balanced by his striking skill in being clued up on world current affairs, the rising cost of living, political scandals - and the fact that *Hinge and Bracket* were in fact just two old men in dresses and wigs. Of course he had to reveal this earth-shattering secret to me whilst in the company of nearly all of my fellow classmates, who promptly joined in with a chorus of incredulous *"how could you have not known?!"* type sniggers. As the universe imploded all around me, I wondered if I really could be the only boy that hadn't known that men could also be women and women could also be men.

"What did Terence mean?" I asked Mum, perplexed, that evening after school. I couldn't understand it. But Mum had a simple explanation for me. She awkwardly yet simply let me know that the men who were dressing up as women, were, as she eloquently yet very basically put it, *"funny"*. I already knew *that*, *Hinge and Bracket* were hilarious to the point where I needed a wee during every commercial break, despite not understanding half of their jokes, being just shy of six years old. But Mum meant another kind of *"funny"*. I asked what she meant. There were two kinds of funny? Despite my insistent demands for a more detailed explanation, Mum quickly dropped the subject by telling me that I didn't need to fret about such things. For I was a boy and I had the prettiest girlfriend in school.

*

Yes that's correct. I now had a girlfriend. Well, when I say girlfriend, it was more akin to the fact that somehow, inexplicably, I was now 'holding hands' with Fiona Coleman, the significance of which was the equivalent to a full-on relationship in pre-pubescent terms. And this was a love story that overshadowed the rival romance of Prince Charles and Lady Diana and would give my Nan Shirley's dog-eared and well-thumbed *Mills and Boon* novels a run for their money.

It had all started, as all the strongest romances do, when Fiona took pity on me during art class, as I accidentally snorted *Fairy Liquid* up my nose during some bizarre painting exercise that involved blowing it through a straw over a smattering of paint to create random patterns. As I leapt around the classroom in pain, it was Fiona who came to my aid amongst the backing soundtrack of hysterical laughter. Escorting me to our teacher Mrs. Marx, it was through her kindness that Fiona and I bonded as the last dribbles of *Fairy Liquid* evacuated southbound from my nostrils as at the same time I realised that I had stumbled upon a sure-fire method of Terence finally being able to rid his nose of his fucking bogie.

*

Fiona was as pure and wholesome as *Snow White* - minus the high-pitched warbling to little birds or hanging out with a group of hard-working midgets who were in desperate need of a Trade Union. Day after day, Fiona would rock up at the school gates to be despatched by her Mum in a different flowery dress and headband to match. Her wardrobe clearly rivalled that of Princess Di. And *I* was the lucky boy that was holding her hand. I - and only I - was Fiona's treasured 'hand-holder'. I should have been smugger that Fiona and I were 'together'. In little infant straight boy world, she was a hottie - the prettiest girl in school whose attentions were vied for by a myriad of boys and thugs in the making, often resulting in jealous scraps in the playground during fervent games of Kiss Chase. But deep down in my subconscious, thoughts and memories of a certain Boy in a Green Parka still lurked. Still, these were now resigned to a dark recess of my mind that should have been labelled *'Confusing Thoughts to Never, Ever Entertain Again. Never. Ever'* and so I pushed forward with my equally baffling union with Fiona, one which left the other boys perplexed, especially as to why Fiona would pick a nerdy little 'clever clogs' who was always being rewarded with *Mojo* sweets from the headmistress for good work. No-one liked a 'clever clogs', especially one whose best work yet was getting to hold hands daily with Fiona, albeit unrewarded with a *Mojo*. In this day and age, our relationship would be suspected of being a business deal, the wholesome wife being forced to smile brightly and keep up appearances to deceive the world about her husband's true inclinations. Poor Fiona, she was an unwitting beard to a gay boy at six years old and she didn't even know it.

Nevertheless, our courtship was positively blossoming, going from strength to pre-pubescent strength, mainly consisting of course of the perpetual holding of hands whilst our respective parents exchanged *"Aw, aren't they cute?"* kind of smiles. And cute we were. A cuteness that was milked to its full school-endorsing potential by our teachers who chose to parade our courtship at the Harvest Festival that Autumn, the peculiar yearly ritual when parents' cupboards all over Dagenham would be raided for out-of-date tins of food to be donated in cardboard mushroom baskets to elderly people in care homes, clearly to hasten their imminent demise with the forced consumption of stale baked beans and powdered *Bisto* gravy that was five years out of date. It remains undocumented exactly how many old people went on to pass away from the dodgy tinned food served sweetly to them in a *"well you can't say no to us"* kind of way by the cute six year old couple from Leys Infants.

*

My commitment to Fiona was such that one day, it was rewarded handsomely when she decided to lend me her treasured copy of the book *The Water Babies*. Maybe it was because Fiona realised that she and I mirrored the characters of Tom and Ellie, the *Water Babies* themselves, with Tom having to prove his morals so that he could be allowed the company of Ellie until they could be eventually returned to human form at the end. But what was moral about a young boy who was gay-despite-not-knowing-it-yet letting a girl believe that he was her boyfriend? Even though he was unaware that what he was doing was wrong?

Anyway, do not underestimate the significance of this book for Fiona. It was a step up from the *Mr Men* and *Little Miss* books we often shared, of which there should have been editions titled *Mr Little Closeted Homosexual* and *Little Miss Fag Hag*. But Fiona now had a prized copy of *The Water Babies* and she carried it everywhere with her, to the point where she could recite the whole text off by heart at any given request to do so. Getting your hands on her personal copy of *The Water Babies* would have been addressed in the equivalent to an infant pre-nuptial agreement. This book was hers and no one was ever allowed to touch it, let alone borrow it from her. So when, one playtime, Fiona declared that she would like to lend me the book for me to read, it was as if time suddenly froze in shock. Other kids gasped and stared. Even the teachers had looks on their faces that suggested the whole fabric of reality had suddenly been torn asunder from under their sensible shoes. As Fiona handed me the book, our relationship had become official. We were now the power couple of Leys Infants. Charles and Di were lowly peasants compared to us.

*

The crowning moment in our relationship was at Christmas 1980, when Fiona and were being selected as the postman and postwoman, a shoo-in after the recent success of our attendance at the Harvest Festival. Being chosen as the Christmas Postman and Postwoman was an honour that was sought after by all the kids at school, the anointing of one boy and one girl to be given the hallowed task of going from classroom to classroom delivering their peers' Christmas cards to their respective teachers for allocation. Or to be more precise - to be the cogs in this particular festive brand of an infant popularity machine. Yes for the Christmas cards distribution was a sure-fire way to indicate how popular you were amongst your classmates. It was nothing but a cruel contest, inflating the egos of the popular cool kids whilst embarrassing - no, *humiliating* - the less fortunate. The results were as predictable as the Oscars.

After the delivering of the Christmas cards to the teachers had finally been completed, I was relegated back to my seat in my class, where I would reside, desperate for my name to be called, even just once, hoping that despite the fact that none of the cards in my delivery bundle bore my name, maybe Fiona had delivered the cards meant for me. Of course, this wasn't the case and only the same classmates (namely the heart-throb Cooper twins) were rewarded every time, whilst I was left to feign smiles of being genuinely pleased for them as they sauntered up to Mrs. Marx's desk getting showered in Christmas card after Christmas card, until their desks were drowning in a sea of card, envelopes, stickers of baubles, cute reindeer, drawings of Santa, paper cut-out Christmas trees and glitter - of course, glitter. By the time the Cooper Twins had a worn a groove in the floor between theirs and Mrs. Marx's desks with their frequent trips of adulation-receiving, their desks were left resembling a tacky Christmas grotto built with the bricks of sheer popularity. Meanwhile, I, as well as just a couple of others, just stared at the bare wood of our desk lids, hoping for even just one card to break up the monotony of wood grain, paint splatter and crayon stains. Maybe it was the envy at my union with Fiona that has caused the short supply of Christmas cards this year.

But with the inevitable lack of cards on the day, the next day would always yield another phenomenon - the Afterthought Cards of Sympathy - which would, like clockwork, come rolling in to placate the deflated and disappointed egos of the less popular. Well, when I say rolling in, it was only ever just a couple at most, namely cards from girls who felt sorry for me the day before. Even the pig-tailed divas who had barred me from the wendy house gave me cards. The Afterthought Card of Sympathy was better than nothing and I did appreciate them. But I didn't need cards, for I still possessed something far more valuable. I had Fiona.

*

Mine and Fiona's epic kiddie romance continued all throughout the first half of 1981 where together we engaged in such fun childish activities such as making egg cups for the upcoming Royal Wedding and more bizarrely, designing posters for cigarette brands, sponsored by the cigarette companies themselves in an era when no-one even considered the harmful effects of nicotine, which meant it was easier to rope young children into promoting it. Needless to say my Nan Shirley helped me win with my abstract design for *Benson and Hedges*. My winning streak also continued into the summer when, during the school summer fete, I weirdly guessed the exact number of sweets in a jar and was rewarded with the said jar of sweets as well as the toy of my choice from the white elephant stall. I plumped for the toy till instead of the toy car, much to Mum's dismay. I had inadvertently erred back on the wrong side of 'normality 'again as toy tills were meant for girls and toy cars for boys, the subliminal message of the desired destiny for the children of Dagenham being pre programmed into their minds where the girls had to become checkout operators and the boys working in the Fords car factory. It was an indoctrination that had already been hammered home months earlier when in February 1981, the Ford's car factory became the view from my bedroom window. Mum and Dad had completed a house swap, exchanging our council flat in Dagenham East for a council house that happened to be two doors away from my Nan Shirley. We had returned back to the street where I spent the first part of my infancy and now I was growing up with a view of the industrial chimneys of the desired - and wholly expected future workplace of my male peers and I. It was a grim daily reminder of where I would probably be ending up, peeking over the rooftops and looking in through my window. Maybe it was the dread of this destiny that led to the events that would see the tragic end of my hand-holding with Fiona.

*

The terrible betrayal had occurred during the 1981 six weeks summer holiday at Fiona's sixth birthday party. Charles and Di's honeymoon period was over - and very soon, so too would ours be. After a long period of 'courtship', Fiona and I had never kissed, not even once. The hand holding was par for the course but neither of our lips had ever met, not even for a simple peck of affirmation for our union. Egged on by Fiona's parents, clearly working a sideline in arranged marriages on top of their day jobs, it had been decided that The Kiss would finally occur at Fiona's birthday party via a game of Postman's Knock. Postman's Knock had always baffled me in its assumption that postmen gleefully went around kissing housewives on their doorsteps and had to be re-enacted by children in all its illicit glory. And considering that my Mum's funny word for a vagina was *"letterbox"*, which only confused me even more as to what exactly the Postman delivered to our house every day.

Anyway, but now, Fiona's birthday version of Postman's Knock was about to commence and had gathered quite the crowd, kids and parents eagerly slurping fizzy drinks and munching on crisps in fervent expectation. It was decided that a boy would kiss a girl first and so the chosen girls - including Fiona - were all selected and lined up against the living room wall.

It was like an identity parade to pick out who was the beard with the gay boyfriend, with everyone unaware it was the poor Birthday Girl herself. Naturally, it was my turn first to play the postman. I was incredibly nervous, more so with dozens of pairs of eyes on me, eyes which now darted horizontally back and forth between Fiona and I - and the route between us and our lips, which as the crow flies was less than four feet. I started to move towards Fiona. Her lips puckered, my own puckered and de-puckered repeatedly in response like a flailing goldfish gasping for air. Kiddie saliva was about to be exchanged, there was no getting away from it. Three feet... two feet... Fiona closed her eyes, leaving her lips still rigidly puckered waiting and ready. One foot away... There was football style chanting now, hands punching the air. I was seconds away from scoring. Fiona's lips were in my line of vision; all I simply had to do was line mine up to hers, which should be a relatively easy feat with all the frenzied egging on from all sides. Her face was inches away now... But suddenly, as if my body had been taken control of by a remote operating unit, I inexplicably veered left at the very last second - just as Fiona opened her eyes, wondering why The Kiss was taking so long to materialise - and I planted a smacker on petite blonde Donna Baker, who stunned with the unexpected turn of events and my lips glued on hers, ended up looking like a sex doll with her mouth perfectly round and open in shock as she stood propped deathly still against the wall as I pulled away. There was complete silence in the room. Even the house flies would have dropped dead in shock. The air could be cut with a pair of Fiona's crimping scissors. Everyone was staring daggers at me. Seconds later Fiona burst into tears.

    I couldn't explain myself. I had made a girl cry instead of kissing her – and on her birthday no less. I was as mortified as a six year old could possibly be. I tried to desperately explain why I had suddenly decided to kiss Donna instead, for me it had been a weird instinct in not wanting to give the crowd what they were expecting of me, to instead shake things up and go against being labelled as predictable. Something inside me had instructed me not to kiss the person I was meant to, but to plant my lips on someone else instead - but there was no way I could convey this reasoning without sounding mildly bonkers. Instead I left Fiona devastated, my in-laws incensed and I was nothing but a cheating infant. I was quickly ushered out to my Dad's waiting car like a dirty politician being whisked away to safety after the exposure of his terrible misdeeds.

    Needless to say, it was the end for Fiona and I as I lost my trophy girlfriend and my 'beard' became stubble. Fiona quickly moved on to one of the Cooper Twins, a boyfriend that was more befitting for her than the boy with a confused infantile attraction to other boys which had somehow manifested itself in kissing a girl who wasn't his hand holding beard.

*

Despite my betrayal, Fiona and I remained friends throughout the final year of primary school, at the end of which we would be going our separate ways to different junior schools at opposite ends of Dagenham. As the final day at Leys Infants dawned, Fiona unexpectedly presented me with a parting gift. It was a *World Cup 1982* key ring sporting a cute mascot that was an orange, brought back from her family holiday in Spain. But football?! I had not the remotest interest in football or any other sport for that matter but it was the thought that counted. The thought that maybe Fiona did know all along that she had been holding hands with - and refused a kiss from - a boy who was gay although he didn't really realise it yet. Maybe this football key ring was her way of surreptitiously trying her best to convert me back to the straight and narrow before it was too late.

And then we said our final goodbyes. I would like to be able to look back and remember an emotional farewell, with swelling emotional orchestral music at the school gates, but there wasn't. There was just a mutual *"bye then"* and the handing over of the key ring and that was that. The key ring was a message.

Don't be gay, not in this town. Be a football hooligan and read The Sun.

To this day, I still have that key ring, my oldest surviving possession, a poignant symbol of 'the norm' for a boy that I would spend the next couple of decades fighting and going against.

3 - THE WOO-WOO AND THE OPAL FRUITS

1982 – 1984 (aged 7 – 9)

James and Fiona were both a distant memory by the time I started William Ford Church of England Junior School in September 1982. Well it had only been six weeks but in kiddie years, six weeks might as well have been six months.

The clue was in the name that William Ford Church of England was a religious school but none of my family were remotely god-fearing, except it seemed for during my parents' arguments when the name Jesus Christ would be bandied back and forth in shouty tones, usually with an extra middle name that I always had to pretend I had never heard. Meanwhile the promise of eternity spent in Hell was conveniently only threatened as a punishment for not wanting to eat the Saturday dinners of boiled potatoes and offal whilst Heaven was of course reserved for those who willingly ate my Mum's vegetables that were overcooked to the point of liquidation. The whole concept of Heaven and Hell baffled me, as I wondered which husband my Mum's Nan, Great Granny Kay, would be reunited with in this unproven afterlife. She had been married - and widowed - twice and had loved both of her husbands equally so when she eventually died, I wanted to know which one she would get to spend eternity with on whichever fluffy white cloud was reserved for her. Was it a first come first served arrangement of which hubby number one would be the victor? Or would she have to hang out with both in some kind of celestial threesome? None of it made any sense to me, especially at such a young age. Anyway despite our secularism, William Ford was the only school that I wanted to go to, mainly because my on/off best friend Martin was also going there. I didn't know what to expect in this upgraded environment where I would spend the next four years of my school life, maybe only hoping that there would be no more Incidents with Chocolate

Sponge Puddings or Postman Knock Kissing Debacles to define my time there.

*

      As my first day at William Ford came around, Nan Shirley was waiting on her doorstep two doors down; to begin what would be a daily ritual from her, to give me sweets to eat on the way to school, those weird boiled sweets in a circular tin that were covered in a white powder. I am sure that in today's over-zealous society, she would have been reported to Social Services for potential crack dealing to kids but in 1982, it was just a friendly sugar rush from my Nan to help kick-start each day at Junior School.

      As my Mum escorted me on the ten minute walk to my new school, I was concerned to find that all my new male peers were accessorised with West Ham United sports bags, presumably because West Ham was the nearest Premier League football team to Dagenham, a consequence of which meant that Dagenham was a town where most men over the age of ten seemed to wear West Ham football shirts and reek of *Skol* lager. So it shouldn't have been that much of a surprise to me to find that my new classmates and I were now of the age to be indoctrinated into supporting the same football team as our parents. And now here I was, confronted upon my arrival at the school gates by a whole army of mini West Ham United fans. I panicked. I hadn't even considered that my inaugural day at junior school would involve the social suicide of not having the right football sports bag. The clue should have been in the Football 82 key ring that Fiona had given me six weeks before and which I still carried around in my pocket. Desperate to fit in and not be bullied, I asked my Mum to go on an emergency mission that lunchtime and please buy me a football bag. She came back at the end of that day with a Tottenham Hotspur FC satchel. It would have to do.

      My path to gayness was being curtailed by a road block of forced football-loving macho activity but I felt like a fraud, parading around the playground giving the illusion of being into football when I was not remotely sporty in any way, something which my peers sussed out straightaway, hence me, always without fail, being the last one left standing when teams were picked for sports. Despite hating football, I steadfastly kept up the illusion that I was a devoted supporter and potential hooligan in the making, namely by partaking in the craze that year of filling up the Football 82 Panini sticker album. My pocket money was endlessly spent on purchasing the packs of stickers from the local newsagents but I would only ever end up with endless 'doubles' of some obscure footballer from an even less unpopular team, the stickers that were never in demand when it came to doing 'swapsies' with other kids in the playground in our competitive efforts to be the first to fill the whole album. Even at seven years old I suspected that it was all some sinister marketing ploy to make us naive football-indoctrinated children buy more and more packs of stickers to fill the coffers of the Panini Sticker Corporation or whatever evil genius was behind it all. However, weirdly, I became the only kid at school who was only the manager John Lyall away from completing the West Ham page, which was the key to being accepted by my football loving peers. But his sticker never materialised, nor did my desire to ever like football. So in defeat, instead I decided to partake in the other craze sweeping school, that of collecting the *Garbage Pail Kids* cards, which kind of summed up where I stood on the ladder of social hierarchy, knowing that collecting and swapping cards of misfits and outcasts was much more suited to me, rather than aggressively kicking balls around.

*

Aside from collecting the *Garbage Pail Kids*, there was also something else that I became obsessed with. Stationery.

If Heaven did exist, then I wanted it to be filled with cupboards and cupboards full of stationery, preferably new and unused. Oh how I loved the feel of my new pencil case, pens and exercise books. Over the coming years the best thing about starting a new year or new school was the brand new stationery that I could get, as I would excitedly accompany Mum to Woolworths to make sure that I got the right ones. However, this love of stationery led to my first junior school incident of causing more public disorder, something which, by now, I obviously had this unyielding knack for.

I was a well-behaved boy, a good egg, but yet I had this unexplained penchant for unintentionally causing trouble. This particular disruptive episode shall be known as The Incident with Mrs. Darby's Stationery Cupboard.

*

The events unfolded during a Maths lesson in the first year where Mrs. Darby, a rotund, stern, unsmiling dictator presided over her class of seven year old pupils like a Miss. Ratchett with a thick Essex twang. I had reached the last page of my Maths exercise book so requested a new blank one where I was despatched to Mrs. Darby's high security stationery cupboard with the pant-wetting excitement of a child entering Santa's Grotto. Unfortunately, upon sliding open the cupboard, I was to find that one dictatorship skill that Mrs. Darby lacked was being able to keep her stationery cupboard in any semblance of a tidy and sensible order. Now I was a bit OCD when it came to tidiness, so was quite dismayed to now be confronted with haphazard piles of mismatching exercise books and pencils scattered willy-nilly, that, to paraphrase my Mum's judgement on how Dad left the bathroom, looked like *"a bomb's hit it."* So being the bit of a 'goody two shoes' that I was, I thought it would be a good idea to impress Mrs.

Darby and maybe get her to crack a smile of gratitude, by taking it upon myself to tidy up this mess of a stationery cupboard, re-sorting the exercise books into carefully categorised and logical, matching piles and segregating pens according to their colour. I was sure that Mrs. Darby would be more than grateful for my sterling efforts. However, of course, it would backfire spectacularly.

When Mrs. Darby discovered the stationery cupboard's extreme makeover, she yelled and bellowed like a fire-breathing dragon, immediately halted the lesson, made all us kids line up at the front of the classroom, as, armed with a very long ruler, she angrily demanded a confession from whoever had possessed the sheer audacity to re-arrange the stationery cupboard, sending all my classmates into a bewildered confusion as to a) why would anyone get into trouble for doing such a thing? And b) who the hell would want to re-arrange a stationery cupboard anyway?

I had no choice but to own up. But I felt I had to try and justify my actions by criticising Mrs. Darby for the woeful way she had mixed up the lined exercise books with the plain ones, had the green pencils in the same pot as the red ones and let's not even get started on how she had stacked the boxes of rubbers in a way that was more precarious than the Leaning Tower of Pisa. Predictably she wasn't impressed and I got into big trouble, reported to the headmistress and also to my parents who were as equally baffled as I, for not getting into trouble for truancy, fighting or picking my nose during Assembly but instead for my skills in the impeccable re-arrangement, sorting and categorising of stationery. That combined with my reluctance to embrace football and my obsession with tidiness, I am surprised my parents hadn't yet twigged that their eldest son was taking more baby steps to that eventual coming out of the closet - an impeccably arranged and tidy closet of course. Not that I knew of course that I was even *in* any closet, I still had no inkling of what I really was. Everyone else though was getting clue after clue about my sexuality to the point where Lionel Blair on *Give Us a Clue* would be able to just hold up a picture of me and the panellists would correctly guess *"GAY!"* within half a second. But I still didn't even know such a thing as gay existed – only that men could dress up as women if they wanted to. Until one day, a few weeks later, when I finally heard The Word. The one syllable label that not only would be a high scoring word in *Scrabble* but was also the definition of all my weird feelings towards other boys. Of what I was.

Queer.

Luckily it wasn't me that this word was directed at in an accusing manner but in this instance, Toby Curtis was on the receiving end, an extremely awkward perpetually red-faced chubby boy who languished even further down the ladder of kiddie social acceptance than I did. Which was not an easy feat when many points for me had already been lost because of a

Tottenham Hotspur bag and a dodgy sense of fashion courtesy of my Mum. Nevertheless, Toby had been selected as the easy target for a gang of thuggish seven year old bullies, a cocky trio known as The Three Ds (Darren, Danny and Dave) who were now labelling Toby a real life *Garbage Pail Kid* - and worse than that - queer.

   One playtime, I had found Toby screaming for help in a corner of the playground as his tormentors threatened him with wooden lollipop sticks that had been carved into dagger-like weapons. They were trying to get him to admit that he was this thing called queer. Upset at Toby's distress, I still didn't know what queer meant or why Toby was being tortured into saying he was this word. The Three Ds pulled me into their ranks and egged me on to join them in this harassment of Toby, pulling another lolly stick-come-spear out of one of their West Ham football bags and handing it to me.

"Go on, tell him he's a queer!" they spluttered, trying to spur me on.

"He's a what?" is all I could meekly respond with.

"Queer!"

"I can't call him that" I protested, seeing that a small warm puddle of wee now radiating across Toby's school trousers.

"Why not?!" questioned 'Head D' Darren, in an accusatory tone.

"Because I don't know what that word means", I confessed.

They all looked at me in disbelief. Even Toby looked at me with an incredulous look on his face.

"You seriously don't know what queer means?" they chortled as I shook my head.

"It means you want to kiss boys instead of girls".

In that instant someone had inserted the keys into the thick steel doors of my vault of confusion and swung them open with a slam that crushed my innocence. Suddenly my experience with James the Boy in The Green Parka came to mind, like a long forgotten family friend popping up on your doorstep suddenly saying *"Coo-ee! Remember me?!"*

"What?" I asked, wanting exact clarity on this. *"Queer means you like other boys like as in fancy them?"*

"Yeah" the Three Ds all nodded in unison, *"Like Toby does. He's queer."*

I looked at Toby. He was trembling now, his face now redder than it ever had been. Did we have more in common with each other than either of us realised? I knew he didn't like football either and was also an avid collector of the *Garbage Pail Kids*. But unlike me, as far as I was aware anyway, he hadn't yet caused a scandal with stationery. Therefore I was far higher up on the queer scale than he. And yet he was the one being picked on.

"Leave him alone" I said, the words vacating my mouth before my mind could catch them up. The Three Ds - and Toby - all looked at me in surprise as I handed back the sharpened lolly stick, unwilling to take part in a pre-puberty queer-bashing of some kid who might be just as confused as I was.

"*Queer!*" they shouted, but this time it was not directed at Toby, it was aimed at me.

"*Are you queer too? Do you kiss boys too?*" they interrogated me like I was on the witness stand in a court. Before I could fathom any answer I was literally saved by the bell to be returned to class. I helped pick Toby up as he composed himself and thanked me. I was his hero. I was *The Littlest Hobo*, the heroic TV dog that would make me cry like a baby each time he waggled off into the sunset rather than collecting his medal at the end of each episode. But I was no hero. I was a seven year old boy who finally had a word for his attraction to other boys - and had now seen firsthand the trouble it would get him into.

*

My recurring nightmare started soon after, the bad dream that would go on to torment me on a regular basis throughout the rest of my childhood. It was always the same scenario - me being pinned to my bedroom floor as a dark monstrous entity bore down on me, faceless yet terrifying, trying to suffocate me as I struggled in vain under its gargantuan weight and tried to scream but with no sound coming out. The only way I could wake from the nightmare was to call for my Mum and Dad three times. As an adult now, I now know what the monster in the dream was, it was my perceived Monster of Abnormality. And it was trying to get me. For deep down I knew I 'queer', I was something that was strictly forbidden and repulsive to others and which would find me on the receiving end of very pointy lollipop sticks without the pleasure of getting to eat the lolly beforehand. Mum already thought there was something wrong with me, as since I was born, I had this strange affliction of rolling my head from side to side to get to sleep. Maybe I was subconsciously trying to roll the queerness out of myself and now the creeping awareness was magnifying that, just like *Hinge and Bracket*, I might also be "*funny*".

*

What I was about to discover though, was that there was already 'funniness' that had grown moss-like on my family tree. The first rumblings of gayness already existed within my own vast network of relatives although the truth of it had been hidden deeper than the non-existence of the Tooth Fairy or Father Christmas. It was my Dad's brother Uncle Jimmy and his 'friend' Billy who were the guilty party. Up until now, I hadn't remotely twigged that Uncle Jimmy's friendship with Billy, his "best friend" who accompanied him everywhere and actually lived in the same house as him, his siblings and my paternal Nan, was actually a much deeper companionship, one which, behind closed doors, involved the swapping of a lot more than just Football 1982 stickers. The true nature of Uncle Jimmy and Billy's bond was a family secret on a par with the true nature of Mum's Christmas presents to my Auntie Reenie which were bath sets given by

Reenie to my Mum the previous Christmas, subsequently rewrapped and given back as presents the next Christmas. The knowledge of this present ping pong was always met with a polite feigned smile of gratitude and never spoken of. Just like Uncle Jimmy and Billy's homosexual relationship.

It was a Sunday afternoon gathering around Auntie Reenie's house where I found out that Uncle Jimmy and Billy were my family's equivalent of *Hinge and Bracket*, minus the wigs, dresses and prime time slot on TV. Auntie Reenie was showing off her new purchase of a cushioned foot stall called a pouffe and was resting her feet up on it when one of my Uncles joked for her to *"get her feet off Jimmy and Billy"*. Much hilarity ensued about the pouffe and the poofs, not realising that I was in the doorway watching everything. I had heard the word poof before as an equivalent to queer, adding to the descriptive repertoire that also included 'funny'. So at hearing Uncle Jimmy and Billy be called this, my curiosity was peaked as I stepped into the living room and asked:

"Are Uncle Jimmy and Billy queer?"

"Where did you learn that word?" responded Mum, visibly appalled. Another Uncle, drunk on cheap lager and therefore loose with his words and more so his manners, went on to gleefully, despite Mum's protests, give me a lurid description of Uncle Jimmy and Billy's *"favourite game"* that somehow involved putting their willies inside each others bums. I was more than confused. I didn't even know how birds and bees had sex, let alone adult human beings and certainly not two men. My mum was a prude who would come up with bizarre words for anything to do with sex or sexual anatomy. Sex was called *"rudies"*, a penis was a *"donker"* or *"ding-dong"*, and of course, a vagina was a *"letterbox"*. I thought I had an inkling of what went where but now Uncle Jimmy and Billy's own particular version of *"rudies"* had thrown what I thought I knew hurtling out of the confusingly shaped window.

The upshot was that Uncle Jimmy and Billy were boyfriends - and had been so since being teenagers in the 1960s, when they met and fell in love in an era when being gay was illegal and any gay activity was invisible and taking place underground. Billy's family then discovered he was gay and disowned him, after which my paternal Nan took him in and gave him a home. Which wasn't easy when you had nine kids already in the house.

Billy was no angel though. Now in his forties, he was an extremely effeminate chain-smoking alcoholic who possessed ingenious methodical approaches to sourcing whatever drop of booze he could get into his mouth. His most scandalous crime, which had created a huge family row between all my Dad's siblings, was when Billy raided Uncle Frank's wardrobe, located his stash of liqueur chocolates that he had got for Christmas, pricked a hole in them with a needle, sucked the alcohol out of them then replaced the now soggy chocolates back into the box, as if the booze had magically teleported *Star Trek* style out of their insides.

Billy actually scared me, he reminded me of *Worzel Gummidge*, the TV scarecrow that regularly gave me bad dreams because of his ability to unscrew and replace his head. Billy's own brand of frightening me was at my paternal Nan's eightieth birthday party when he got blind drunk and kissed my hand, which resulted in my nine year old self spending the rest of the party hiding from him under the buffet table. It was clear why Mum said that she didn't want me to end up like him. Whether she was alluding to being an alcoholic or *"funny"* was never made clear, though I could deduce neither figured in her aspirations for her first born.

Nevertheless, I had now put two and two together. Was I queer? Was I a boy who fancied other boys? Was I, like Uncle Jimmy and Billy, a 'poof'? Would I end up a camp alcoholic sucking the liqueur out of boxes of chocolates or could I go the showbiz route and form a new trio with *Hinge and Bracket* calling myself *Handle* or *Door Knob*?

Regardless, I now knew that not only could men pretend to be women and that two men could like and fancy each other, they could also have 'rudies' together in a way that was far different to my previous guesswork that they must just rub their willies together. The anatomical workings of being 'queer', a 'poof' or 'funny' were at a loss for me to fathom. Not being worldly wise about sex except for accidentally watching sex scenes on telly which always looked terribly uncomfortable, I needed an explanation of where a willy was really *supposed* to go. And that's why I ended up paying to see Stacey Waters' vagina.

To use the term other seven year olds used, a vagina was a *"woo-woo"* and Stacey Waters' own woo-woo was available for viewing, like a new des-res semi that had just come on the housing market. Even at seven years old, Stacey was a bit of a slag and a troublemaker and I'm sure I was the last boy in school not to have already seen her woo-woo. She was a primadonna, a temptress and a bully who often had social services involved when she was playing truant or actually running away from home. Other girls were terrified of the power that Stacey wielded. Even more powerful, entrancing boys under its spell, was her woo-woo.

Being able to see it was subject to negotiation with Stacey, so I had brokered the deal in the school library, with Martin in attendance, helping with the bargaining of the finer points of the verbal contract that would involve trading sweets in exchange for the witnessing of a girl's woo-woo. It was hardly a transaction that required reams of paperwork and caveats as Stacey simply demanded an entire pack of Opal Fruits as her payment. I haggled, reluctant to give her the whole pack. After bartering for a while, she finally settled on wanting just the orange and red ones. She, like anyone else, never wanted the green ones. The deal was done.

I was quite nervous to see Stacey's woo-woo and recruited Martin to accompany me, feeling safety in numbers should it suddenly come alive or something and attack me. We found a shady corner in the playground, ironically the same spot where poor Toby Curtis had been bullied for being 'queer'. I handed over the orange and red Opal Fruits to Stacey, which she counted out, dare I try and diddle her, then, satisfied with the sugar intake payment, she lifted her skirt, like the unveiling of a masterpiece, or rather, the drawing of the curtains in my Nan's living room.

I was distinctly unimpressed at the hairless mound that had been revealed before my eyes. It looked just like the smooth mound of plastic that I would find down below when I undressed an Action Man or cousin Kim's Ken Doll, which was the only way my seven year old self had been able to so far address any puzzling gay feelings.

"*Oh. Is that it?*" I said with an air of unappreciative nonchalance. Stacey looked at me blankly, her skirt still hitched skyward, as if expecting me to burst into applause or faint at the sheer marvel of it. Martin seemed entranced, practically drooling to pay homage to the *Opal Fruits* slogan of *"made to make your mouth water" but* I just shrugged. Yes, I shrugged at a girl's vagina. My subconscious was already telling me in no uncertain terms what I had already started to suspect. I really had no interest whatsoever in girls - or their woo-woos - and certainly never wanted to venture this close to one again.

4 – SHOULDERPADS, TV HUNKS AND RAFFLE TICKETS

1984 – 1986 (aged 9-11)

My family could have easily been described as close-knit. Woven together tighter than Nan's home-made jumpers, we were a family tree whose branches were numerous, with a family member sprouting up on nearly every corner of Dagenham - and in some cases, three or more relatives on the same street. There were aunts, uncles, great aunts, great grandmothers, second, third and fourth cousins removed more times than Great Granny Kay's dentures. Nan Shirley's living room often resembled a doctor's waiting room, with a revolving door of relatives and elderly family friends popping in to gossip, chain-smoke, down Rich Tea biscuits dunked in milky tea and compare ailments as well as generally put the world to rights. My favourite of these regular visitors was my Nan's friend Esme, a Thora Hird lookalike who would always bring me a *Milky Way* chocolate bar to devour whilst she and my Nan discussed at length the effect that ageing had on bladder control.

The knock-on effect of having such an immensely large family was that there was always a party to be thrown. Not just birthdays and the annual Christmas shindig that was always only slightly less crowded than the Live Aid concert, any excuse at all justified the holding of some kind of drink fuelled and pineapple/cheese stick-eating celebration. Dad just won three quid on the horses - let's have a party! Grandad's big toenail has finally grown back - quick, get the invites sent out! Nan's perm didn't deflate in the wind today - go ask Auntie Janet to make her famous chicken vol-au-vents for the buffet! These were parties that sent the family social calendar into a PMT-esque meltdown, shindigs that warranted exciting shopping trips into nearby Romford for my Aunties to buy *"something fancy"* from the market stalls or the C&A department store there whilst Mum would treat my brother and I to 'new tops' from the *Kays* catalogue. Nothing brought the family together better than a good old knees up which involved *Chas and Dave* style sing-alongs and the passing around of vile-looking pots of jellied eels. These family parties were a regular ritual on the same level as the nightly 'drawing' of the curtains and 'leaving the big light on' whilst we slept. Then, in late 1984 and into 1985, another family ritual developed - that of the communal viewing of the American super soaps *Dallas* and *Dynasty*.

We already had family film evenings thanks to a knock off VCR and pirate copies of Hollywood movies, provided by my one of my paternal Auntie's dodgy husband who was a supplier of stolen goods. Whenever I asked where the shiny new VCR or portable telly came from, it was always met with a quick changing of the subject after being reprimanded that *"it's rude to ask where something came from"*. Well, that explained my lack of knowledge of 'The Birds and the Bees'.

But for me, films were to pale into insignificance compared to the glitz and glamour of the American prime time soaps. Mum had already been an avid viewer of *Dallas* for years but now, at nine years old, I was of the age where I could also appreciate it and so Mum now had a viewing companion on Wednesday evenings at 8.10pm on BBC 1. But whilst Mum was devoted to *Dallas* and *Dallas* only, my Nan also liked the camper glamour of *Dynasty* that was on Fridays. Soon, I got sucked into both, gawping at the screen like a wide-eyed innocent in awe of the crazy worlds that were so far removed from Dagenham life, it was impossible not to get caught up in them. My Nan and Grandad's house evolved as the viewing lounge of choice for this quality family time on Wednesday and Friday evenings, (minus Mum who preferred the comfort of her own living room two doors away) as we tuned into BBC 1 to be transported to a world of shoulder pads, cat fights, impossibly large hats and torrid love affairs. The routine had been fine-tuned like clockwork. Grandad would *"go down the offy"* at 7.45pm with me in tow, to stock up on *KP crisps*, *Revels*, *Maltesers*, a huge bottle of *Coke*, *Babycham* for Nan and cans of *Skol* lager for himself. Catering *Dallas* and *Dynasty* nights was clearly serious business. Nan would have her packet of *Benson and Hedges* cigarettes at the ready and squeeze out a wee at approximately 8.05pm as the lack of advert breaks on the BBC did not help with any bladder emergency that would result in the potential missing out on any shock plot development. The phone would be taken off the hook and by the time the opening credits rolled, we were all set and ready for our fifty minutes of over the top camp entertainment. I would lie on the floor on my stomach in front of the TV, legs up in the air behind me, not dissimilar to a position from Auntie Carol's *Jane Fonda Workout* exercise videos which I sometimes partook in with her, whilst Nan and Grandad would devour their multitude of cigarettes so rapidly like two *Pac Men* that sometimes we could hardly see the screen. The lungs of minors were not even an afterthought. In fact, Nan and Grandad smoked so much and so often that when the time come to redecorate their living room, the removal of the ceiling tiles revealed them to have become a ghastly yellow/brown colour compared to the white edges of the tiles that had never been exposed to the unrelenting clouds of nicotine pumping like chimneys from out of their mouths. It put me off smoking for life and to this day I have never smoked a single cigarette, always visualising that mustard colour of my Nan and Grandad's living room ceiling tiles. But anyway, despite being a secondary smoker in my grandparents' living room, I was also inadvertently starting to feel guilty about leaving my Mum to watch *Dallas* alone. My problem solving skills led to a solution to watch *Dallas* with my Mum on Wednesdays and *Dynasty* on Fridays with my grandparents. Then *The Colbys* arrived which threw everything into disarray.

Grandad would remark to Nan Shirley on each and every cliff-hanger with a *"Ooh, that's dodgy, Shirl..."*, which was either a comment on Sue Ellen or Alexis's latest misdemeanour or a vocalised observation on his ten year old grandson lapping up every moment of these campfests.

Looking back, I can't help but marvel at how my grandparents could never work out I was gay. Of course, I hadn't quite 100% worked it out for myself yet either. Until the next clue for me came through being exposed to the first openly gay TV character on prime time telly in *Dynasty's* Steven Carrington. At ten years old, I was enraptured by his love story with his on/off boyfriend Luke, blind to my grandparents' uncomfortable shifting on the settee and deaf to my Grandad's commentary on the *"dirty poofs"* in the gloriously PG-rated tame love scenes between two rich good-looking men in Denver. Whilst slutty Alexis was getting all the hardcore cock action, her shoulder pads only less bigger than the list of men hopping in and out of her bed, poor Steven's closest encounter with intimacy with another man was a quick cuddle that was more befitting for a kiddie's Disney movie. Imagine my disappointment when Steven then started fancying women again and shacked up with nutty Claudia, a storyline which could do nothing but only heighten my own confused feelings. The message from the Carrington Mansion was clear, fancying boys was just a phase, a terrible family-wrath-inducing one at that, and desiring girls was always the true way forward. Nevertheless, Steven Carrington had been a step up from the usual representation of gays on TV whose Sexuality Was Never Discussed. He was handsome, he briefly had a boyfriend and he had shot straight into the Top Ten of my Confusing Crushes on 1980s Male TV Characters.

For a young boy possessing an unexplained magnetic draw to the same sex, the TV shows of the early 1980s were packed with handsome characters that certainly didn't help to quell the weird feelings inside me. Whilst my Mum was salivating weekly over a hairy chested detective called *Vegas* who made her feel *"all hot and bothered"*, I, in fact had my own whole cohort of equally hairy chested counterparts who were leaping heroically out of our TV set to enter into and wander inside my imagination where they gave me confusing looks and weird vibes. The interior of my mind resembled a cruising ground with all the shirtless men gathered there but unable to make the first move.

As of late 1985, my Top Ten Confusing Male TV Character Crushes from the past three or so years were, in reverse order:
10) Bobby Ewing in *Dallas*
9) Richard Gere in *The Thorn Birds*
8) Jan Michael Vincent in *Airwolf*
7) Face in *The A Team*
6) Steven Carrington in *Dynasty*
5) Scarecrow from *Scarecrow and Mrs King*
4) Romano (TJ Hooker's sidekick) in *TJ Hooker* (climbing higher after an episode where he had to pose as a male stripper)
3) Lorenzo Lamas from *Falcon Crest*
2) The male detective in *Cagney and Lacey* whose shirtless hairy chest was the highlight of the opening credits.
1) Jeff Colby in *Dynasty*

Of course Jeff was my Number One. Straighter than straight but incredibly mesmerising, there was just something about him that gave me odd butterflies in my belly when I watched *Dynasty*, wishing I could comfort him as that selfish harlot Fallon treated him like dirt. Being only ten going on eleven years old, it was not a sexual attraction of course, just weird, inexplicable and very, very confusing feelings, towards Jeff Colby and all the other men on TV. Might I add here that I drew the line at fancying David Hasselhoff in *Knight Rider*. It was the permed hair that put me off. Even at my young age, I knew that kind of curly bouffant was only suitable on my Nan. I could only help but wonder if Mr. Hasselhoff held his firmly in place with a whole can of *Silvikrin* like my Nan did.

Meanwhile, as well as my doe-eyed staring at hunks on TV, my taste in literature and music was also clueing up the whole world except me that I was more than likely 'of a different persuasion' than most other boys of my age.

My choices of reading material were my Aunties' trashy and racy blockbuster novels that I would borrow from them without their knowledge. They were meant-for-adults sagas by the likes of Jilly Cooper and Jackie Collins, the 'heroine in distress' stories of Sidney Sheldon novels or one particular favourite; *Lace* by Shirley Conran, which was also a mini-series on TV at the time with the campest line of dialogue that I loved to quote endlessly: *"Which one of you bitches is my mother?"* Unfortunately by secretly reading the book beforehand I totally spoilt it for myself as to which of the aforementioned bitches was indeed the mother. Aside from outlandish plots and camp dialogue, I was also immersing myself in luridly descriptive text that featured the use of words that most of the time; I had no clue as to what their meaning was. When I should have been reading my *Brer Rabbit* or *Rupert Bear* books or whichever other anthropomorphic animals were all the rage for young children, instead I was giving myself an inadvertent education of all things carnal which were being provided by literary corkers such as *'Angie gasped as she set her eyes upon Tyler's mighty phallus'*. What on earth was a phallus? It sounded like a model of car but in this chapter, Angie and Tyler were in a hotel bedroom not on a motorway and this phallus thing was bursting out of Tyler's trousers so I was more than baffled. I didn't have a thesaurus to hand so had to rely on innocently asking my Mum, naturally during a family party, if she knew what a phallus was, which confused her as equally as me as she had no idea either but made 'Uncle' Billy in earshot practically faint with shock.

As for music, every Sunday was now spent in front of my Auntie Carol's stereo, armed with a fresh blank cassette tape as I recorded the songs from the Top 40 on BBC Radio 1, my fingers having to spend two hours hovering above the pause and record buttons with the need for ultra-precise and quick reflex timing to make sure that I only got the songs that I wanted, without getting any of the DJ's inane chatter at the beginning or end of each tune. Of course, the songs I pilfered from the Top 40 were always the ones that raised eyebrows as to my liking of them - the latest Cher or Bonnie Tyler anthems or Whitney Houston power ballad. It was hardly surprising that I was a lover of the Emotional Power Ballad. After all, Mum and I were avid listeners of the *Our Tune* segment on Radio 1, a not-so-cheerful kick to the day where, together, she and I would listen and both cry our eyes out at the stories that would always, more times than not, end in death. *'Tracey and Simon were married after a whirlwind romance, they were going to live happily ever after... until...'*

"I bet she dies", I would guess.

"I bet he dies", Mum would retort. Regardless nine times out of ten, someone died.

Mum didn't yet realise that she could have had her own *Our Tune* story what with the sexuality of her son. I can imagine Simon Bates telling it now, getting all choked up at the tragedy of it all as the emotional *Our Tune* theme warbles away on the verge of acoustic tears in the background:

'Valerie's first born son was the apple of her eye. She had his life all mapped out, wife, kids, a job for life at Fords. Until one day, the tragic event occurred. She found her son drooling over Jeff Colby, listening to Bonnie Tyler and reading Jackie Collins. Yes, her son was THAT way. He was funny. A poof. A queer. This song is for him.' Cue *Holding Out for a Hero* blaring across the radio waves as the listeners across the country all sob into their morning teas. But hey, no ending of death in this story!

I was terrified of death. Happily unaware of its existence as a very young child, until I finally learnt that one day, I would cease to exist forever. Just the thought of it sent me into mild panic attacks where I would lock myself in the bathroom, unable to comprehend the enormity and finality of such a frightening concept, something far, far worse than my Monster of Abnormality that stalked my dreams at night. My fear of death was not helped at all when in 1986; a new, appallingly scary advert suddenly appeared on our TV screens, advertising something called AIDS. Of course this was not an advert in the sense of advertising a new-fangled product to persuade us to buy, this was something that apparently could be got for free. With an image of a darkly looming tombstone and a foreboding voiceover telling us *"Don't Die of Ignorance"*, it was an advert that petrified the living shit out of me, even though I had no clue what this AIDS thing was. The only clue I could surmise that it was some kind of awful disease a lot, lot worse than Nan's varicose veins, Uncle Frank's gout or Billy's alcoholism. Mum and Dad of course assuaged my terror by informing me that this AIDS virus was nothing I needed to fret over as it was something only affecting *"funny"* men. But these were the same men that I had the makings of, that despite not truly knowing it, at the same time, somewhere deep down I knew that this AIDS advert could be directed at me. I tried to pretend that I had never seen it and would never think about it, much in the same way that I couldn't allow myself to think about dying.

*

Anyway, I had something far worse in life to currently fear - that of going up to Senior School, which, rewinding now back to mid 1985, was a mere year away. For years since I was a kid watching *Grange Hill*, Dad had told me that when I got to Senior School, I would at some point get my head flushed down the toilet like a goldfish's corpse. It was just another one of my Dad's doom-laden comments. In the family he was nicknamed 'Look on the Bright Side Larry', an ironic label to attend to his always mumbling of something negative. Despite me correcting his grammar to say that it was physically impossible to flush my head down the toilet unless it was severed, all Dad would do was shrug and say *"You'll see"*. Was decapitation really a common occurrence in Senior School? And why would someone want my head to get up close and personal with a *Harpic Toilet Duck* and faint traces of schoolboy faeces and urine anyway? Could it be that The Thing I Was Denying to Myself would be the cause?

I should say that despite my subconscious suspicion that I might be something that any senior school bullies would have a field day with (and hoping that the Three D's wouldn't be following me to my new school), I hadn't exactly made it any less obvious that I was a little Larry Grayson or Kenny Everett in the making. For starters I was putting on impromptu drag shows for my paternal Nan who, because of an operation, was recuperating for a few weeks at our house. Wanting to innocently cheer her up and skilfully improvising with various items of my Mum's clothes and an array of household objects, I impersonated in turn, Bet Lynch from *Coronation Street*, (the living room leopard skin rug for a coat and red milk bottle tops for earrings), Alexis from *Dynasty* (my Mum's nightdress and washing up sponges for shoulder pads) and finally Dame Edna Everage (Mum's best party dress and a purple cushion cover for the hairdo) all of which were met with a polite enthusiasm from my Nan laced with a sideline of suspicion of my true tendencies. She wasn't daft. She had more than enough experience as Mother of a Gay Man, being the mother of Uncle Jimmy and sort of surrogate mother-in-law to his partner Billy. No doubt she had a qualification in it and could easily pass the Telltale Signs a Family Member is a Poof exam.

Question One: Your ten year old Grandson is putting on a drag show for you. Is he:
a) Just innocently imitating Dame Edna
    b) A poof
    C) A poof
    d) A poof

It's not that I was a camp child, not in the slightest but it seemed I was well on the way to becoming Dagenham's only - and youngest - drag queen. I could have blamed it on two things - the resounding success of my star turn as the Tin Man in our school play's version of *The Wizard of Oz* - or the desperate need to bravely come to terms with the incident that happened soon after with the Christmas raffle tickets.

The Wizard of Oz production had occurred first in the final week of school before breaking up for Christmas 1985. Of course having no clue whatsoever in the irony of the Tin Man being a friend of Dorothy, I had decided to audition and somehow was chosen. I would be starring opposite Stacey Waters who had been inexplicably selected to play Dorothy. God knows how she managed to get the part, I could only wonder if it was maybe in part down to the magical powers of her woo-woo that by now most of the school's boy population had seen - or maybe it was the threat of violence from her parents that was somehow a deciding factor. Needless to say, Stacey went into full-on primadonna mode as the star of the show, swanning about, bossing everyone around and only stopping slightly short of demanding a basket of puppies in her dressing room. Being more troublesome to direct than Emu's appearance on the Michael Parkinson show, Stacey responded to her critics by, on the night of the play itself, throwing a hissy fit and refusing to turn up. With only a couple of hours to go until curtain up, the show's company managed to persuade meek class brainbox Hadassah Descombes to take on Dorothy's role, knowing that she would be able to learn all her lines in less than two hours. And she did. But alas it would be for nothing. For as the audience assembled in the hall and the lights were about to go up, Stacey swanned back in, reclaimed her role leaving poor Hadassah's moment of stardom to languish on the sidelines along with the only boy left in existence who hadn't yet seen Stacey's woo-woo.

The show was a fabulous success, the highlight of which (for everyone else anyway) was when I had to sweep up the scarecrow (a female version played by blonde vixen Kelly Owen) into my arms during her 'scared of the lion' scene, a rescuing of the damsel that met with nods of approval from my parents in the audience and the assumption - and constant teasing - that I had finally found a new girlfriend to replace Fiona.

However, any attempt to milk the afterglow of stage success was soon to be thwarted by The Christmas Raffle Tickets Humiliation, which would leave me with a fear of having an audience of more than three people for pretty much the next thirty years.

It was my competitive streak that did it, the desire to win that would be my undoing in front of an audience of approximately four hundred adults and children. It was the last day of Christmas term three days after *The Wizard of Oz*. As was tradition at Christmas at William Ford, its pupils were ritually sent out armed with raffle tickets, dispatched like Fagin's little helpers to accost our nearest and dearest with doe-eyed pressure to part with their hard-earned wages to buy one or preferably a whole book of the tickets in the vain chance of winning a prize sourced from the back shelves of Woolworths that they had no hope in winning. We were like an army of little chuggers tugging at the skirts and trousers of our family members and their friends, raking in funds for our school, which looking back now was clearly spent by our teachers on booze, cigarettes and in the case of one particular teacher, the latest top-shelf copy of *Escort* magazine.

To give us children added incentive to sell, sell, sell as many tickets as possible, it was announced that this year there would be a prize given to the child from each year that had sold the most raffle tickets. The hallowed prize would be presented on stage at the Christmas Assembly on the last day of term, with an audience consisting of every teacher and child in the school, every child's parents, the cleaning staff, dinner ladies and it wouldn't have surprised me if they had also roped in the local tramps to bolster numbers so that there would not a spare seat in the house. With such a crowd in attendance, I was determined to win. I needed the glory of being a winner, to bathe in that spotlight on stage as my peers and their hangers-on applauded my success. My star turn as the Tin Man had prepared me in good stead for this moment. My parent's gratitude at publicly sweeping a girl into my arms live on stage would fade into insignificance compared to the thunderous appreciation I would get at being the Fourth Year Pupil Who Has Sold the Most Christmas Raffle Tickets. It would be like the Oscars. I had to think about getting a speech prepared. Something witty and endearing, yet humble.

However, this year I had serious competition. My main rival in this challenging fund-raising was Kirsty Montgomery, a new pupil who had transferred in from another school for her final year. She was smug, self-confident and knew how to get her way. Even Stacey Waters felt threatened by her. And Kirsty had a killer weapon in her arsenal - her family. All three hundred and forty-eight of them. Yes, Kirsty was Irish. Imagine if all of *The Waltons* had married all of *The Brady Bunch* then each one went on to have a dozen kids, and those kids went on to have another dozen kids. Not to mention the ones that got divorced, remarried and had another dozen kids. This was the size of Kirsty's family - the Carringtons and the Ewings all rolled into one with no doubt more long-lost relatives popping out of the woodwork on a weekly basis to replace any that had died, been deported, gone missing or more than likely - been imprisoned. And each one was a guaranteed raffle ticket purchaser. I shouldn't have been that worried, for I was of Irish stock myself, my Dad's side of the family were of Irish heritage and he himself had nine brothers and sisters which meant I had a myriad of cousins. The problem was that most of them lived out in the wilds of Essex and were only ever glimpsed at weddings, funerals or any other family event that provided a free bar and buffet.

Regardless, I put in a sterling effort, selling as many tickets as humanly possible, thrilled each time I had to ask the teacher for a new book of tickets because I had run out. Often I would bump into Kirsty and try to elicit her current tally but like her manners, she kept her cards close to her flat chest. The only way any of us would discover the outcome was at the Christmas Assembly.

It came around quicker than I had anticipated. I guess nothing made the days tick away so fast as the nerve-wracking pressure to foist tickets on as many people as possible.

Everyone gathered. We got the hymn singing out of the way. I looked back to check my parents were there. There they were, squashed in at the back with Aunties Janet and Carol. I smiled and waved, excited at how proud of me I was going to make them.

It was time for the results. The First, Second and Third Year Pupils Who Had Sold the Most Raffle Tickets were announced and awarded in turn, ascending the stage in glory then descending again, waving their prizes triumphantly at their adoring public. And then, finally, it was time to announce the winning Fourth Year Pupil Who Had Sold the Most Raffle Tickets. The tallies had been counted and verified and the winner is...

I scrunched my eyes closed and actually prayed to God that my name would be the one uttered. I prayed that it would indeed be like the Oscars and the presenter of the award (in this case Mr. Brown) would rip open the envelope and inadvertently smile satisfied to himself that the name written inside was the one he secretly wanted to win.
I heard my name.
I couldn't believe it! I had won! I sprung to my feet immediately, like a meerkat popping up from the horizon. I was so elated at my victory that I bowed. I actually bowed to the sea of kids sat cross-legged all around me, to the teachers, the parents, the dinner ladies. Not for one second did I wonder why they all stared perplexed back at me, wondering what on earth I was doing. I looked around for Kirsty, wanting to see her reaction. I would be gracious about it, give her one of those sympathetic smiles. I couldn't see her. Maybe she had fled in tears.
I clambered over the row of crossed legs and squeezed out into the gangway and made my way to the stage, still giving the odd *"screw in the light bulb, clutch the pearls"* type wave that the Queen does, into the audience whose every pair of eyes were now darting amused between me and the happenings on the stage.

For climbing up onto stage at the other side of the hall - was Kirsty. I looked at her appalled. What was she doing?! Being a brazen thunder stealer?! *I* was the winner; it was *my* name that had been called out. Mr. Brown had given that satisfied smile that *I* was the victor. He had! Kirsty was now up on stage, gravitating towards Mr. Brown who seemed to be welcoming her as the crowd applauded. What? Something was clearly amiss here. I quickened my pace, leapt up on to the stage. Kirsty and Mr. Brown turned to look at me, stunned, as if I was a streaker that had suddenly invaded a crucial football match.
"What are you doing up here?", asked Mr Brown.
What a stupid question I thought.
"To get my prize Sir."
Kirsty was now staring at me in angry disbelief, furious that I was casting this unexpected shadow on her fifteen seconds of fame.
"But you're not the winner. Kirsty is."
I was aghast - as aghast as an eleven year old boy could be.
"But you called my name, Sir."
Mr. Brown shook his head. *"No, I didn't. I called Kirsty's. Now if you could go back and take your seat."*
At that precise moment, the entire crowd erupted into laughter. Every man, woman and child in the room roared in hysterics at the little boy in the diamond jumper and purple trousers, who obviously needed his ears de-waxed for thinking that his name sounded remotely like Kirsty. Even my Mum and Dad and Aunties were trying hard to suppress their amusement.

Suddenly the long walk back to my space on the floor seemed akin to walking the entire length of the Great Wall of China. It was my very first walk of shame, which would have a different context in later life as an adult but for now, as a deeply embarrassed eleven-year old boy, my nightmare Monster of Abnormality now had an even more evil twin, the Monster of Humiliation. My penchant for public disorder and degradation had happened again. My Dad was right, a boy like me *was* someone whose head was going to get up close and personal with the inside of a toilet on his ascension to senior school.

5 – PLEASE DON'T FLUSH MY HEAD!

1986 – 1988 (aged 11 – 13)

It was September 1986. I was eleven years old going on twelve. It was my first day at senior school. I had been dreading it all through the six weeks summer holiday, wishing somehow that I could stretch the space-time vortex and make the six weeks last forever. Which of course, if that was indeed possible, the downside would be that I would forever remain as a nerdy and shy eleven year old boy hiding a secret that was relentlessly banging on the door to my consciousness, rather like Jack Nicholson in *The Shining*, until it would eventually burst through into my brain with a wicked toothy grin taunting *"Here's 'funny'!"*

Now, on this cool September morning, I was standing outside the gates to Dagenham Priory Comprehensive, a school whose reputation was notorious all throughout Dagenham, in fact across the whole borough, for it was a school which made Strangeways prison seem like the wendy house from Leys Infants. I pondered whether it would be better to just go in and offer up my head straightaway for a bout of toilet flushing to get the inevitable over with before registration. I was after all, a lamb being led to the slaughter when even my school uniform consisted of zero fashion sense. I was the kid with 'jack-ups' (trousers drifting around the ankles) and white socks with black shoes, which I would come to learn on this first day was an extreme fashion faux-pas, one that would see me on the butt end of so much ridicule. How was I supposed to know that even a school uniform had to be worn a certain way? I wasn't even mildly aware that you could wear your school tie rebelliously with the thin side showing.

Within my first hours here, I realised that I had no chance of fitting in with the cool kids but instead was grateful to be welcomed with open arms into a fringe group, who would hang at the periphery of popularity, noses squashed against the window, convinced their invites to coolness had got lost in the post. They were a motley but friendly crew of outcasts. Dougie Brooks was a human 'before' advert for dental hygiene with snowdrift-like mounds of tartar on his lower teeth and breath which could paralyse insects from ten feet away. Then there were the 'It Boys'; a trio of Indian geeks named Sarjit, Injit and one actually called just It, a random Chinese lad with the unfortunate name of Arthur Cok, Daniel the only black kid in school, Sandy who lived in a caravan that clearly lacked a bath or shower and lastly, Julie the token ginger. We were a PC collective of ethnic and social minorities, of body odour, halitosis, disastrous hair, questionable fashion and in my case, repressed queerness. We were the Freaks and Geeks, long before such a group would ever be deemed hipster or cool. But I felt safe with them.

Sidelined from the higher echelons of popularity, day-by-day we sought refuge in our own shady spot in the school grounds where we would chat about the nerdy topics of the day, but in reality were hiding from our predators. For each one of us had an unofficially assigned tormentor. My particular nemesis was a boy in the year above me called Ben Taylor, a cocky, freckled wide-boy who, clearly projecting his own insecurities towards the explosion of sunset-red ginger hair atop his head, would ridicule my big ears (which I had inherited from my Grandad) much to the delight of his devoted minions. He would also complement his insults with a live action show, in which he would actually grab hold of my ears and 'fly' me around the playground calling me *Dumbo*, before 'peanutting' my school tie and despatching me back to my buddies who compared notes as to how my ordeal matched up to the their equivalents at the hands of their own bullies and whose own terror was outbalanced by the grateful relief that their ears were of normal size and thus it wasn't them that Ben had picked on.

My Dad had been right all along. Senior school *was* as terrifying as *Grange Hill*. The rose-coloured formative years had now given way to an animal kingdom-esque survival of the fittest battle. There were bullies, contraband cigarettes, monthly incidents of arson, not to mention the poor terrified teachers who would suddenly go off sick and sometimes never return, as was the case with French teacher Mrs. Kitchener who whilst trying in vain to teach that *'Voulez-vous coucher avec moi ce soir'* was not the only French that us kids needed to know, would be bombarded with rubbers as if she was being stoned to death medieval style. Meanwhile nervous breakdowns were the order of the day for history teacher Mr. Patel who got his turban knocked off to be used as a football and geography teacher Mr. Croxley who was ridiculed and bullied by kids for his *"Jesus Creeper"* look - aka wearing socks with sandals. Meanwhile, back in the world of actual kid-on-kid warfare, hardly a day went by when there wasn't a punch-up or organised fight in the playing fields after school, spectacles that ticket touts could have made a mint from, such was the excited demand for a ringside seat. Even worse was the vicious girl-on-girl gladiator style combat. These skirmishes were less spontaneous than the male equivalents as the girls would first spend a few minutes pre-fight removing their earrings, tying their hair up into tight facelift-inducing ponytails and rearranging the multitude of rings on their fingers to create makeshift knuckledusters. Proceedings could then finally begin whilst the teachers had retreated to a safe corner, pretending (and too scared) not to notice.

Yes, senior school was a harsh new reality, more so for a young boy nearing his teenage years with a growing realisation that he really, truly, probably is queer. Dagenham Priory was no place for a gay boy. I thought of Toby Curtis and wondered what it was like for him at whatever senior school he had ended up in. I genuinely hoped that he was doing ok.

I did have one potential ace up my sleeve though which I hoped would be a particularly potent power of persuasion to my new peers that maybe I was cooler than they gave me credit for. And this trump card was Fiona. Yes, Fiona Coleman, my 'beard' from infancy that I had not seen for over four years had re-entered my life and was now at Dagenham Priory too, her beauty having blossomed even further in that her crown as Most Desirable Girl at School was still atop her now sans headband head.

Although Fiona was in the same year as me, she was in a different form class thus our paths would only cross at break times or in the one weekly Maths lesson that brought different classes together. Break times though were completely off limits in trying to approach Fiona, who, in record-breaking time, had somehow gathered her own slavishly devoted band of female followers, a precise number of girl sycophants that could have easily formed a girl band to rival *Sister Sledge* or *Bananarama*.

A sideways glance from Fiona was the only acknowledgement of my presence in her environs, but I wanted everyone to know that I had an existing connection with her, that we had been the Charles and Di of Leys Infants, that I had the honour of having been her first ever boyfriend. I would omit the details about The Postman's Knock Kissing Debacle although now aged eleven, the going around kissing girls left, right and centre might count in my favour in the aspiration to climb the ladder of coolness.

And so, during the amalgamated Maths class, I suddenly decided to confide in my desk buddy Paul, as he was drooling over Fiona, that she and I had been boyfriend and girlfriend in primary school. Paul of course, lacking any skill in decorum or social niceties, promptly announced my wild claim to the whole class, at which point silence descended and Fiona was asked to publicly corroborate the past existence of our infant bond. My fingers grasped the Football 1982 key ring in my pocket ready to show her, to remind her. She just laughed and flat out denied it, her sycophantic posse chortling and gasping that I had the audacity to suggest such a ridiculous thing. According to them, alien abduction would have been more believable. After all, I was the boy that had just got into trouble in English class for having to write a story of our choosing and who had opted to plagiarise *Dynasty*, with a word for word retelling of the scene in which nutty Claudia burns down the La Mirage hotel and foolishly dies because of it. Our English teacher Mr. Good's unimpressed reaction told me that whilst he must have been a *Dynasty* fan himself, having recognised that this was the source of my 'work', he was still furious to the level where I was summoned to the headmaster's office and forced to face the wall, no doubt so he and Mr. Good could snigger out of eyesight to me. Facing the wall was always a peculiar punishment, all it ever did was reveal that the school walls needed a good new lick of paint.

So I didn't bother to try and argue the truth of my claim about Fiona and I. Fair enough, maybe Fiona was finally getting her long-overdue revenge for The Postman's Knock Kissing Debacle on her sixth birthday. Or maybe she had very, very early onset dementia and just didn't remember. Not for the first time in my life so far, I was left humiliated but once the fuss had died down, Fiona, making sure she was unseen by anyone else, just gave me a knowing nod and slight smile, as if to say sorry but she had her social status amongst her female peers to preserve. A status that would have instantly diminished had a past involvement with the class nerd came to light. I completely understood. I barely ventured anywhere close to her proximity after that.

*

As the first couple of years of senior school dragged on by, my true sexual preferences were also being dragged kicking and screaming like a petulant child towards the closet door whose hinges were starting to wobble precariously. As my gay feelings started to increase exponentially, my natural reaction was to become even shyer, if that was even possible. Despite my repeated knack for causing all kinds of trouble, intrinsically I was a introverted boy and hardly a social animal at all. At the regular family parties at my Nan and Grandad's house, I would now be sat alone in the corner, a place of retreat that was eventually put to good use by my Aunties Janet and Carol when they relocated me next to the hi-fi stereo and made me DJ. I relished this task of having an excuse to be alone, making sure the music kept flowing, putting on vinyl record after vinyl record and would always take requests, well in reality being nagged by my Aunts to put on *Oops Upside Your Head* which would send all the adults inexplicably plunging to the floor in sudden excitement to pretend to be in what looked like a mimed version of a rowing boat. Then there was *Agadoo* which involved the pushing of pineapples and shaking of trees, even though I knew that pineapples did not grow on trees, as well as whatever other cheesy novelty record was currently always being played at suburban working class house parties across the country.

Naturally, I would sneak in some tunes of my own liking, namely the latest Cher or *Heart* record which would invariably each time bring the dancing to a complete halt and give various Uncles a well-timed opportunity to head into the kitchen to try and grope the boobs of various buxom female family friends or obscure cousins that, now all grown up, had *"a right pair of knockers on her"*, said in a way that was in no way appropriate for someone you were a) related to and b) had babysat a few years previous.

Anyway, another upside of being DJ meant that I wasn't being forced to get up and dance. I wasn't a dancer, I took after my Dad in that respect, he doing his Dad dances which involved sporadic punching of the air like he was Rocky Balboa. In-between putting records on the turntable to keep the party going at full tilt, I would sit in my spot, analysing the way different members of my family tripped the light fantastic, or in the case of some inebriated elderly relatives, tripped full stop. Cousin Kim's dancing was the need-a-wee shuffle with her feet rooted to the same spot as she swayed from side to side. Grandad would dance like he was galloping and riding a horse and Nan Shirley would wave her hands in front of her as if she was swatting flies during an epileptic fit. Mum never danced at all, she would instead get to the party three hours early (easy to do when you live only two doors away) so she could bagsy the prime spot on the settee and not move one inch all evening, just waiting for me to pass by so that she could hand me her empty glass for me to refill for her, or a bare plate thrust into my hand to be topped up from the buffet, with a detailed order of four cheese and pineapple sticks, two pork pies and one of Auntie Janet's chicken vol-au-vents, dictated to me like I was Mum's personal waiter. Worst case scenario was when Mum needed a wee so she would recruit me to mind her seat for her that was being enviously eyed by various female relatives of a certain age who needed a rest after yet another bout of the *Hokey Bloody Cokey*. I could have just put *Oops Upside Your Head* on again so that they could rest their bums in the imaginary rowing boat on the floor. One time though, my seat warming for Mum went tragically awry when Great Aunt Edna manipulated me into vacating Mum's seat by faking a fainting fit. Sensing Mum's imminent post-wee wrath, I fled back to the safe haven of my DJ spot, watching from afar as my Mum returned to partake in a Mexican style stand-off with Edna, who had miraculously recovered as soon as she sat down but now had to endure Mum just towering over her, giving her 'evils' until Edna's fear translated into her own urgent need to urinate at which moment, Mum promptly and victoriously reclaimed her throne whilst shooting daggers at me for letting her down.

I never liked to let Mum down. I was the apple of her eye, and according to my younger brother, her favourite. It's true, I was unashamedly a 'Mummy's Boy'. But at this particular party, I would indeed let Mum down, not by the

Seat on the Settee Scandal - but by the consumption of my very first alcoholic beverage.

To be honest, I hadn't even known it was alcohol that I was gulping down. Auntie Carol had after all, just told me that it was this new fruit juice from the supermarket, when in actual fact it was a Harvey Wallbanger, courtesy of Carol's mischievous need to bring me *"out of my shell"* at twelve years old. Three faux 'fruit juices' later, I proceeded to spectacularly vomit all over the hi-fi just as sneaked-in-to-the-playlist Cher was warbling that she had *"found someone to take away the heartache"* when I had simultaneously found something to take away the contents of my stomach. Poor Cher never got to finish her song which was a blessed relief for some. Meanwhile, Mum was livid as she had to finally forego her seat on the settee and march me home, where she at first forced my head down the toilet to bring up more torrents of sick, fulfilling Dad's prophecy of my head flushing, only not in the way that I had been expecting. I was then unceremoniously despatched to bed, which Mum placed a bucket beside in case more aftershocks of retching were to take place during the night. It was the same bucket that I would jokingly bring to my Mum every Sunday evening to *"catch her tears into"* as she sobbed at every episode of *Surprise, Surprise,* namely the predictable reunions with long-lost relatives who had clearly emigrated to Australia for good reason. Which was an attractive option for me at the moment. Mum would always bawl as Cilla Black launched into *"the unexpected hits you between the eyes"*, as now, instead, the unexpected ramifications of her twelve year old son being intoxicated was hitting the bucket upstairs, over and over again. Surprise, surprise indeed.

*

As the final months of 1987 came around to celebrate my thirteenth birthday and thus becoming An Actual Teenager, it had been decreed by various members of my family that I needed to start showing a proper interest in girls.

Up until now, no-one had ever addressed my lack of engagement with the opposite sex since my infantile union with Fiona. I was only thirteen but in Dagenham, boys of this age were supposed to have at least felt a boob by now. Of course, by now I knew what sex was, well between a man and a woman anyway. And thanks to my friend Daniel, I also knew lots more that I wished I could blank out. This had come courtesy of a porn video called *Tangerine Dream* which Daniel had found hidden in his Dad's wardrobe and which was now providing some lunch time viewing for me, him and Dougie Brooks. A fish and chips lunch was probably not the best choice to be devouring here as we watched agog at some fat bearded man pulling something string-like out of a woman's vagina, before licking it, sucking on it and re-inserting it as she moaned in pleasure - or quite possibly pain. Even Jackie Collins wouldn't have written filth like this. *"That's her ovaries"* claimed Daniel smugly; referring to what apparently had just been repeatedly pulled in and out of the poor woman's fanny like a cross between a cheese string and the world's worst yo-yo. I was dubious. Dougie looked traumatised. We rewound the video and paused it for a better look but the juddering freeze frame did nothing to clarify whether it was indeed the poor woman's ovaries that Fat Bearded Bloke was snacking on. We would later find out of course that this was physically impossible but for now, I was left convinced that I would burn in Hell for witnessing such a depraved thing.

And so, unaware of my *Tangerine Dream*-infused education of the supposed pleasurable-but-actually-looks-painful workings of a woman's vagina, various members of my family commenced a series of elaborate set-ups with young girls. It was a fierce competition between my Aunts and Uncles as to who could set me up with a girl first, regardless as to whether she was in, out of, or had completely skipped puberty. Oh this is Jenny, Cousin Pam on your Dad's side's cousin's daughter's auntie's niece with the big boobs. Don't worry you're barely related, go cop a feel. One time, Auntie Carol upped the ante by trumping Auntie Janet's choice of the younger daughter of her friend, by actually bringing along a young female refugee from El Salvador called Dominique. How and why Dominique and her family were seeking refuge in Dagenham was never explained. A kiss or juvenile grope with me was the only important issue. Go on, she's just escaped a war-torn country, a quick sympathy tongue sandwich will make her feel better! My bedroom's free upstairs, go on, up you go, I won't tell your Mum.

This endless sourcing of potential female matches for me was a human trafficking version of Auntie Reenie's 'Tea Towel War' with her neighbour Kath Wagstaff. For some unknown reason, Reenie and Kath were engaged in a long standing feud that had now evolved into one-upmanship of placing tea towels from ever more exotic destinations on their neighbouring washing lines to try and outdo and install jealousy in each other. Reenie's tea towel from Devon would be overshadowed by Kath's tea towel from France, which Reenie would retaliate with via a tea towel from Benidorm which was humiliatingly shot down with Kath's tea towel from Florida. Neither Auntie Reenie nor Kath had actually been to any of these places, the tea towels only procured on their behalf by holidaying friends and relatives.

Now with the need to get me At Least Feeling a Boob after my thirteenth birthday, tea towels had been replaced by nubile young girls. *"This one's from Barking!" "Big deal, this one's from El Salvador, beat that!"* The pressure to get my first girlfriend since Fiona was unrelenting. I wasn't even safe from the pimping on our annual holidays to the family caravan in Weymouth with the egging on to go chat up any girl of around the same age (give or take a year or two) who even glanced at me or breathed the same air as me within a ten metre radius. Imagine their delight when a girl actually asked me out in the amusement arcade. I made an excuse and turned her down of course, not telling that instead I was being mesmerised by a boy who was part of another family staying two caravans across from ours. In the end, the only way I could get my family off my back was to pretend that I had a massive teenage crush on Lesley, the long-legged twenty-something holiday rep on site who sauntered around the holiday camp in very, very short shorts and was also being simultaneously worshipped by my Great Uncle Derek in a much more pervy way. At night, I could hear him masturbating in his room, the squeaking of the caravan alerting me to the presence of Lesley in his imagination.

My pretend love for Lesley was a gamble but that was not a problem considering my entire family were devoted gamblers. For my brother and I, a vast majority of these holidays to Weymouth were spent in the doorways of bookmakers waiting for Mum and Dad to re-emerge whilst back at home, Mum and Dad were always 'down the betting shop' or we would spend regular Saturday nights at Walthamstow Dog Stadium watching greyhounds chasing after a mechanical rabbit, one that they could never catch, in the same way that I was seemingly unable to catch a member of the opposite sex. But then if I was a greyhound in one of these races, I would have been the unenthusiastic shy one languishing at the back, coming in last, for I didn't want to catch one at all. Because I was the thing that no-one ever talked about.

But in late 1987, it turned out that they *had* to talk about it - or rather the whole nation did - as the unthinkable happened - a gay kiss occurred between two men in BBC soap opera *EastEnders*. I was already a massive fan of the show, having watched it since the very first episode only two years before. In fact, the whole family were addicted to it and family Christmases now consisted of an extra ritual, that of gathering around the telly to watch the Christmas day drama in fictional Walford. And now, in November 1987, my family and I watched as the character of Colin revealed himself to be homosexual and shared a kiss with his new boyfriend Barry. Now this kiss wasn't a tongue sandwich or even the meeting of lips, it was just a simple peck on the forehead, a step up from Steven Carrington's cuddle with his boyfriend in *Dynasty* a couple of years earlier, but still, just a touch of lips planted on frown lines was all that two gay men on prime time TV were allowed to exchange. Well, according to *The Sun* and other hysteria-inducing tabloids, the whole nation was in uproar, collectively projectile vomiting at such a terrible sight on their TV screens, locking their children away in the attic to shield them from such predatory sexual terrorism, as well as complaining in their thousands to the BBC to clearly atone for having no life of their own to live. It was just A Kiss on a Forehead. A reaction of such an apocalypse-inducing catastrophe did nothing to encourage me to take another baby step towards opening that closet door. For I had now witnessed for myself, yet again, the rife and prevalent homophobia within the society I was growing up gay in. The introduction of Section 28 by Maggie and her cronies was bad enough but now, even just a simple peck on the forehead between two male TV characters was enough to supposedly bring about The End of the World.

I had already survived The End of Days once already that year when earlier in the Summer, *The Sun* (of course) had printed a front page headline that the world was going to end on a sunny day in August due to a once-in-a-billion years alignment of the planets that would somehow cause a gravitational pull that would rip the Earth apart. Not realising of course that it was clearly a Slow News Summer for *The Sun* and combined with my existing fear of death, I believed every word. And when the fateful day came around, I said a tearful goodbye to my Mum and Dad and went upstairs to my bedroom where I lay down and waited for The End. But of course, like the admittance of my true sexuality, it never came.

*

1988 eventually made its grand debut and with it, my confusing crushes on good-looking men were developing to the point where I was now gathering keepsakes of all my forbidden feelings, mementoes that were being honed and collected thanks to an increase in my pocket money. I had already purchased videos of *Top Gun*, purely because I fancied Tom Cruise, and *Dirty Dancing*, which involved repeated play-and-pause viewings of Patrick Swayze's bare bum to the point where the tape would start to spool. My number one prized possession though was Robin Beck's number one hit song *The First Time*, which was the theme from the *Coca-Cola* advert and the seven-inch single of which sported the most dreamy college hunk I had ever laid eyes on. Well, three quarters of his face anyway as prominence on the cover was given to some beret-clad girl about to glug a bottle of coke. I would kiss the image of this unnamed guy nightly before bed in a bizarre *I Think I Might Be Gay and If I Am, I Really Fancy You* kind of ritual. Still three-quarters of this drop-dead gorgeous guy's face was enough to represent all that my subconscious really wanted, although of course I would never, ever admit that out loud to myself, let alone anyone else, the only evidence being Tom Cruise, Patrick Swayze's bum and the now mushy-with-saliva cover of *The First Time*. And then along came *Neighbours*.

It was the little teatime Australian soap opera, a twenty minute daily serving of dodgy acting and wobbly sets, that somehow in 1988 took the whole nation by storm. Everyone was crazy for it. Of course I wasn't immune to the *Neighbours* obsession and had started watching it inadvertently after rushing home at lunchtimes to set the VCR to tape *Knots Landing*, and ending up with *Neighbours* and quiz show *Going for Gold* on the tape as well. Because of this, I was already addicted to *Going for Gold*, the game show hosted by Henry Kelly that featured contestants from all over Europe. I always wanted the English one to win. Reading *The Sun* was having that kind of effect on me.

And then I discovered the world of *Neighbours*, all sunshine and loveliness and populated by these Australian dreamboats called Scott Robinson and Mike Young. Little did I know that this equally little show would be the catalyst that would sow the seeds for my eventual departure from Dagenham five years later.

It wasn't hard to get obsessed with *Neighbours*, such as was the random storylines whose most important purpose was to get the likes of Scott and Mike running around without their tops on. But somehow my lust for Jason Donovan and Guy Pearce became offset with a weird crush I suddenly developed on Kylie Minogue. Charlene from *Neighbours* had suddenly become a pop star, namely so that I could finally learn that her surname was not pronounced Mine-a-goo like I thought. She was the diminutive Aussie temptress storming to the peak of the UK Top 40 with her debut single *I Should Be So Lucky* which I raced out and bought after feeling all giddy watching Kylie frolic in her inexplicably bubbly bubble bath in the song's video. I had even bought my weekly copy of *Smash Hits* so I could learn all the lyrics. But what did this strange crush on Kylie mean? It felt just as weird as all my boy crushes. Had my feelings towards other boys really been 'just a phase' and all I had needed was a Aussie soap vixen-come-pop-diva to tempt me back to the path of normality?

I was of course, nothing but a manipulated new disciple of a gay icon in the making who was summoning her gay followers. The 'crush' on Kylie was in fact subliminal recruitment by her, sitting in her bubble bath, blowing the foam of gayness at the screen for us to breathlessly catch. It's okay, Kylie, I was getting the message. I had *I Should Be So Lucky* on 7 inch. Seven inches of pure gayness sitting in my bedroom. You've got me. You can now continue honey trapping countless other confused teenage boys into thinking they have a crush on you when in actual fact the whole 1988-89 discography of your hits is in fact one long letter from you pleading with us to come out. I had your letter, being read to me telepathically from inside a whole bathtub of *Matey* bubble bath. You are telling me that *I Should Be so Lucky* to be brave enough to come out of the closet, I had *Got to Be Certain* whether I fancied girls, boys or both because you are not impressed with the frenzied back-and-forth *Locomotion* movement of my confused feelings. I have to *Put My Hand on My Heart* and tell myself the truth otherwise there will be *Tears on my Pillow*. Although you *Wouldn't Change a Thing* about me, it was still *Never Too Late*. *Je Ne Sais Pas Pourquoi*? I wish I could answer that but I don't know any French because my French teacher is too busy being stoned to death by rubbers. But never mind, I will embrace by gayness *Especially for You*. Well, eventually.

I actually kept a scrapbook of all things Kylie and Jason, the pride of place picture being one of them photographed together on a beach on Bali, during the height of their romance. Kylie was topless and Jason was just in his Speedos. I would gaze at this picture daily. But it wasn't Kylie's boobs that I found titillating; it was the bulge in Jason's trunks. By the end of 1988, the print on Jason's trunks had been worn away from the picture and my sexuality was determined to burst through the fraying threads of my blanket of denial, the glint of glittery gay sunlight peeking through the crack in the slightly ajar closet door. And as the last year of the 1980s dawned, I would soon find myself falling in love with another boy. My best friend in fact.

6 – THE TEENAGE GIGOLO

1989 (aged 14)

In early 1989, a new Australian soap opera arrived on British teatime screens. Billed as ITV's rival to *Neighbours*, which by now was the show that all the kids - even the cool ones - were obsessed with, *Home and Away* was a sexier version that was set by the sea so featured Aussie hunks wearing not much more than swimming trunks for most of each episode. Needless to say I became a devoted viewer from episode one. As a fourteen year old boy, my hormones were already starting to rage and with the arrival of *Home and Away*, were now actually bellowing into a full-on meltdown what with the daily dose of Australian hunks in trunks parading across the new portable TV set that I had got for Christmas from my parents the previous year. A television that was of course, safely ensconced in my bedroom which meant I could enjoy the delights of *Home and Away*'s finest in complete privacy. It was therefore only fitting that I had my very first orgasm after viewing one particular episode that featured some kind of surf competition. I guess I could thank ITV for me now discovering the delights of masturbation. And I'm pretty sure I wasn't the only secretly-gay teenage boy in the country who was now wanking in perfect time to the warbling theme of *"Closer each day..."*

I had been sexually awakened. Desires were now rife inside me. And with that came my first real yearning for other boys. But first I had my own alluring image to work on. The hunks gracing the screen in *Home and Away* presented a fantastical idea of the aspirations that I had to become one of them. I was a six foot tall fourteen year old boy who was pasty, thin, gangly and riddled with spots. I had even overheard some kids at school secretly refer to me as The Beanpole. So seeing the shirtless older teenage boys on *Home and Away* with the perfect abs and chiselled bodies only made me feel worse about my own physical appearance, not to mention my complete lack of style.

But nevertheless, I was determined to push forward with my self-styled transformation, to finally throw off the shackles of nerdiness and become something a lot more beguiling. I started wearing my school tie on the thin side and drastically re-styled my floppy mop of hair into a slicked-back quiff, created by Auntie Carol's private hairdresser Trevor, an overly camp bohemian sporting a ponytail and a single earring who would set up his travelling salon in my Nan's kitchen and whilst cutting my hair, would regale me with tales of how he had time-travelled back into his great-great-grandmother's living room. I didn't care what a nutter he was, he was giving me the fancy haircut that would be another step towards my Aussie hunk-esque transformation. It was worth enduring his probing questions about my interest (or more precisely my lack of it) in any girls at school. It was clear that he suspected I was a younger version of him, minus the time-travelling. Obviously trying to out secretly gay teenage boys was a nifty sideline to a short back and sides and adventures in space-time.

It didn't matter though, for I now had a radical new haircut, kept in place with a surfeit of nuclear green-coloured hair gel sourced from the local pound shop. I felt cool, but not yet cool enough. Something else was required. I needed an earring. Single stud or small hoop earrings were all the rage amongst the most alluring boys at school, as if their earrings possessed magnetic capabilities to pull devoted followers slavishly to their side. More than that, sporting a single earring seemed to have this magical way of elevating your social status instantly from the bottom rung of the ladder straight up to the upper echelons of peer-worship in less time than it took to shoot a tiny hole through your fleshy earlobe. Indeed the acquisition of an earring had worked wonders for Gary Britton. Formerly the slightly simple kid with a penchant for alighting his strange cloud-like bouffant with a succession of Bunsen burners, Gary had one day rocked up in class with his left ear now adorning a tiny stud earring that glinted in the sunlight and could have almost been accompanied by swelling orchestral music as he entered the classroom to impressed gasps from our classmates. By the end of the day, thanks to the new Jewel in His Ear, Gary had been absorbed into the welcoming and hallowed arms of the Cool Boys Club.

The Cool Boys Club was a relatively small clique. Its members were trouble-making cocky blonde Stevie Pope, (forever organising fights with his rivals), John James, (sporting the same name as the actor playing Jeff Colby in *Dynasty* but with a much less hairier chest), Jimmy Miles (barely ever seen due to constant truancy, no doubt just to maintain his air of mystery) and presiding over them all - Stuart Pincer, the self-aware school heart-throb who would swagger through the school like a cowboy in a Western, the envy of boys and the wet dreams fodder of girls. The Cool Boys Club was like a Tory cabinet, all white men, no ethnic minorities allowed, and I'm sure, definitely no gays. I should note here, that I was far from defining myself as gay. I was still deep in denial, despite my lust for TV hunks. I had feelings that I could never admit to anyone, let alone to myself, convincing myself that they had to be *"just a phase"*. And these forbidden feelings were manifesting themselves now into my application for membership into the Cool Boys Club.

And if it could work for Gary Britton, it could work for me. I had to get my ear pierced. It was as simple as that. Of course, I didn't dare ask for permission from my Mum. It was bad enough when she saw I was sporting a blackhead, I could only imagine her reaction at a small piece of cheap gold attached to my ear. Nonetheless, I wanted an earring.

And so, one afternoon after school, I told a fib that I would be late home because of an after-school study session and took a detour to a backstreet newsagent in Old Dagenham Village, in the shadow of the church where Mum and Dad got married. It was the same newsagents where I sometimes accompanied my friend Daniel on his frequent sojourns to shoplift a copy of *The Sunday Sport* so he could fascinatingly mull over the weirdly huge boobs attached to even weirder women to be found inside. So whilst a baffling display of newspaper mammaries were to be found freely advertised here, ear piercings were not. But Daniel had told me that they were unofficially provided if you asked nicely.

So here I was. I took a deep breath and entered the newsagents. It was like going into a drug den to make a dodgy deal. I nervously asked the poodle-permed woman at the counter if I could have my ear pierced. Without even an affirmative response to my simple query, Poodle Perm just shouted *"BRENDA!!!"* like a personalised spoken car alarm triggered by a heavy downpour. For a second I wondered if Brenda was some kind of authority to march me out of the shop but suddenly, the tatty curtains to the back room were aggressively parted and out squeezed Brenda herself, a terrifying looking woman, with barely any teeth and a cigarette dangling from her lips that was more ash than actual cigarette.

"One or both?", she growled at me.

"One or both what?", I gulped, confused.

"Yer ears, stupid!"

Customer service skills had obviously eluded Brenda in life.

"Er, just one."

"Three quid. Stud?"

Realising she was not referring to what I hoped to become, I nodded. She disappeared back into the back room for what seemed like an eternity whilst Poodle Perm gave me a *"Your mum is so going to freak out at you for this"* wry smile.

Brenda finally reappeared with a tiny folding chair, and what seemed to be a small gun in her hand. She wasn't quite James Bond with her weapon, more like his foe Jaws with her sad remnants of staggeringly cigarette-stained and blackened teeth.

"*Sit*", she barked, suddenly going all Mary Woodhouse on me.

It was all over in seconds as she pinned me into the chair, grabbed my left earlobe, and fired the gun into it, creating a hole which promptly had a small stud earring jammed into it.

My torture session at the hands of Brenda was over, the magic key to the Cool Boys Clubs was shining in my left earlobe and now all I had to do was weather the reaction from my Mum.

Understandably, she hit the roof. I was always a good kid, barely ever got shouted at by my Mum, whereas my younger brother was always on the receiving end of her angry tirades. As much as I loved my Mum, she did have a fearsome temper on her which was sometimes downright scary. The arguments she and my Dad had were legendary, leading me to sometimes scream at them to get a divorce, convinced that they did not love each other. One particular epic argument that I bore witness to and is forever etched in my memory was when Mum's nagging of Dad needing to use a napkin whilst eating his regular post-pub chicken chow mein resulted in said chow mein dumped over my Mum's head, the noodles in her hair giving off a Medusa vibe complemented with curry sauce streaking down her face. My Mum had retaliated by hurling the empty plate at my Dad and World War 3 had erupted in a suburban living room in Dagenham. Anyway ChowMeinGate was now being superseded by EarringGate and this time, I was the cause of the anger. At first, Mum demanded the earring's immediate removal but, remembering the sole piece of advice that Brenda had given me whilst I was recoiling from the horrors of her teeth, I gleefully informed Mum that if the earring was taken out within the first week, it would get infected and ooze pus like a scene from *Ghostbusters*.

The earring stayed. It did the trick and within days, I had somehow wormed by way into the Cool Boys Club, well a faction of it as it seemed my new membership had timed with a drastic upheaval in its structure. Jimmy Miles had finally been expelled and some fight over a girl had torn Stevie Pope and John James away from Stuart so Stuart was now clearly vulnerable and in need of new cohorts. Enter moi!

Cut to a few weeks later and somehow Stuart the School Stud and I now seemed to be best mates. He was the first best friend I had since Martin Schofield had disappeared into the vortex known as going to a different senior school.

Mine and Stuart's friendship was surreal and inexplicable, even more of a mismatch than my 'hand-holding' with Fiona in Leys Infants. It was like a cheesy Hollywood buddy movie, the shy quiet nerdy virgin forced to team with the wisecracking ladies man. And Stuart certainly was a ladies' man. He was voraciously sexually active for a fourteen going on fifteen year old boy. Never a day went by when he didn't regale me with the tales of his latest conquests, told with such box-ticking (in more ways than one) glee, that I half expected his bedroom wall to have some police-style rogue suspects chart covering it, adorned with the faces of the entire teenage female population of Dagenham with each one crossed through with a 'been there, done that' tick and marks out of ten. Well he was a teenage boy after all, as was I, our hormones were off the charts and whilst mine could only be channelled elsewhere by staying up late secretly watching limp willies in saucy German movies being beamed in from our newly acquired satellite dish, Stuart's hormones were being bandied around the whole of Dagenham, being spent in his own and various teenage girls bedrooms, the backs of alleyways and that old cliché of behind the bike sheds.

But Stuart was my hero. I adored him. I hung on his every word. For I was now madly in love with him.

*

Deep down, I knew from the start that it was a love affair doomed to be forever unrequited. He was straighter than straight, brazenly confident with his sexuality that could easily be misinterpreted and blindly misconstrued by his secretly-yet-still-not-fully-aware-that-he's-gay-best-mate. Parading around naked in the sports hall changing rooms might have seemed like horseplay to Stuart, but for me, it was increasing my love for him. I channelled the passion of this unrequited love into trying to beef myself up with the aid of a bedroom multi-gym ordered from Auntie Janet's *Kays* mail order catalogue. Oh, how I loved studying the pages in the *Kays* catalogue, spending an inordinate amount of time around my Nan's house absorbed in the pages of the male underwear section, admiring the bulges inside the cheap pants being sold. Or course the titillation from this was counterbalanced by an even deeper realisation that I would never get the lithe, muscular bodies of the models wearing the pants. But still I tried to soldier on. But whilst I was busy struggling with a pec-deck crammed into my bedroom, something else was threatening my love for Stuart. Or rather, *someone* else.

Dave Barclay was another flower in bloom, albeit a thorny one puncturing my unrequited love bubble with Stuart. Formerly one half of a double act with uber-geek and *Doctor Who* obsessed outcast James Wilson; Dave had unceremoniously dumped his best friend and set his sights on replacing him with Stuart. Dave was relentless in pursuing a best-buddy friendship with Stuart. He was actually becoming a clone of him, dressing like him, styling his hair the same way, even emulating Stuart's swagger so that when they sauntered across the playground together, it resembled some weird synchronised dance move from a cheesy *Stock Aitken and Waterman* video. In fact, Stuart and Dave were turning into the pop duo *Bros* with their now near-identikit looks and mannerisms. And I was the third member of the band whose name nobody could remember and who clearly never really fitted in with the two hot brothers. A love triangle had formed. Of course Dave wasn't in love with Stuart like I was, as he was just another lad possessing an overly-sociable penis, as together, he and Stuart laid waste to many a teenage vagina in sexual adventures that ranged in variety from fingering Tracy McCarthy, getting hand jobs from Denise Potts and the gift of 'bombay rolls' from Julie Loveday, which were in this case the gift that did not stop giving, which meant that Julie's boobs must have been suffering from serious chaffing due to all the penises that had been massaged between them. I was confused as to why the latter was called a Bombay Roll. It resembled nothing like an Indian dish. This juvenile exploring of body parts and sexual activity occurred mostly in Stuart's lounge on school lunch breaks as I was relegated to being the bouncer in the hallway, keeping watch through the window for Stuart's mum coming home whilst also escorting inside a succession of teenage girls desperate for a go on the Stuart-Dave Penis Merry-Go-Round as well as other boys that *"wanted a go"* with Tracy et al. I felt like a madam in a brothel with Dado rails and woodchip wallpaper. *"Your name's not down; you're not getting a bombay roll from Judy. What's with the attitude? Well you're certainly not getting to finger Tracy now!"*

Weirdly, I felt I was missing out on all the vaginal exploration and stress-ball like groping of boobs and thus somehow found myself weeks later 'going out' with Joanne Albright. She had decided that she fancied me and asked me out, not directly of course but in true teenage style by getting her friend Leanne Cresswell to badger me into saying yes. Lisa managed to corner me at exactly the right time, when my defences were low, after being exhausted from my watch shift at the latest roman orgy in Stuart's house. So I said yes. Fuck! I had just agreed to go out with a girl! Panic!

However, according to others, Joanne was clearly a lesbian in the making as she dressed in boys clothes and had a boy's haircut (it later turned out that she was). She must have known I was clearly gay so a lavender relationship ensued as we both unwittingly helped conceal our real and of course unspoken desires. Of course none of this was ever addressed and we were happy with keeping up the pretence of our union. Well, when I say union, the truth was that our pathetic relationship involved not once being in each other's company. We even passed each other once after school and just said hello to each other, clearly not the workings of a boyfriend and girlfriend. Needless to say, it lasted just over a week until I got dumped - via proxy of course from Leanne Cresswell who nonchalantly informed me of the dissolution of mine and Joanne's 'romance' in that Joanne *"didn't want to go out with me"* with anymore. Well, we hadn't gone out anywhere together anyway. I tried to feign upset but could barely conceal the relief at the end of my non-relationship.

*

Meanwhile, all the Benny Hill style shenanigans that Stuart was partaking in was resulting in him getting a bit behind with his school work and needing to catch up fast. Obviously the amount of time spent fingering and getting bombay rolls from the local strumpets was taking a toll on his education. And so, as was expected of the nerdy-yet-devoted best friend, I offered to help. No ulterior motives whatsoever. None. Okay, maybe just a little one. For this was my chance, to spend quality one-on-one time with Stuart, to bond again and cast out the negative influences of Dave. Stuart suggested that we have homework evenings in his bedroom every Thursday. I could even sleep over if I wanted. Of course, at this last suggestion, I think I might have actually exploded in my pants. Sleep over meant sharing the same bed, meant us in just boxers and T-shirt at the absolute maximum. It was mildly ironic that Stuart and mine's quality boy bonding time had been facilitated by his relentless pursuit of the other sex.

Needless to say the anticipation I felt for the impending arrival of our first Thursday evening together was on a par with people that queued up days before to bagsy a prime spot for the local sale in C&A.

Stuart only lived two streets away, a mere two minutes stroll, yet on that first Thursday evening, I still arrived fifteen minutes early. Prior to this I had been stressing over whether to shave the little sprout of bumfluff off my chin and what fashion choice to plump for from my limited wardrobe choices. I needed to wear something casual yet something that made me look cool. Now, let me re-iterate that my personal fashion sense was dubious to say the least, even worse than the togs my Mum chose to dress me in when I was younger. Clearly the particular gay gene that imbued you with a delightful sense of style had not yet manifested itself in me. Still, I took comfort in the fact that I wasn't alone. It was 1989 after all and *Stock, Aitken and Waterman* songs were not only clogging up the Top 40 but they were also influencing the dress sense of many a teenager up and down the country. Thanks to this I actually owned a pair of dungarees. Yes, a pair of dungarees. Ordered of course from (as were my most of my ill-fitting clothes) my Auntie Janet's *Kays* catalogue, these hung off my wiry, thin frame leaving me resembling the love child of that bloke from *Dexy's Midnight Runners* and one of those scary women inmates from *Prisoner Cell Block H*. Of course I couldn't see this and when selecting this as my outfit of choice for Date Night - sorry - Homework Night, yes HOMEWORK night - with Stuart, I decided I looked as cool and desirable as Jason Donovan or Marti Pellow. Rick Astley, not so much.

And so I made my way to Stuart's, arriving, like I said, a whole fifteen minutes early, despite his house being less than a two minute stroll away. His mum, June, answered the door. She smiled that she had been expecting me. I took this as a good sign of Stuart's enthusiasm for my arrival. She stated that he was in the shower. Blimey, he was even freshening up for me. June and I made polite small talk in the living room for what seemed like an eternity, consisting mainly of in-depth conversation starters such as *"How's school?"*, *"Did you see EastEnders on Tuesday?"* and *"I saw your Mum in Woolworths last week"* which of course was not a question at all as June worked in Woolworths, where I often sent my Mum with my pocket money and a list of the 7" chart singles that I wanted, so June seeing her there was not that much of a shocker that warranted a conversation but smacked of desperate filler to take up the remaining minutes until Stuart emerged from the shower like a resurrected Bobby Ewing in *Dallas*.

Finally, Stuart materialised into the living room, his hair still damp. My heart leapt in tandem with me leaping out of the armchair at the sight of him. Like it was his turn to be the madam in a brothel, he summoned me upstairs. As we ascended each step one at a time, me trailing behind him, Stuart told me that he had something that he wanted to show me. I visibly gulped.

We entered his bedroom-meets-boudoir and he shut the door behind us. The air was electric. Maybe all the girls that had been given the gift of his penis were just an experiment. Maybe he really wanted.... Stuart opened a drawer and took out a... can of *Lynx* deodorant. Apparently - and unbeknownst to a boy like me - this was THE must have for any cool and 'with it' boy. It was new, it was exotic. Everyone was wearing it. It was a flavour called *'Marine'*. *Boots* had sold out. It was just a fucking deodorant. Nevertheless, Stuart was thrilled that his armpits now reeked of *Lynx Marine* and were thus now the trendiest-smelling armpits in Dagenham, if not the whole of Essex. He asked if I wanted to try some. Me? He was willing to share this hallowed sought-after merchandise with *me*? This one can of contraband goods with a street value of many a teenage boys' reputation? And so there we were for the next few minutes or so, sharing, sniffing at and spraying *Lynx* between us, like two addicts in a crack den. We were bonding. Dave seemed an imaginary nemesis now. Stuart and I were back together. Eventually, after our armpits smelled so Marine-like that the world's oceans would be jealous, we kicked back and relaxed, watched *The Bill*, did a token amount of homework then it was time. Bedtime. I was staying over. I was about to share this single bed with the boy who I was in love with. A tiny single bed. There would be unavoidable skin-on-skin contact. It would be top and tail of course but that didn't matter to me.

Stuart undressed and reclined on his bed in just his boxer shorts and a gold chain draped around his neck, looking like some stud that had leapt out of the pages from one of my secret Jackie Collins novels. I gingerly followed suit and slipped out of my dungarees as we both got under the covers. The tension emanating from me was palpable. It was at this moment that two things happened. First, Stuart decided to tell me of the simply wonderful blow job that he had received from the thirty-five year old mother of his friend Paul. Apparently, he had been at Paul's house whilst his mother was hoovering in just her skimpy negligee, as you obviously do in the company of teenage boys, one thing led to another and before you could say Dustin Hoffmann in *The Graduate*, Stuart's dick had leapt over the age barrier and illegally into the mouth of a woman over twenty years older than him. It was when my mouth dropped open, appalled at this confession, that the second incident occurred - as the bedroom door flung open and Stuart's younger sister Amy screamed the house down at the sight of us, in the manner of a young girl finding an imaginary monster under the bed, by shouting at anyone who could hear that Stuart and his mate were in bed with each other!

I didn't sleep a wink that night, perturbed by how bad Stuart's feet smelt wedged against my face and with the foreboding knowledge that Amy's discovery and slight over-reaction would be related back to her Mum who in turn would relate it back to my Mum in the environs of the Top 40 chart singles section in Woolworths. I had to keep Mum away from Woolies, even forsaking the next errand bestowed by me on her to purchase the latest Kylie single for me in the effort to silence the impending gossip. I failed miserably.

After school the next day, I came home to find my Mum ashen faced and wanting *"a serious talk"* with me. It would be the first time that anyone would directly ask me if I was gay. Of course I still wasn't even sure if I was gay myself - I just had inexplicable feelings of what I thought was love towards my best friend - and anyway, the word 'gay' wasn't actually used in this little chit-chat. For as always, my mum's word for gay was 'funny'. The conversation went like this:

Mum: *"So I saw June Pincer in Woolworths."*
Me: *"Oh?"*
Mum: *"She told me that Amy found you and Stuart in bed with each other."*
Me: *"So? We were just top and tailing."*
Mum: (disgusted face) *"Oh my God. What does that mean?! Are you and Stuart... you know..."*
Me: *"Are we what?"*
Mum: *"Funny."*
That word again.
Me: *"Well I don't tell good jokes but Stuart's are hilarious but a bit dirty."*
Mum: *"You know what I mean. Are you and him, you know, like Uncle Jimmy and Billy? A poof."*
Me: *"As in something that Auntie Reenie can put her feet up on?"*
Mum: *"You know what I bloody mean!!! ARE YOU A POOFTER?!"*
Me: (cue hissy fit) *"That's sick! How could you think that about me?! We're just mates!"*

And that's when I ran upstairs crying, for many reasons. Not just for being put on the spot like that but it was the first time that I realised that I might actually be *that way*. Maybe I *was* like Uncle Jimmy and Billy. I was in love with another boy. It was The Boy in the Green Parka rebooted and recast for a now teenage audience. It was the love that no-one talked about, the feelings that I was not allowed to be feeling. I was different but I didn't want to be different. I hoped these feelings would go away, that all teenage boys fall in love with other teenage boys or even their best friends at some point in their adolescence. That it was just normal. And more than anything, I just wanted to be normal. I didn't want to be the kid with the jack-ups or my tie on the fat side; I didn't want to be in love with another boy. Maybe it wasn't love at all. Teenagers didn't know what love was. It was just an unexplained infatuation, like an illness. Like the belly ache I got at Cousin Kim's birthday tea party a couple of years before, a sudden bout of something painful that went away as quickly as it arrived. As I lay sobbing into my pillow, my Mum remained downstairs, undoubtedly still with that shocked look of fear etched onto her face that her son, her first born boy could be *that way*.

Subsequently, I started to pull away from Stuart. Our friendship slowly but surely started to fizzle out. I deliberately sidelined myself as Dave swiftly took my place; gluing himself to Stuart's side like some growth defect as together they continued sowing their seed wherever some girl's soil was fertile enough. I retreated into the safety of another fringe group that had splintered off from the original group of 'Uncools' who didn't want me back, still reeling from my betrayal at defecting to the world of acceptance. But now I was back with my tail waggling between my legs. This new group consisted mainly of girls and James Wilson still lamenting the loss of Dave. But I felt safe with them.

*

Then one day, a couple of months later, just before the six weeks holiday of 1989, I happened to bump into Stuart whilst walking through the alley back from school. He was on his own. No sign of Dave. We said hello and chatted amiably, like a divorced couple exchanging awkward pleasantries at a mutual friend's wedding. We were clearly not the best friends that we once were but it was friendly enough. Little did I know that I was to imminently be the only witness to a meeting that would irrevocably change Stuart's life forever. A young girl was standing by a wall further ahead, smoking a cigarette. She was fifteen years old, predictably dressed very inappropriately for her age, heavy-make up, huge budgie swing earrings dangling from her ears like two trapezes. Maybe it was the way that she was sucking so furiously on her cigarette that drew Stuart's attention. Regardless, it was love at first sight, demonstrated by the following romantic exchange that I, and only ever I, had the pleasure of witnessing, like a bewildered innocent bystander roped in off the street to witness a tacky meeting of

minds in a location that had a faint whiff of stale piss and *Skol*-flavoured vomit. It was that romantic. As we passed the girl, (her name was Kerry) Stuart winked and leered at her and delivered his heartfelt opening chat-up line:
Stuart: *"Oi. Do you fuck?"*
Kerry: *"Yeah. Wanna fuck then?"*
Stuart: *"Yeah."*
And that was it. So fuck they did. A fuck that would result in Kerry getting pregnant and Stuart becoming a father at fifteen years old, destined to leave school, reside in a council flat in the local grim concrete estate known at the 'Lego Flats' and working at the Fords car factory until retirement. His fate was sealed but it was a fate that he had seemingly wanted. For me, I considered myself to have had a lucky escape. The vortex of Dagenham Doom had well and truly trapped Stuart and years later I would hear that he was still living in those depressing Lego flats now on his third kid by a different woman. My love for Stuart was over; I was still in denial about my sexuality yet subconsciously casting my net further afield. The rise of *Neighbours* and *Home and Away* had planted the first seeds of a journey that would make me want to find the world outside of Dagenham.

7 – VIVA ESPANA!

1990 (aged 15)

It was the first proper view I had of the wider world outside of the UK. Well, when I say view, it was actually quite difficult to ascertain whether that was indeed mainland Spain out of the window, as I was currently trapped behind a curtain at the back of the plane, sitting helpless and coughing in the midst of a thick pea-souper fog of cigarette smoke, being billowed from the highly anxious mouths of my Nan Shirley and Auntie Reenie, like they were single-handedly operating the *Top of the Pops* dry ice machine from what was left of their lungs.

Nevertheless, my excitement at my very first foreign holiday was palpable. The annual sojourn to the family caravan at Weymouth had still taken place earlier that summer, this time to coincide with the 1990 World Cup which meant hours of enduring football matches on the TV as the male members of my family labelled Gazza *"a poofter"* for his crying on the pitch. It was the kind of family holiday of which I had clearly outgrown as I was now yearning for different kinds of adventures in holidaying. I was subconsciously extricating myself from the bosom of my family as my independent spirit started to surge inside of me. Not to mention my constant worry of what I deemed to be my family's homophobic tendencies as the nugget of homosexual truth fidgeting restlessly in my consciousness grew larger each day. I was only fifteen years old but already I was realising that I desperately needed to forge a long term escape plan from Dagenham. This was also exacerbated by the school work experience programme a few weeks before where I was assigned to the Ford car factory of all places. Aaargh - it was happening! The Dagenham powers-that-be were clearly manipulating its young male population with this particular form of mind control that coincidentally placed them where they were expected to earn the pitiful crust until their early death from a machinery-related accident or sheer boredom, whichever blessed relief would be lucky to occur first. And now here I was, spending a two week taster session inside this impossibly large factory that seemed to have Tardis-like qualities in its deceptively endless environs. It was a completely heterosexual environment with the typical male species found slaving away inside having clearly missed a few steps in the evolution from their primate ancestors as they swaggered around in greasy overalls that more times than not kept their beer belly tightly confined, leering over the very few women that I ever saw working there, relegated to canteen servers and secretaries. It was clearly a 1950s time capsule with the men doing the work whilst the women served their food and noted their demands. Trying to feign interest - and even worse - join in the crude discussions about women's breasts and each other's *"birds"* during every tea and lunch break was excruciating to the point where I deduced that if I grabbed hold of poor *"Mandy with the great tits"* from the canteen and shagged her over the soldering board, I would be offered a job for life. Mind you, from the way that Mandy suggestively handled the spout of the coffee machine to expertly relieve it of its warm liquid, it was more than clear that her and her generously-sized mammaries had already done the rounds around the factory quicker than you can work out how to correctly spell gonorrhoea. The lurid graffiti in the toilet cubicles confirmed this, making for compelling reading during my regular bouts of hiding in there like Anne Frank to escape the relentless blue-collar heterosexuality. But the felt-tip scribed adulation for Mandy's vagina adorning the flimsy cubicle walls paled into insignificance compared to the other graffiti beside it - that of accusations of various blokes being 'cock suckers', 'bum fuckers', 'shirt lifters', 'fudge packers', like a homophobe with Tourettes had spewed up word vomit, accompanied by child-like drawings of penises, bums and the act of inserting one into the other. It was homophobia presented right in my face, inside what was supposed to be my tiny retreat. There was no escape from it, from the realisation that these drawings and accusations could have easily been directed at me. The only way to get away from them was to flush the loo to give the illusion that I had actually had a shit and push open the door to rejoin the bowels of hetero-hell on the factory floor. It was a jarring foreboding of what might lay ahead for me should I embrace my true sexuality. And it terrified me. However, on my very last day of work experience and during my final session of cubicle-dwelling hermitage, I noticed something else accompanying the cutely illustrated playground homophobia - it was a hole carved into the partition between mine and the neighbouring cubicle, temporarily stuffed with a tissue-shaped ball, like a paper mâché recreation of the boulder that blocked the entrance to Jesus' cave of resurrection. Beset with curiosity, I carefully pulled away the tissue blockade to reveal the entirety of the hole, the circumference of which could coincidentally accommodate an average sized penis (and would be more of a snug fit for the more well-endowed).

It was the first glory hole I had ever seen - and here it was, glaring with pride of place in the middle of the most heterosexual work environment known to man. I couldn't help but peer through – only to be greeted by something else inexplicably coming back from the dead - that of a flaccid penis in the shadow of a Jabba the Hutt sized beer gut, sensing the sudden glorious opening of the hole, as it twitched, protruded and extended like R2D2's horizontal periscope towards the hole and my widening eyeball. It took approximately two seconds for me to quickly do the Pretend-I've-Had-A-Shit loo flush and hurriedly escape from the toilet, not wanting to find out who the mysterious floating penis belonged to and realising that perhaps the Fords car factory was actually populated by repressed gays, projecting their secret desires into anti-gay graffiti in-between putting their willies into a hole that bore a lesser risk of getting a splinter from than big-boobed Mandy's.

Maybe there was more to Dagenham homophobia than met the eye, as the looming (and slightly cheesy-smelling) penis meeting my own eye served to prove. Two weeks of working in the Fords car factory had been two weeks of my life that I was deliriously happy to be finally over, but conversely, the experience had also helped me push forward with my determination to get the hell out of Dagenham as soon as I was old enough. And the first step in my escape plan was soon being presented to me when Auntie Carol decided to organise a September family holiday to Spain.

*

Carol was a sun worshipper, always slathering on coconut smelling *Hawaiian Tropic* in Nan's back garden if the sun came out for more than ten seconds. Mum had refused to come on the holiday because she *"hated the heat"*. Which was true because if the temperature crept up above ten degrees, she would have the electric fan out whilst she repeatedly exclaimed how *"close"* it was. Dad had never ventured abroad. This was a family whose idea of foreign climes was taking the District Line three stops to Barking. So in the end, it was my brother, my Nan Shirley, Aunties Carol and Reenie, Cousin Kim and I that comprised the party of holidaymakers. Reenie was already salivating at the thought of purchasing a new tea towel for her ongoing war with neighbour Kath Wagstaff.

And now here I was, on my very first plane trip to sunny Spain, wedged at the back in the smoking section of the Monarch Airlines charter flight to Malaga, trapped in an undulating *Benson and Hedges* flavoured thick mist because Nan and Auntie Reenie could not last more than two minutes without a cigarette, which had shrunk to thirty seconds with their combined nerves of their first ever plane journey with an equation that roughly equalled smoking one entire pack of cigarettes for every half second of turbulence. It didn't help that, thanks to trying to adopt the latest fashion trend, I had ditched the dungarees and was now resplendent in a turquoise shell suit (purchased from *Kays* catalogue of course!) and was therefore a highly flammable fire risk.

It was my first proper foreign holiday. I didn't count the school day trip to Boulogne in France in March earlier that year. My paternal Nan has died the week before aged eighty-six and her funeral had ended up being held on the same day as my debut excursion to the fringes of continental Europe. In the end, Mum and Dad decreed that I should still join my peers in France as my Nan would have wanted to me broaden my horizons. I couldn't help but remember her face when I had performed my impromptu get well drag show aged ten. Maybe all along she knew I was destined for a world wider than what Dagenham could give me. She had been after all, mother to Uncle Jimmy so knew first hand of the tell-tale signs that your child was of a 'different persuasion'. I wished I had spent more time with her through my childhood but appreciated her blessing from beyond the grave for me to get my first taste of another country.

Boulogne was a let-down though. Even though it had felt momentous to get my very first glimpse of a foreign land from the P&O ferry, the day consisted of wandering around with my classmates posing outside of and tittering at sex shops whilst I felt a nagging guilt that I should be at my Nan's funeral. The only educational experience that I gleaned from the whole trip was that I found French guys to be a damn lot more desirable than the English.

But now six months later, I was to imminently land in Spain. My knowledge of the country was quite limited, my expectations of it pretty much formed from the TV sitcom *Duty Free*, so I imagined it to be full of waiters with comedy moustaches and horny husbands cheating on their wives.

Finally, two and a half hours after taking off from Gatwick, we disembarked in Malaga to the feeling of the warm air blasting us as we stepped off the aircraft. It was like when you open the oven door to check if your dinner is being cooked through and get blasted in the face by the heat. I'd never been this warm in my life and immediately I was elated at the feeling of being out of England in what felt like a proper foreign country.

We had rented a sixth-floor holiday apartment in a block in central Benalmadena on the Costa Del Sol, a place with basically transpired as Dagenham in the sunshine, full of sunburnt English holidaymakers and ex-pats that were in the delights of a foreign land but had to still feel at home by patronising the English cafes and bars and shops that sold copies of *The Sun* that were two days out of date. There was no such thing as the internet. You had to make do with two day old sensationalist headlines and third page tits and be happy about it. Within minutes of unpacking, we were dragged to a local shop so Nan and Auntie Reenie could stock up on more (and ludicrously cheap) cigarettes, most of which, I was informed, were to be smuggled back to Dagenham inside mine and my brother's suitcases to be sold for a profit down the local pub. Always sensing a bargain – and no doubt to also increase profit margins back in Dagenham - Nan and Reenie settled for about two dozen packs of a cheap Spanish brand called *Swing*, which aptly described the frenzied motion of their arms as they tried to scoop up as many fags as humanly possible, taking out a whole shelf of souvenirs and four bottles of sangria in the process, causing sheer carnage in the shop as the poor shop owner, a hunchbacked fraught-looking woman, screamed at them incoherently in Spanish. It was a suitably chaotic start to what would turn out to be a memorable holiday, still talked about and chuckled over to this day.

For me, the holiday would prove to be the next step in the awakening of my sexuality, which was inevitable as I started to clock the handsome Spaniards everywhere. Forget the French hunks spotted in Boulogne, they were limp baguettes compared to the sizzling tapas on display here. I wish I had known earlier that tanned hunks often wearing not much more than a pair of short shorts could be found just a couple of hours flight south from England. I had been transported inside a more bronzed version of the male underwear pages of the infamous *Kays* catalogue. It was all too much for me and my burgeoning sexuality. By the second day, I had started a ritual where I would feign thirst by the pool so I could sneak back up to the apartment and masturbate in the locked bathroom. I had evolved since my first wank after the episode of *Home and Away* at the beginning of the previous year. Now it was occurring more than once a day, twice, even three times. And here in Benalmadena, the Spanish sun and the native men were making my hormones go all *One Flew Over the Cuckoo's Nest* kinda crazy inside of me.

On the third day of the holiday, I was locked inside the apartment bathroom as usual, quickly knocking another one out when I heard my Auntie Reenie's voice scream *"WANKER! YOU DIRTY FUCKING WANKER!!"* I froze, quickly looked around in a panic in case I had left the door open or there was some unexplained see-through portal into the bathroom. I certainly wasn't making any noise, wincingly restrained in my cries of pleasure as I pictured an identity parade of trunk-clad Spanish lotharios. *"HE'S STILL DOING IT! THE DIRTY OLD BASTARD!!"* The use of the world *"old"* finally clued me up that I was not the guilty party here. I zipped up and raced out of the bathroom to find Auntie Reenie leaning out of the apartment window, shaking her balled fists furiously and screaming obscenities to the ground six floors below as the rest of the family hooted with laughter. Confused as to what was happening, I squeezed beside Reenie and stuck my head out of the window, following the direction of Reenie's furious gaze and downward torrent of appalled abuse to see a middle-aged Spanish man sat in his open-top car on the street below, cock gleefully out and being aired in the hot breeze, as he wanked himself off whilst looking up and winking and smiling repeatedly at Auntie Reenie. If this was how Spanish men chatted up women, it certainly wasn't working with Auntie Reenie. I thought Reenie should have been more flattered to get this much cock action in her mid-fifties. Finally she tossed one of her hair rollers down at him and he finally got the message and sped off. As his car disappeared into the urban sprawl of Benalmadena, I couldn't help but feel quite thankful to him for the irony of his public wanking session masking my own simultaneous exercise in the bathroom. It was apparent now that there was a lot of wanking going on in this resort - private, public or otherwise. And who could blame them with all the hunks that populated this town.

    Auntie Reenie might have been immune to the dubious charms of the locals but Nan Shirley certainly wasn't. At sixty-seven years old, she still had a boundless energy that in this case was manifesting itself with her flirting cougar-like with sexy Miguel the apartment block concierge approximately forty-five years her junior. Maybe it was her elderly lust for this younger man combined with too much sun and a dodgy paella that led to her infamous 'Shit in the Lift' incident. The unfortunate turn of events for Nan's bowels had transpired whilst walking back to the apartment after an evening of watching amateur flamenco dancing in a local bar. At first complaining of feeling *"a bit dodgy"* followed about twenty seconds later by a sudden more desperate exclamation of *"I'M GONNA BLOODY SHIT MYSELF!"*, a *Carry-On* style race ensued to get Nan back to the apartment in time before the shit literally hit the fan, in this case, the frilly plastic Spanish one poking out of Nan's handbag that swung precariously close to her rear end.

    We finally hurried into the apartment lobby, escorting a mortified and now bow-legged Nan past a bemused Miguel as she now started wailing that she wasn't gonna make it in time as we reached the lift. As the lift could only take three people at once, my brother and I drew the short straw of being the ones to get Nan safely up six floors before the Spanish equivalent of Mount Vesuvius erupted in her drawers. This six floor journey should have taken less than thirty seconds but Nan saw fit, in her blind panic, to crazily jab at every floor button, confusing the poor lift so that it stalled between floors whilst my brother started screaming as he caught sight of the first trickle of diarrhoea vacating Nan's behind and trickling down her leg like the oil in the 1980s Castrol GTX advert. Finally managing to cajole the lift to its six floor destination just as the air inside turned toxic with swear words and the smell of geriatric shit, we literally got Nan into the apartment with seconds to spare before all manner of brown hell was unleashed in the bathroom, my brother and I only being able to listen in horror to the sound effects that would have sounded at home in a 1970s disaster movie. Minutes later, Nan finally emerged from the bathroom, holding up her drawers which she had physically blew a hole right through, the sight and tragedy of which made her burst into tears. She couldn't face Miguel again after that.

I shouldn't have laughed at Nan's unfortunate mishap as the very next day, I got sunburnt from top to tail after falling asleep in the sun with no sun cream on and spent the remainder of the holiday hobbling around Benalmadena like a burns victim in a Burka. The ramifications of which put paid to my daily poolside admiration of 'SuperTrunks'.

As far as I was concerned, 'SuperTrunks' was all mine. Cousin Kim was crushing on a local hunk with his leg in plaster who lived in the house opposite and who we came to nickname 'Senor Crutch', Auntie Reenie had attracted the attentions of The Benalmadena Wanker, Nan and her bowels were now on the rebound from Miguel whilst I was dreamingly pining after a particular muscular, hairy chested, specimen of a dreamboat, always seen strutting around the pool in the smallest pair of lurid trunks in existence, as if his genitals were shrink-wrapped in Day-Glo cling film. I was a bag of nerves whenever he walked close by and had mastered the skill of using sunglasses to mask my drooling stares at him and all his gorgeousness. And then I got burnt. Which meant that my poolside cruising was suddenly off the menu.

Instead, I was relegated *Rear Window* style to the shady corner of the apartment balcony, taking turns reading the latest Jackie Collins novel with continuing to worship SuperTrunks from the safe haven of six floors up, via the telephoto lens on my camera. Upon returning home, my excitement was palpable at getting the developed photos back from Boots, a visual record of SuperTrunks to last until the end of time. Imagine my crushing disappointment at SuperTrunks instead being rendered as a blurry figure, not unlike the supposed photo of BigFoot or Nessie.

Our sojourn to the Spanish sunshine had been a holiday that had an effect on us all, but the week spent in Benalmadena was enough to ignite my desire for sunnier and more further away climes, a turning point in a road that would eventually see me flee the UK in just under three years time.

8 – THE DOUBLE HANDJOB IN THE YELLOW SKODA

1990 – 1993 (aged 16 – 18)

Operation Escape from Dagenham wasn't going to come cheap. I needed an after-school job, something to bring in the pennies to squirrel away, something that would elicit fevered excitement at seeing the account total in my Nationwide Building Society passbook climb higher and higher. I was realistic in knowing that it might take me a good few years, more unrealistic maybe was the expectation at what these savings might actually eventually bring me. All I knew was that, thanks to *Neighbours* and *Home and Away*, Australia was now calling. And when I say calling, I mean it had metaphorically phoned me saying *"Hi this is Oz. I'm big, hot and full of danger but you know that you want me. And seeing as you are clearly a big old poof, you need to get your skinny, pasty arse over here to truly realise it. You know that I have lots of hot men in the vein of Brad Willis from Neighbours. You want one? Then come and get one!"* At which point I would hang up and sulk that I actually needed to be able to afford to go and get one.

The idea of going to University never interested me. Not one member of my family had ever attended one and I wasn't going to break the mould in this case. Like my parents, grandparents, aunts and uncles, all I wanted to do was get out into the big wide world and learn from life itself.

And so, immediately upon my return from the Chaotic Holiday to Spain, I discovered that a brand new ASDA store was conveniently opening a mere ten minute walk from my house and was recruiting en-masse. And thus I applied for a part-time evenings and weekends job there, happy to take anything that might be offered me. I had tried to apply for other jobs before, or rather was coerced by my Mum into trawling around the shops and market along the local High Street trying to half-heartedly convince every retailer that having a shy, gangly teenager on their staff would be great for business.

But now with a possible adventure to Australia as an incentive, I sold myself as best as I possibly could in a non sexual kind of way at the ASDA interview and was given a job as a Produce Assistant, known more commonly as working on the Fruit and Veg department. My hourly wage was £2.90, a pitiful sum that meant I might get to Australia just before my death bed but it was a job and it was a start and a week later, after completing training at ASDA Gravesend where we learnt such complicated tasks as to how to correctly and aesthetically arrange apples in a basket, I burst onto the shop floor at ASDA Dagenham resplendent in a green and white striped apron and hat to match. I would come to learn that, of course, this uniform, just like my school uniform, could also be worn in a more rebellious way with sleeves rolled up and the hat's green band having a magical ability to just disappear, as demonstrated by my colleague Luke, a wide-boy heart-throb with hair like Michael Bolton who was a walking, talking advert for testosterone and whose sexual exploits were of a size that was as biblical as his name.

In fact the Fruit and Veg department had a whole trio of heart-throbs as Luke was complemented by Tall Blonde Mark who looked like he had just stepped out of *Home and Away* and Barry, a mischievous lad who reeked of confidence and who had aspirations of joining the army, wanting also, like me, to pull out his own Get Out of Dagenham For Free card from the pile. Meanwhile, the female contingent of the team consisted of three teenage girls whose names all began with J - Jo (sweet and wholesome), Jackie (so quietly spoken she was practically mute) and Julie (motormouth) and finally elderly Myra who seemed permanently bemused to be surrounded by so much youth.

ASDA was a steadfastly hetero place to work, albeit far from being aggressively so like the Fords car factory but still, it was a workplace where being gay was a thing that was never talked about to the point of it not existing at all. As a result, my surroundings were blowing up a snowdrift outside the door to my closet, leaving me unable to get out. But I was having so much fun earning my first wage, I didn't even think about the Feelings Deep Inside Me. In-between delicately arranging those apples, I was flirting harmlessly with Jo, gossiping with Julie, awkwardly talking 'fit birds' with Luke and Mark, and hiding in the chiller with Barry for surreptitious bouts of eating the stock of chocolate peanuts whilst listening to whoever was partaking in Shag of the Day in the storeroom behind (usually Luke). Shag of the Day was a common feature of life at ASDA, this being a supermarket where the raging libidos of the staff were spent far quicker than the money from the purses and wallets of the customers. The teenage fingering and bombay roll fumblings of school were now replaced with proper sex and endless scandalous affairs that made the extra-marital copulations of *Dallas* and *Dynasty* seem like an episode of *Rod, Jane and*

Freddy. Even customers were not immune to the sexual atmosphere - and especially the charms of Luke, Mark and Barry who were getting surrounded on a daily basis by their own devoted followers, giggling schoolgirls and randy housewives who were shopping on our Fruit and Veg section to get their recommended apple a day as just an excuse to drool over Luke's bum that he had re-tailored his work trousers to hug as tight to as possible. Meanwhile the only entourage I had surrounding me with their own brand of idol worship were the BABs - aka the Bargain Aware Biddies - who possessed magical *Supergran*-like abilities to spot my roll of Reduced Stickers from seven aisles away and have me surrounded within ten seconds flat, pushing, shoving and grasping at the air as if I was Jesus who was cannily only handing out the fish and bread that had been drastically reduced by 2p because it was going out of date. It was a corporate successor to the harvest festival from my infant school days. Clearly the only things that were still fresh and in date were the staff's sexual exploits, the perpetual hotbed from which no-one was safe, not even me, for as a consequence of living a faux-heterosexual life, I was constantly being egged on to pass comment on a multitude of female customers' tits by the rabidly randy duo of my twenty-six year old manager Tim and 'One Ball Bobby', the forty-ish senior manager with a single testicle who would forever be leering Benny Hill-like at the younger female members of staff but could usually only make full use of his singular ball in the dark recesses of the warehouse with a variety of horny, mostly married, middle-aged women from the Deli Counter. Needless to say One Ball Bobby would overcompensate for his lonely testicle by being the first to somersault over the checkouts and play the hero during the regular bouts of what came to be known as 'Macho Minute'.

'Macho Minute' was the phenomenon that occurred whenever staff member Elsie Norman was called to the Customer Services counter. But Elsie did not actually work at ASDA, as nor did she exist. For she was just the code name called to alert the staff that there was a shoplifter on the loose, and most times, trying to make a daring escape across the car park outside. Hearing Elsie Norman's name over the tannoy would immediately send all the male members of staff, eager to prove their manliness and impress the ladies, leaping over checkouts and giving chase across the car park like they were in an episode of *The Sweeney*. Meanwhile, I would hide.

It was no coincidence that Elsie Norman's summons to Customer Services miraculously increased tenfold during summer when there was a higher proportion of scantily clad female customers shopping and flirting. In fact, Luke's sudden dismissal came about when he was rumbled for deliberately creating over a dozen fake calls for Elsie Norman, just so that he could show off his athletic till-jumping prowess and Super Magical Tight Bum to his hordes of female admirers. Poor Elsie became strangely uncalled for after that, until one day when the familiar request *"Would Elsie Norman please come to Customer Services?"* came through, an old lady tottered over and was taken aback to find herself suddenly surrounded by a dozen out-of-breath men desperate to play the hero. Her name was Elsie Norman. Poor Elsie was left disappointed that these dozen men were not panting for wanting to get into her drawers but were just the competitors in 'Macho Minute'. The code name was changed to something more obscure after that. Tabitha Allsop didn't have quite the same ring as Elsie Norman and was quite a mouthful for Becky on the Customer Services counter to announce over the tannoy but according to One Ball Bobby, Becky was no stranger to dealing with a mouthful.

*

It was the sexual activity and subsequent sacking of my supervisor Susie Newsome that would end up benefitting me greatly and pushing up my bank balance with gusto to get me nearer to that plane to Australia. I was already working as much overtime as possible, which we were permitted to do - and get paid for every single hour we worked with 'double time' for Sundays. Our clocking in cards dictated our hours and thus our wages. Barry introduced me to a little scam where we could clock each other's cards out if one of us worked later than the other, to give the illusion of working even more hours than we did. It was naughty but apparently everyone 'in the know' was doing it. Then, one day in Spring 1991, suddenly without warning, Susie was fired for stealing, a crime which transpired had been going on for months and was uncovered when Susie was caught in the act loading her car with her latest stash of pilfered goods and whilst trying to make her escape, got the tongue-twisting fictional Tabitha Allsop summoned to Customer Services and thus Susie received her very own 'Macho Minute' as a send-off. I felt a little guilty. I had stolen a few hours, but Susie had stolen vast quantities of cans of whipped cream, chocolate sprinkles and strangely, *Dairylea Triangles*, for, it eventually transpired, to be used in regular fetish evenings with a teenage lover. You couldn't blame her really. After all, she, like I, was working in a place where the in-their-sexual-prime hormones of teenage boys and older women were meeting and converging in the aisle where fresh chickens met triangular shaped cheeses that could be easily stolen to fit perfectly in Susie's vagina but not so much in her job description.

Tim offered me Susie's job. A full-time commitment which would mean me leaving school. My GCSE's were already complete and I was six months into my A-Level studies. But the lure of a full-time job and thus more money and thus that Plane to Australia was just too great and so I quit sixth form to be promoted to a full-time ASDA Produce Supervisor at just seventeen years old. School was over; I was out in the working world and earning money, which I was squirreling away towards my eventual fleeing from Dagenham. Nothing was going to stop me.

Not even my love for Phil Miller.

*

  Phil Miller was a new recruit on the Dairy department which was the closest neighbour to the Fruit and Veg where I worked and lurked. Phil wasn't a wideboy or a lothario, he was, like me, a little bit nerdy, a tad on the shy side. All I knew was that my heartbeat gathered pace a little whenever I saw him and I had to do my best *Cagney and Lacey* impersonation to try and get any clue as to whether he was straight or gay, knowing full well the odds were firmly stacked in favour of him being on a different department in terms of sexuality too. Predictably he turned out to be straighter than straight, so I tried to bury my feelings for him and we instead became firm friends, joining forces with Jo and two other new recruits Ant and Daz to form a solid group of mates. The five of us became inseparable. We were the Famous Five, Phil, Ant, Daz and I were the Merry Men and Jo was our Maid Marian. We were *Penelope Pitstop and the Ant Hill Mob*. We were the Scooby Doo gang of which I was the only one who could logically be Velma. We even had our very own annoying Scrappy Doo, the somewhat unwanted hanger-on Jamie Turner who was a seventeen year old dirty old man, a re-incarnated Sid James from the *Carry On* films who would guffaw and pant every time something remotely resembling sex talk was uttered in his vicinity. Even the mention of the word boobs would send him into potential cardiac arrest and heavy breathing that put my Nan's own heavy breather phone caller to shame. Nan would get this call once every couple of weeks, and when asked what she was wearing, would answer *"my cardigan cos it's cold"* then say she needed to go for a wee, which always took so long, that by the time she finally made it back to the phone, her hyperventilating admirer's excitement had no doubt subsided as Nan came back to an empty line and dial tone. I never knew whether this was a deliberate tactic of hers or not. She always had her own way of dealing with awkward situations.

  I dreaded to think of what she would make of what was going on between Jo, Ant, Daz, Phil and I. Now when you put together one sensible girl and four boys in their mid teens and thus at their sexual peak, with a spaghetti junction-like tangle of feelings joining us all, some things are bound to happen. After all, Jo was besotted with me, Daz was into her, I was in love with Phil but strangely jealous of Daz being into Jo, and Ant was into porn. Even Cupid himself would get a migraine trying to work it all out.

  But for me, everything revolved around Phil. The buried feelings I had for him had now been exhumed again for another autopsy. I wanted to be his Boy in the Green Parka or rather now The Boy in the Green Apron. The criss-cross of feelings between the five of us eventually manifested itself somehow into naked sleepovers at Phil's house, where innocent games of strip poker would end up with all the boys running around sans clothes like we were filming one of those tame German saucy movies that I used to secretly watch very late at night on satellite TV in the late 1980s, soft core titillation to be found on obscure channels called *Sat 1* and *RTE* with dubious reception and incoherent plots that involved nothing but jiggling boobs, flaccid willies and simulated sex where the forced panting was the only part of the language that I seemed to understand.

And now Phil, Ant, Daz and I were making our very own extremely homoerotic versions with an added female into the mix. We were one girl and four straight boys (well three straight and one secretly gay). It was homoerotic foreplay without the promise of sex afterwards presided over by a teenage girl whose nervous giggling just masked the fear as to how her parents would react should they ever find out that their daughter was spending her evenings surrounded by naked eighteen year old boys engaging in homoerotic horseplay. These shenanigans occurred with increasing frequency, leading to regular bouts of camping in our colleague Joan's back garden; despite all our homes being less than five minutes walk away.

It was like an early 1990s version of *Brokeback Mountain*. Four boys, one tent, the pitching of which was no match for the pitching of the erections inside our pants. The running order of Camping Night was always the same. Firstly, talking about 'birds' which would somehow lead to a suggestion from Ant that we take our clothes off, after which we would wrestle naked then engage in a wanking competition. A side-by-side engagement of hands to penises (only our own of course, this homoerotica firmly drew the line at touching each other's cocks) and when asked who we were imagining, I could never truthfully answer that it was Phil, so quickly had to blurt out the name of whoever was supposed to be the hottest 'bird' on TV at the time but always drew a blank which would then make me panic and say Pam Ayres when I should have said Pamela Anderson. If these *Homoerotic Adventures in Tents* was a title written by Jackie Collins, I could only imagine her choice of words to describe them. *'The smorgasbord of engorged phalluses tore the fabric of the tent asunder'*. At least I finally knew what a phallus was.

But Phil was the only one currently residing inside my Wank Bank, a residency that whilst he was blissfully unaware of, he still did nothing to combat what with the naked sauntering around. Unluckily for me, Phil was having an intense bromance with Ant. It was Stuart and Dave all over again, the object of my affection being stolen away by someone infinitely cooler than I was. Once again, unrequited love was taking my feelings and framing them in a picture that could be only be looked at and never purchased. It was a pattern that had started with James the Boy in the Green Parka in infant school, Stuart Pincer the Teenage Gigolo in senior school and now again with Phil the Boy in the Red Apron in my first job.

I should have known by now that unrequited love, especially that of the teenage kind, never ends well so I started to try and deliberately sideline my growing feelings for Phil by pursuing Jo, who was in turn being pursued by Daz, a strange little love triangle which culminated in Jo living up to her new nickname of MOMO (Mistress of Many Orgies) by being the perpetrator of a double hand job inside Daz's yellow Skoda.

Phil and Ant were both not present for this latest exploration of teenage hormones, as Daz had driven Jo, Jamie Turnbull and I for a late night drive around Epping Forest, a night-time drive being best for disguising the fact that the transport of choice was a yellow Skoda. We parked the car on the incline of a hill, kept the engine running for warmth (it was Winter) and somehow, Daz and I ended up reclined in each other's arms on the back seat together, with Jo sandwiched in-between us. It took a few minutes for Daz and me to realise that our hands were starting to wander as the stroking of each other veered away from being purely platonic. Suddenly realising what was happening, we both quickly sat up straight (in more ways than one) and flustered Daz suddenly dared Jo to give him a handjob. And me. Both of us. Jo just shrugged and said ok and so unzipped became our trousers and out came our penises. To say the whole exercise was extremely awkward for all concerned would be an understatement. Jamie was still in the front seat now being given a treat like you do with an obedient puppy, until we saw that he was wanking too, all realised the absurdity of the situation and the fact this was taking place inside a yellow Skoda. I suddenly flagged, a girl's hand around my penis just wasn't doing it for me whilst Jamie watched and wanked simultaneously in the rear-view mirror. My penis suddenly became the half-mast flagpole above Buckingham Palace which no-one could remember whether it meant the Queen was home or not. In this case, the flag was at half mast precisely because a queen *was* present. Meanwhile, Daz came in five seconds flat, all over Jo's hand to which she promptly screamed as if not expecting the obvious end result of a penis being massaged in her hand, her oral shock at which sent Jamie flying across the front seat, knocking the handbrake off, which promptly sent the car and all us half-naked teenagers inside it, rolling down the hill like we were in an episode of *Last of the Summer Wine* where the horny old men always seem to end the episode by rolling down a hill in a bathtub. Only in this case it was an unfashionable yellow Skoda, the interior of which was being decorated with the splatter of Daz's semen that Jo was desperately trying to flick off her hand as the car slid out of control and we all tried to grab hold of the only gearstick actually worth grabbing onto and bring the car safely to a stop.

There was a weird vibe between us all after that. And on top of it all, our colleague Joan was sussing out that I was gay and that maybe I was in love with Phil. She never vocalised her suspicions but I knew that she knew, the tell-tale sign being the looks she gave me whenever I was in Phil's proximity. It was becoming clear to others around me that I was into other boys. And yet still, now at eighteen years old, I could never admit it to anyone, especially as I was being witness to the homophobic treatment of the other gay man now working on the Fruit and Veg department at ASDA.

His name was Dean Fleeceman. He was a couple years older than me but whilst I hid my sexuality behind a straighter-than-straight facade, Dean's own homosexuality had manifested itself into an extreme campness, one that could leave no doubt in anyone's minds as to his preferring of the same gender. Dean was already a troubled soul, which was only being made worse with him being the butt of homophobic digs about his sexuality. He could have been Toby Curtis, recast *Dynasty* style with a new actor after several years away. I should have done more to defend him. But this time I wasn't the hero. I didn't step up to save Dean in the same way I did with seven-year old Toby a decade before. I was now fully aware that I was gay, that Dean and I shared a common bond. And yet I didn't want to endure Dean's fate. At seven years old, my innocent self was the hero. At eighteen I was the coward, hiding behind a veneer of heterosexuality in a staunchly straight work environment that I was happy to hide my gayness within, now that I was finally part of 'the gang'.

But it wasn't right. My in-crowd membership was a fraud. I was their mate, their 'bro', but I knew that if I revealed my true self - and my love for Phil, my fate would be that of Dean's - sidelined, sniggered at and teased mercilessly. Nothing felt right anymore, it was time to go. I had to go in search of the clichéd 'Real Me'. What I would find, I had no idea. But the journey had to be worth it. I just didn't know when I would leave.

That answer was soon given to me when a controversial new initiative was introduced in which every staff member had to rotate shifts on the checkouts. That was the final straw. I had ended up working on a checkout in a Dagenham supermarket. Destiny had up-ended and been delivered the opposite way round and I had become the checkout girl. Only I didn't have a husband who worked in the Fords car factory. Dagenham was trying to poke fun at me. Dagenham could go fuck itself. I checked my savings; I had six thousand pounds which at the current exchange rate, equalled twelve thousand Australian dollars which to me seemed A Bloody Lot of Money. It was more than enough. It was time to leave Dagenham. A few weeks later, I was officially unemployed and on a flight to Australia.

9 – WE'RE NOT IN KANSAS ANYMORE

1993 (aged 18 – 19)

It was Sunday 22nd August 1993. Also forever known as the day I left Dagenham. I was two months shy of my nineteenth birthday. I had to be up at 6am for my journey to Heathrow Airport but got home at 4am after one final night out with my friends. I just lay wide awake on my bed for those two hours, consumed with a heady cocktail of booze, excitement, anticipation - and a little bit of fear. After all, leaving everything behind - home, family, friends and job - to embark on an adventure across the other side of the planet was nothing less than daunting with a capital D. But the Real Me was to be found out there and the search for him had to start somewhere.

Less enthusiastic about my departure, was of course, my Mum. Over two decades later, I still feel guilty that I wasn't more sympathetic towards her distress at her eldest son leaving home for an indeterminate amount of time. I hadn't even given her much notice that I was cutting the apron strings and letting them fly in the tail wind of a jumbo jet bound for a country over ten thousand miles away. She had refused to believe me until I produced the round the world flight ticket and Australian visa in my passport. And now, as I lay on my bed on this rainy Sunday morning, waiting for the clock to hit 6am, I could hear Mum crying in her bed next door and being comforted by my Dad. When I finally emerged from my bedroom, my backpack all packed and slung over my shoulder, Mum instantly appeared in her bedroom doorway, sobbing uncontrollably, snot running like a gooey waterfall out of her nose and down onto her nightdress.

"My baby, my baby, please don't leave me", she cried.

Naturally being an eighteen year old boy, I thought this was the most overly dramatic thing ever, despite my own knack for creating drama since my infancy. I hadn't even got out of the front door and Mum was already asking me when I was coming home. I honestly had no idea. It would be at least a year, hopefully a lot longer, or if my dream came true of finding the beefcake of my dreams in Australia, I might not come back at all. Of course I didn't dare say such a thing to Mum, she was enough of an emotional wreck as it was. My Dad was emotionless, though that was just his way. But I would later learn that he also cried once I had gone.

So I said my goodbyes and left the house, passing my Nan Shirley who was waiting on her doorstep, also in tears, to give me a last round of her powder-covered boiled sweets like she did when I was a young boy on my way to school.

Daz, Ant and Phil drove me to Heathrow Airport, the journey to which was weirdly silent. None of us knew what to say and Phil couldn't say anything, being deep in the realms of slumberland on the back seat, his head resting on my backpack. I couldn't help but smile at his sleeping face in the rear-view mirror. I still loved him but it was a love that could never be returned. Leaving him behind felt oddly right.

I said a final goodbye to the boys at Heathrow and disappeared into the lift up to Departures where the doors opened and despatched me into a whole new world - one in which I was entering alone, but one that contained endless possibilities. Dagenham already felt like a bygone era.

*

Two days later (via a brief stopover and bout of culture shock in Bangkok) I arrived in Sydney. I had a year-long working holiday visa for Australia and a round the world plane ticket but Sydney was always going to be the place to start - the destination that I had read was a Gay Utopia, a city that was teeming with 'funny' men just like me, a metropolis where men held hands and could love one another. And a place where men could cruise for sex with each other outdoors, overlooking a nudist beach on Sydney Harbour. Ah yes, they could do that too. This little titbit of information had already been circled with the highlighter pen in my mind. We'll come to that later.

So this was it. I was finally here. In Australia. My long-held dream that *Neighbours* and *Home and Away* had kick-started was about to come true. I could already imagine how it was going to play out. There I would be, sitting nonchalant on the beach, having just devoured the latest raunchy Jackie Collins or Sidney Sheldon blockbuster when the Brad Willis from *Neighbours* lookalike would emerge from the surf, his surfboard dripping in conjunction with the water running off his abs. He would clock me, there would be electricity and before we knew it, we would be making love on his surfboard *From Here to Eternity* style and live happily ever after.

Now the fact that I could not swim would be only a minor problem in realising this dream. An accident on my first school swimming lesson aged nine had put paid to that, when I had collided with Samantha Moore in the pool and gone under the water where I panicked and flailed and had to be fished out with a stick and net like a dead goldfish. I was too afraid to go back in the water after that and would get my Mum to write me notes to get me out of swimming. Anyway, ten years later, the lack of swimming skills would only be a minor inconvenience compared to the others that would prevent my surf dude love affair from ever becoming reality.

*

I met my new Scooby Gang of fellow backpackers on my first night in a Sydney backpacker hostel located near Central Station. Bohemian football fan Sandra from Cambridge, party girl Michelle from Nuneaton, madcap Geordie Debs from Newcastle and trainee accountant Gareth from London were my new friends and together with a strangely silent girl from Manchester called Angela and a Scottish compulsive liar called Lisa, we ended up renting two neighbouring flats on Curlewis Street, Bondi Beach for a bargain rent that equated to less than £20 a week each. I was ecstatic that within the space of a few days, I had gone from living in the family home in Dagenham to a flat on Australia's most famous beach. I was living the dream. I was eighteen about to turn nineteen and I was having the last laugh on the school peers that had mocked or bullied me. I was sure that Ginger Ben Taylor must be already working in the Fords car factory by now. But here *I* was in Sydney, the result of my refusal to consign myself to a life spent in the same town where I grew up. I was grabbing life by the balls even though I also wanted to be grabbing other balls too. But hey, one step at a time. If I played my cards right, I could be the gay version of Scotty Walker, another backpacker the same age as me, who lived with us for approximately two hours and who had a mission to shag a woman of every nationality but was stuck on finding a Japanese woman. Not finding one hiding in our flat's airing cupboard he promptly left to go Japanese-hunting elsewhere. Tokyo might have been a good start.

A couple of weeks after settling in, I landed myself a part-time job in a gift shop called *Miscellaneum* inside the Pitt Street Mall in Sydney's Central Business District, the location of which meant I could take diversions on the way home to surreptitiously visit the famed Oxford Street, the self-styled Gay Centre of Sydney, a road lined with gay bars, gay shops, gay cafes, gay coffees, gay trees, gay lamp posts, gay pavement slabs, you name it, it was gay. I had never seen anything like it, I had never ventured to London's Soho and the streets of Bangkok had only been lined with temples, tits and discarded ping pong balls and firecrackers that had been shot out of a myriad of fannies like a Thai remake of *Tangerine Dream*.

Sydney's Oxford Street was something else entirely. I would start at the beginning City end and walk all the way to Bondi Junction, savouring all the gayness around me but still too petrified to even dip my toes in and become part of it. Instead, all I would do was meander up and down the length of the street, too afraid to engage eye contact with any gay men, too scared to even step foot into any gay bar, convinced my entry would be akin to something not unlike stumbling into a Wild West saloon where everyone stops drinking and stares/hisses at you to leave, at which you flee like a child who has just accidentally walked in on his parents having 'rudies'. I was Just Not Brave Enough. Not even courageous enough in fact to go into a gay bar with the safety net of my group of friends, when one night Sandra had suggested we go to gay bar Kinsellas that she had heard was 'fun'. I made an excuse and refused to go, inadvertently leaving Sandra to think I was homophobic. I was just too terrified that other gay men in the bar would take one look at me and suss me out in an instant, outing me to all and sundry before I was ready. So I felt that I couldn't really explain to Sandra that my supposed homophobic tendencies were in actual fact the deep desires to become the very man that the real homophobes feared so much. These desires were now rife within me, an unstoppable force that I had to find the courage to finally act on, and then as a result, finally come out as a man's man.

*

And this is why I found myself at Lady Jane Bay, the name given to the small scenic cove facing West on Sydney Harbour's North Head, consisting of a tiny nudist beach with rocks above and a winding path cutting through some wild bush land. It was also the most notorious cruising spot for gay men in the whole of Sydney, if not Australia and had switched on its gay magnet, retuned its settings to attract Young Skinny Closeted Teenagers from Dagenham and thus was pulling me in with a gravitational tug that most small planets would be jealous of. It wasn't the easiest place to find, there was no internet in existence and Googling was just Go Ogling with a forgotten space. Lady Jane Bay was just casually mentioned in a guide book that it was a nudist beach with a warning that it was frequented by gay men. As if the danger level of encountering a gay man was up there with meeting a great white shark or redback spider. Eventually I located it after looking it up in a copy of the *Sydney Street Directory* and tearing the page out to pocket and refer to as I hunted this mythical place down.

It was blindingly obvious when I eventually found the winding path that led there, as suddenly lone man after lone man would appear and wander around like someone who had lost their friends in a busy nightclub. The quickening pace of my heartbeat counterbalanced the snail-like pace of my feet as I walked As Slowly As Possible, pretending to take in the view so that I could glance down to the nudist beach below, reached by a long metal ladder going down. I couldn't climb down that ladder. I was too scared, too afraid to act on my desires. I had to be left instead as a terrified bystander in the midst of so much furtive homosexual activity, a blushing bride too nervous to do her first dance that would involve a level of intimacy far beyond the requirements for dancing to Chris De Burgh.

The ironic thing was that I wasn't sure if I was interested in casual sex. I just wanted love. Love with another man. But how to find it was another problem and I certainly wasn't going to locate it within the horny environs of Lady Jane Bay, despite my naivety that indeed I would. Which meant that the afternoons when I wasn't working, I would spend here, just wandering, sitting on the rocks, observing but never taking action, just a voyeur and nothing else. I was leading a double life, portraying the hetero lad at night whilst trying to inch further towards man-on-man action by day. But let me say I was happy with this dual existence, despite the terror at the thought of carnally confirming my true sexuality; I was having the time of my life.

*

And then one day, for the first time, a man at Lady Jane Bay spoke to me. He had spotted me 'admiring the view' and followed me along the path. I could see him trailing me, a pursuit that was making me nervous yet excited at the same time. I deliberately stopped at a small jetty, pretending yet again to be a devoted connoisseur of the amazing views across the harbour. As predicted, he followed me onto the rickety planks of the jetty, stood beside me, also took in the view for just two seconds, then turned and asked me outright and without any chance of being misunderstood - if I was gay. I froze. To have The Question put to me so directly suddenly overpowered my senses with a sudden fear. My body was trembling as if alcoholic 'Uncle' Billy had suddenly jumped into it with a very bad case of the DTs. Half of me wanted to run away but the other half of me was like my feet had turned into concrete blocks, like those dreams where you are trying to run but your feet are so heavy, you are making no progress at all. After my Mum's accusations of being 'funny' towards my fourteen year old self, this man was only the second person on the planet to ever ask me directly if I was gay.

I said no. Actually I went the whole hog and spurted forth the cliché *"No. I'm not but I have no problem with gay people"*. He just rolled his eyes, clearly not the first time he had heard this and more evidently, not the first 'straight' teenager he had encountered who had 'accidentally' stumbled onto Planet Cock. As I quickly made excuses and fled from him, I metaphorically kicked myself. Over and over. This was a major step backwards in my attempted manoeuvring out of the closet. I was too afraid to return to Lady Jane Bay after that.

*

The phenomenon that I hadn't expected was that since my first foray to Lady Jane Bay, suddenly the people of Sydney seemed to know I was secretly gay. No matter where I went, incidents would regularly occur where someone would naturally - and without question - assume I was A Gay Man. It was as if Lady Jane Bay had branded me with some kind of tattoo that was invisible to me but clear as day to others to advertise my little sojourns there and thus my apparent homosexuality.

The first episode took place at Palm Beach, the beautiful real-life location for *Home and Away* and the outpost of Sydney's northern beaches. I had taken myself up there on a day off from the gift shop, sunbathed a bit to try and bring at least a little colour to my milk bottle white complexion then decided to have a little paddle in the sea, which being a non-swimmer was the best that I could muster to cool off. Upon emerging from the sea again, I found an elderly gentleman grinning at me in the manner of a creepy ventriloquist's dummy. He said I was hot. I assumed he was referring to my mild case of sunburn. But he wasn't. For when he next suggested, his grin not wavering one millimetre, that I come back to his beach house for *"some fun"* which even I could deduce didn't mean a game of *KerPlunk!*, I realised he had somehow worked out that amongst all the other people on the beach, I was the gay one. How on earth had he sussed me out so easily? Did I have a gay aura that I wasn't aware of? I was hardly a gay sex object and hadn't exactly emerged from the sea with an air of seduction like Ursula Andress in *Dr. No*. And yet this strange man was inviting me back to indulge in his own particular way of cooling off. I politely declined. An hour later when I was waiting for the bus to leave Palm Beach and return to the city, he pulled up in his car and asked again, this time more insistent. I refused. He asked again. I said no again. He then went all *Oliver Twist* on me and practically started begging. I told him to fuck off or I would call the police, albeit worrying for a few seconds whether it would be me that would get arrested for bandying my gay aura around willy nilly all over Sydney.

Whatever my paranoid thoughts were, it was clear that the gay vibe I was giving off was unrelenting. The next incident to prove this happened one drunken night in Bondi when a bar crawl with Michelle, Lisa (despite being teetotal) and Angela culminated with the acquisition of four Aussie hunks, two of which were brothers, to partake in a night-time copulation on Bondi Beach itself where the girls had divided the hunks equally between them (even mute Angela was getting some action) and I had voluntarily relegated myself to the back, waiting for them to finish.

It was like the teenage 'orgies' in Stuart Pincer's lounge all over again, the others copping off further down the beach in front of me whilst I played bouncer. Only this time I had company in the form of Adam, one of the sexy brothers who for some reason had chosen not to indulge in the nocturnal exploring of female tonsils and was sitting beside me in silence, his hand doing the talking as, without warning, it found its way onto my leg.

"Shall we leave them to it and go back to your flat?" he suddenly asked me. I asked him to repeat the question, needing clarification that this hairy chested specimen of gorgeousness with the mop of curly dark hair was indeed gay and that it was a gayness that he wanted to explore with none other than moi. Adam was certainly several steps up from the persistent geriatric ventriloquist's dummy on Palm Beach. He re-iterated his intention and I gasped a yes, astounded that this proposition had come about without even the need to step inside one of those daunting-looking gay bars on Oxford Street. But as Adam and I made our way back to my empty flat and the location of the hopeful imminent loss of my gay virginity, he took a slight detour. To a cash point. Explaining to him that we didn't need money for a cab as the flat was just a very short walk away, Adam just demanded that I pay him fifty dollars. Had he mistaken me for a prostitute? But then realising of course that hookers don't pay their clients for the pleasure of their company, it dawned on me that in this case, my gay aura had morphed into a way for others to make a quick buck. I didn't even know anymore if Adam was really gay or not. I lied and said I had no money but the flat was empty, hoping for a least a shag of sympathy for my lack of funds. He just muttered that I was a cock tease and stormed off into the night.

So now apparently I was not only an Obvious Gay, I was a Cock-Teasing Gay too. Not bad going for a now nineteen year old gay virgin who hadn't even yet kissed another man but certainly wasn't prepared to pay for an exchange of bodily fluids that was going to cost more than a dollar a drop. Instead I had to lay awake that night, having no choice but to listen to Lisa partake in ludicrously noisy sex with Adam's brother Tim which made her sound like she was being tortured and murdered by Chucky. I was too deflated to bother checking if she was ok or not. Thankfully the din was abruptly ended when Sandra and Debs returned home after their own drunken night out, burst into theirs and Lisa's bedroom just as Tim had his lips clasped on one of Lisa's saucer-like nipples, declared that they were tired, pissed as farts and needed their beds so promptly threw Tim out before he had a chance to retrieve his trousers. I couldn't help but wonder if a similar reaction would have occurred had they found me in bed with Adam, which sadly was now only taking place inside my imagination.

Finally the third occurrence of the Unexplained Evidence of My Gay Aura happened whilst working at the gift shop one Saturday when my boss Roz called out to her friend Julie who was passing by the window. Julie came in, excitedly chatting to Roz in a strangely deep voice that gave away that she was in fact, a transsexual. She was the first one I had ever met. A real life version of *Hinge* or *Bracket* or Dame Edna. The old Dagenham kid in me would have pointed, laughed and mocked, in an effort to disguise his own supposed 'abnormality'. But not me, not now. Julie looked stunning as Roz treated her as exactly any other human being without even a hint of any prejudice or transphobia. And then Roz introduced me to Julie, saying I was relatively new to Australia, to which Julie commented, without skipping a beat that she bet I loved the boys to be found in this city. I just nodded, flabbergasted and going a shade of red that outdid the ruby colour of Julie's lipstick. And that is when I knew that Sydney was as far removed from Dagenham as it could possibly be. It was a parallel universe where strange things happened, like a transsexual not having a single eyelid batted at her, where gay men walked hand-in-hand along Oxford Street, where gay residents of the city seemed to know when another gay secretly walked amongst them and finally, even more weirdly, where my doppelganger and I would have a bizarre encounter in a mountain pub.

*

The gang and I had decamped for a weekend away to the Blue Mountains in November 1993, a rural retreat west of Sydney. There we hiked, cycled, bush walked, picnicked by waterfalls and took cable car rides. And drank a lot in pubs. It was an establishment called The Carrington where we found ourselves on our last night. It was my round and I was up at the bar queuing to be served when I felt a tap on my shoulder and turned to find a coarse looking woman sporting a horrifying mullet looking somewhat delighted to see me.

"You came back then?" she growled.

"Excuse me?" I said, baffled as to who she was and where she thought I had 'come back' from.

"You still want that root or not?" was the appendage to her first query. I knew full well that 'root' was Aussie for fuck or shag, having previously been offered one by another less-than-desirable Aussie woman called Janelle who lurked in *The Fortune of War* pub in The Rocks area of Sydney. Like I also did with Janelle, I politely refused this new kind offer of a root. But she was undeterred.

"You wanted one last night."

"Trust me, I didn't."

"Yes, you did, you liar. You were in here last night chatting me up!"

Despite her mullet being hard to forget, I'm sure I would have remembered such an encounter and I was not impressed at being called a liar.

"Listen, I wasn't in here last night. You've got me confused with someone else."

"No I ain't" she persisted, like a stubborn genital wart.

"You were here, I was here and - fuck me!"

At that point her mouth fell open and her jaw dropped as she gawped at the opposite side of the bar.

"It wasn't you, it was him!" she finally admitted, with a sharp rising intonation that indicated that *"him"* was someone I needed to look at. I followed her

gaze and my jaw also dropped to reside with hers on the beer-splattered floor. For waiting in line on the other side of the bar was a man who looked EXACTLY LIKE ME. The same height, the same eyes, the same hairstyle, the same face. It was like something out of *The Twilight Zone*. Mullet-Head looked at me then at him then at me again. I couldn't stop staring at my doppelganger as he clocked me, sending his eyes bulging and his jaw dropping as he stared at me with an equal level of shock. For a second I wondered if I was drunk and actually just looking in a mirror but he was wearing a different shirt - plus I also hadn't even had my first beer yet.

    Who the hell was this man that looked like my identical twin? Had I actually been one of twins, separated at birth whilst one was raised in Dagenham and the other sent to Australia? If so, my parents had a lot of explaining to do. Or was he another version of me from a parallel universe? I was already fascinated with the concept of the Multiverse where every little decision we make in life spawns off an entirely new universe following the ramifications of that seemingly tiny choice in life. What if The Incident with the Chocolate Sponge Pudding had never occurred? What if I had joined in the bullying of Toby Curtis? What if I hadn't had that homework sleepover with Stuart Pincer? What if the BBC hadn't bought *Neighbours* and introduced me to all things Australian? But how far could we go back with this concept? Just being alive right here and right now was a miracle in itself. Out of all those millions of sperm my Dad ejaculated inside my Mum, it was my one that made it to the egg. What are the odds? And then the chances of that sperm and that egg getting fertilized and developing, then making it that whole nine months to produce me at the end of it? And all this happening because of that exact time my parents had sex, let alone met? Again, what are the odds? And then the same thing for *them*, the million to one chances of *them* being conceived and their parents meeting and then the same billion to one chances for their parents and their parents and their parents... so you see, it's a miracle I was even here! And now, throughout my life, even just any little change could have set it off in a multitude of different directions. But this was *my* version. Right here. Right now. A secretly gay nineteen year old now in the ramshackle Carrington pub in the Blue Mountains looking at a possible alternate version of himself. Was he gay? Was he out? Was he happy? Or was he a straight version of me, who was happy to spend his Saturdays copping off with the mullet-haired woman in front of me who was so rough, she made a piece of sandpaper feel like a silk sheet? Or was he me from the near future, sent back to give me some advice and tell me to fucking hurry up and get the hell on with coming out and finding love with another man? If so, where was future me from? Living in contented bliss with a strapping Aussie hunk in a beach house? It's at that point that my brain exploded and I made my way through the crowd to find him and get the answers myself. But he disappeared into the busy mass of thirsty people before I could reach him, never to be seen again.

It was the spookiest encounter of my life. But it also felt like a message, it was time to get on with Being Gay, which meant properly experiencing what that entailed. And that's why I made my triumphant return to Lady Jane Bay.

10 – THE HOME AND AWAY STAR AND THE MILK TRAY MAN

1993 - 1994 (aged 19)

I was back at Lady Jane Bay, nestled in my usual spot on the rocky ledge overlooking the nudist beach and Sydney Harbour beyond. In fact, I had now spent so many hours here over the past couple of weeks, that I half expected there to be an indentation in the stone in the shape of my bum. Anyway, as ever, I was admiring the view down below, whilst trying to convince myself that I could be brave enough to venture down there myself. And that's when I heard the patter of footsteps coming up behind me.
"Nice view isn't it?" I heard a voice ask me.
I turned around and if I was a cartoon character, my eyeballs would have comically popped out of their sockets as I scrambled to re-insert them in shock. For behind me was a heart-throb star of *Home and Away*, he being the enquirer of my appreciation of the view, albeit it wasn't clear whether he meant the view of the naked men lying on the nudist beach below or the general view of the waters of Sydney Harbour. I wasn't about to ask him to be more specific as I was too busy agog that this beefy blond Aussie soap star was engaging with me. I knew who he was instantly. He had been in the show for a couple of years now and was currently playing out a high profile storyline dealing with the death of his wife. I tried hard to act like I didn't know his identity and yet didn't have a clue how to respond to his question and so just feebly and nervously replied:
"Ye... yeah. I like to come here to relax."
He smiled knowingly at me and sidled up closer beside me.
"Do you have a girlfriend?" he asked, his second question in this edition of the open air chat show *Wet Dreams Come True* where the host was a *Home and Away* heart-throb and the guest a skinny, trembling with nerves, closeted Essex teenager.

"*No. Do you?*" I replied. Wow, my enthralling banter wasn't going to get me invited back on this show anytime soon.

"*No*" he said, now sitting down beside me, his muscular tanned legs grazing against my scrawny milk bottle white ones, like a lamb doner and chicken kebab rotating next to each other. He kicked off his flip flops and wiggled his perfectly formed and immaculately manicured toes, as if silently reciting the *'This Little Piggy...'* childhood ditty. *'This little piggy went to market, this little piggy stayed at home, this little piggy went subconsciously cruising to the cliff tops over a gay nudist beach and was being picked up by a Home and Away star sporting a visible erection inside his tight jockey shorts. Yes, this little piggy should have definitely stayed at home.'*

I was so busy admiring his feet that I nearly missed the next stage of his conversation.

"*I used to have a boyfriend though. But we split up.*"

Okay, was this little encounter now developing into a therapy session? Being only nineteen, my lack of experience meant I was no Doctor Ruth, but hey, if he needed a shoulder to cry on, mine was right here, perilously close to the mouth-watering stubble on his chiselled cheek that was now eliciting drool from my mouth like a dog with rabies. But I'd heard that drooling was a term of endearment in Gay World.

"*I'm sorry to hear that*" I said sympathetically, waiting for his aforementioned stubbly cheek to tilt sideways like a bronzed Leaning Tower of Pisa and come to rest on my waiting shoulder which was inching upwards now at an angle in excited anticipation. Instead he just turned to look me in the eye, asking:

"*Do you go to any of the bars along Oxford Street?*"

It was clear now where he was going with this.

"*Which ones do you mean?*" I replied, stringing this out now despite knowing what he was getting at. My God, that Adam was right, I *was* a cock tease!

"*You know, The Albury, Midnight Shift, The Beresford...*"

Okay, he didn't need to list every single gay bar along Oxford Street for me to get his drift. His drift was well and truly understood. Mr. *Home and Away* was trying to pick me up.

"*No*", I stated matter-of-factly, without even thinking.

His face dropped.

"*Okay, see ya then*" he retorted bluntly and swiftly re-clad his luscious feet in his flip flops and bounded off like a disappointed kangaroo quicker than I could warble "*You know we belong together...*"

    I was aghast. He had shot off so quick that I hadn't had even a second to explain that No didn't mean *No*. No meant I wasn't lying, I hadn't been in any of the gay bars only because I have been too scared to venture past the step of the front door in all of them. Why couldn't I have just lied and said yes? I had never intended to answer "*No*" again should a hot man ever ask me if I was gay, not after my last encounter here, but Mr. *Home and Away* had confused me by circumnavigating the directness of his query and not getting to the bloody point!

I wasn't going to lie again, I had been lying to myself for years and now a sudden urge to give an honest answer for once was resulting in a *Home and Away* hunk scurrying away from me like I had unleashed a silent but deadly fart. I wasn't about to let him go that easy, the last few minutes having been a slightly tweaked variation on many scenarios populating my teenage Wank Bank that had propelled many an ejaculation aged fourteen. I had to explain the context of my *"No"*, my gay virginity being triumphantly lost to an Aussie soap star was at stake! I stumbled clumsily to my feet and gave chase, catching sight of Mr. *Home and Away* as he disappeared into some thick scrubland further down the path. I was now a demented bitch on heat, scrambling and parting my way through the undergrowth like a horny cross between a younger David Bellamy and a gay Benny Hill until I emerged into a small clearing, battered and scratched with broken twigs and foliage glued to the melting gel in my hair. There I found a quintet of guys, shorts around their ankles, engaged in what looked like to be a human version of the game *Hungry Hippos* with many balls being chomped into many hungry mouths. As they all turned to face the young lad now looking like *Stig of the Dump*, I just nodded politely yet mortified, declined an invitation to become the sixth *Hungry Hippo* and did a quick U-turn. After another fifteen minutes of getting completely lost and inadvertently interrupting a myriad of other half-naked men in various different stages of sexual activity, I finally emerged back onto the main coastal path, having had no success whatsoever in locating my *Home and Away* paramour who had vanished without a trace never to be seen again, apart from on a TV screen at 7pm on Channel 7. As I took refuge in the cubicle of a public toilet to tend to my scratches and de-twig my hair, I took comfort in the fact that at least the whole debacle had been a step up in the evolutionary gay scale from my previous encounter here. Chasing a *Home and Away* star through the bushes might not have been quite laced with dignity but it had sure as hell smacked of increasing bravery. And that would have to do for now. The next step would come when the universe decided the time was right.

*

That ensuing step presented itself quite unexpectedly on New Year's Eve 1993 in a tiny back-of-beyond town called Bega in southern rural New South Wales. Debs had stayed behind in Sydney, Michelle and Angela had departed for Tasmania whilst Gareth, Sandra and I hadn't quite fathomed how we had ended up in Bumblefuck, New South Wales to see in 1994 rather than the glittering bright lights of Sydney. It was all thanks to Machiavellian machinations of tee-total Lisa, who, horrified at the thought of being surrounded by drunken revellers on Sydney Harbour (as was our plan) had fed us stories of double bookings and a burnt down hostel on our post-Sydney travel route which was intended to commence just after New Year. I don't know why we chose to believe her. After all we all knew that Lisa was a compulsive liar, always telling outlandish lie after lie, mostly to exert a sense of superiority over us. If you'd had a job, she'd already had it, if you'd lost your virginity at seventeen, she'd lost it at sixteen. She was twenty-two years old but had so far got two degrees, worked on an oil rig, been the Mayoress of Aberdeen, had an Olympic sized swimming pool in her back garden, was allergic to alcohol but blue *Smarties* got her high, had served in the Navy, fought in the Gulf War (but got sent home because her Daddy was worried about her) - and also had the World Record (in North-East Scotland) for high jumping. I found her catalogue of bizarre lies and her condescension madly infuriating but Sandra thought she was ultimately harmless and wanted another female in the gang and so Lisa stayed with us.

At least we had got to celebrate Christmas on Bondi Beach before we left Sydney. Sandra, Gareth and I had stayed up all night on Christmas Eve to watch the sunrise over the Pacific Ocean on Christmas Day. Staying out was preferable to spending time in our new residence the Biltmore Hotel which we had moved into after our landlord had refused to extend the lease on our flat by just one month. The Biltmore was a comedown, possessing a standard of accommodation that left it as a cross between an old people's home and a mental institution, run by the owner Joe, a middle-aged man who dressed like on overgrown Boy Scout, who was in turn bossed about by Sybil Fawlty with permanent PMT, AKA his frighteningly authoritarian wife Heather. The other residents of the hotel were no better, consisting of a Nazi-esque housemaid who would quite literally throw you out of bed and a motley crew of bizarre misfits who we would encounter at the 'Biltmore Happy Hour', a daily ritual of warm beer and awkward conversation on the same enjoyment level as Chinese water torture. There we had the pleasure of the company of 'Gummy Bear' an elderly man with no teeth who could only drool, an ageing cockney wide-boy who we nicknamed 'Frank Butcher', creepy Ted with the tombstone teeth who would not stop trying to kiss Sandra and finally, ruling the roost from the back of the room whilst chain-smoking in just her highly flammable nightdress, was Noelene, whose sole source of entertainment was to repeatedly keep enquiring as to the activeness of our sex lives. With full lurid details if at all possible. I could have spent hours regaling her with the details of the damp squib that was mine, and one that I was keeping a secret from my friends. The endless near misses with men, the obstacles constantly put in my way, the trying to consummate my gayness but it never coming to fruition. Noelene would have died of boredom.

  I don't know why I was still keeping my homosexuality a secret from my friends. But I had grown up in such a homophobic environment that the truth was that I was just still too scared to come out and be who I really was. Meeting a man, having sex with a man, falling in love with a man, coming out, losing friends, getting disowned by family. That was the chain of events that I could foresee. Maybe it was best that I couldn't even reach that first step of finding a man to begin with. The universe seemed to be thwarting me at every turn. Maybe the universe was actually just protecting me. Maybe I should have listened to it.

*

  And so, after Lisa had successfully convinced us that we had to leave Sydney earlier than planned, on New Year's Eve 1993, we now found ourselves in a quietly surreal YHA hostel run by Irene, a militant-like rotund woman who thought she was the white Bob Marley, with dreadlocks emanating from under her very-soiled Rastafarian bobble hat. It was hardly a thrilling setting for a New Year's Eve party which was just as well because there was no such party planned by Irene. In fact there was nothing much to do at all, made worse by the only other company in the hostel being provided by an odd devoutly Christian couple who we nicknamed the McWeirds and a Scottish father and son duo with identical matching beards who we named the McBeards. After being dulled with the inanity of attempted conversion to Our Lord Jesus and the benefits of facial hair - a conversation for Jesus himself, I jokingly noted to much non-hilarity, the door to the hostel suddenly opened and in walked The Most Beautiful Man I Had Ever Laid Eyes On. Well, I decided on that flattering label after he had the chance to remove his black crash helmet as he rocked up clad head to toe in a leather biker's outfit, like he was the Milk Tray Man with a malfunctioning watch who had arrived in daylight rather than in the dead of night.

  His name was Jarrad. He was in his early twenties, tall, handsome, rugged, ever so friendly - and ginger in a surprisingly sexy way. He was motor biking his way around Australia and had found himself in Bega on New Year's Eve. I was instantly smitten.

  Irene wanted us to spend the evening with her in the hostel, listening to her collection of reggae records but we needed proper entertainment. Unfortunately the one and only venue in town where alcohol was served and anything barely resembling a New Year's Eve party was taking place was the local Royal Servicemen's League (RSL) club. I plucked up the courage to personally ask Jarrad if he wanted to accompany us, timed extremely well with the moment he was squeezing out of his leathers in the male dormitory.

And so we all headed to the local RSL club, leaving Irene with the McWeirds and the McBeards to discuss whether Our Bearded Lord Jesus was into reggae. Well, the RSL party we walked into was a sedate affair that the word party could have sued for misrepresentation of. It was like being back at one of my family's parties but with all the dancing people removed so that all that was left were the settees containing Aussie versions of my Mum and Great Aunt Edna. As midnight edged nearer, a smattering of brave souls actually dared to dance, but not too energetically should the exertion bring about their untimely demise. Gareth, Sandra and Lisa joined them whilst I lurked in a corner chatting to Jarrad, hanging on his every word as if they were skyscrapers that I had toppled over the edge of and now had to cling on to for dear life. The stroke of midnight came.

And Jarrad suddenly kissed me.
Naturally I was astounded. I was rendered mute with the shock of something that I hadn't been expecting at all. He took one look at my face now resembling Munch's *The Scream* painting and quickly apologised, saying that he had got the wrong idea. I had to get out of this habit of giving 'the wrong idea' to gay men that were obviously interested in me. There was an interminable awkward silence as half of me wanted to ask him to kiss me again whilst the other half was panicking that my friends had witnessed the infinitesimal exchange of male saliva that had just occurred. Of all the places that I would share my first kiss with another man, I hadn't anticipated it to be in a Royal Servicemen's League club in rural New South Wales. I wanted to kiss him back. I had to be quick, as everyone in the RSL club had reacted to midnight by eliciting a little collective *"woo"*, the excitement level of which was like they were in a car going over a speed bump and were now collecting their coats and filing out of the door to go home. Obviously in Bega, New Year's Eve parties could not continue once it was no longer technically New Year's Eve. Fuck it, I thought, I'm going to kiss him back. And of course, before I could, the universe course corrected on my behalf yet again as my friends bounded over, killing the moment stone dead.

As we headed back to the hostel, Jarrad mounted his motorbike and rode off into the night, maintaining the air of mystery that defined him - and his kiss with me. He had indeed been my Milk Tray Man, dressed in black, sweeping in whilst I was metaphorically sleeping and leaving me a kiss instead of a box of chocolates. I never stopped thinking about That Kiss. I had locked lips with another man, just a simple peck that had breathed the fire of bravery and realisation deep into my soul. Prince Charming had woken up Snow White from her closet coma. I was Dorothy at the fork in the yellow brick road, at the point when it splits into two. Which path do I take? The well-defined and recommended path of continued heterosexuality? Or would I follow the path of embracing being gay, only to maybe find that there was only a man behind the curtain creating nothing more than an illusion?

A few days later, a parcel arrived for me, forwarded on by my mail forwarding service. It was a Page 3 calendar, a Christmas present from Phil, Ant and Daz back in Dagenham. A tool of an attempt from ten thousand miles away to steer me back towards heterosexuality. I was grateful for the thought but left it behind in the hostel for someone who would appreciate tabloid tits a lot more than I would. For I swore to myself that if another Jarrad rocked up in my life and wanted to kiss me, I would damn well kiss him first.

11 – A 'LAVENDER MARRIAGE'

1994 (aged 19)

Alas, my next kiss with another man wouldn't come about for quite some time. But I didn't mind. I now knew what I would do if and when the opportunity presented itself, but for now my journey out of the closet was put on the back burner whilst I concentrated on my journey around Australia. It was a country I was in love with and I wanted to explore as much of it as possible, every nook, cranny and of course, gay 'hotspot'.

After leaving Bega, the feel of Jarrad's stolen kiss still lingering on my lips, we continued travelling down through New South Wales and into Victoria where we ended up in the Dandenong Ranges east of Melbourne to pick flowers for a few weeks and replenish our funds. It was here that the Bondi Gang finally went our separate ways in February 1994.

Sandra and Lisa decided they were heading west to Perth where Michelle and Angela were also now residing, to settle for a few months and find work. Meanwhile Gareth had decided to stay behind working in the Dandenongs, whilst I impulsively joined a Norwich couple, Phil and Caroline on a road trip around Tasmania. Then in March 1994, with my money running perilously low again, I decided to also head west to Perth where I reunited with Sandra and Michelle - and to a much lesser extent, Lisa and Angela.

I had missed 'my girls' Sandra and Michelle. As a gay man I always felt the most comfortable in the company of women. There was just something that made me feel safe hanging out with them. Sandra, Michelle and I were like Charlie's Angels, embarking on nightly drunken adventures in Perth, ranging from stealing toilet rolls from posh hotels, invading ballroom dances and sneaking into the 1994 World Firefighter's Games then getting thrown out for dancing with the band up on stage.

We were the trio committing the 'crimes', not solving them. We were becoming inseparable.

    I moved into Michelle's little flat on Adelaide Terrace in the city centre, an arrangement that Michelle practically begged from me, due to the pains of her still being lumbered with 'The Dork', the name now given to Angela, the timid girl from Manchester, who Michelle hadn't been able to shake off since her very first day in Australia and who was also living in the flat. There was something very, very off about Angela. All she would do was sit in the corner, mute and barely moving like an endangered koala, just observing everything Michelle and I did or said. She was borderline obsessive about Michelle, creating her own real life version of *Single White Female* or in Angela's case, *Single White Female Who Goes Bushwalking As If Dressed For The Office And Who Leaves Skiddy Knickers In The Bathroom*. Thus my presence in the flat was a blessed relief for Michelle, a male companion that was also wanted after Michelle's date with a guy had gone so horribly wrong that he broke into her flat in the middle of the night, leaving Michelle and Angela to hide under the bed terrified. I was hardly bouncer material though. I would have scurried under the bed too.

*

    Meanwhile I had secured a job in The Most Horrendous Place on Earth to Work working with The World's Worst Colleagues. Running out of money fast and with casual jobs in Perth scarcer than hot men willing to kiss me, I had, in desperation, found myself a job at William J Pascoes chemical factory in the suburb of Jolimont, a happy-sounding name that was a clearly misleading misnomer for the Hell I was about to find myself in. The factory was a place that was an Aussie version of Dagenham's Fords car factory, the workplace that was meant for me but that I had escaped the fate of ending up in - or so I thought - as obviously a tornado had uprooted it *Wizard of Oz* style and unceremoniously dumped it Down Under into a nondescript Perth suburb where it had been renamed and repopulated with the cast of *Prisoner Cell Block H*. If only it had landed on top of - and crushed - its very own Wicked Witches - aka - Marilyn and Kathy, two middle-aged vile, cackling monsters, sporting a grand total of five teeth between them. They ruled the factory with matching oversized Pat Butcher-like earrings and an iron fist that would have been better placed jammed up their planet-sized arses. And here I was at their mercy, their very own trembling Dorothy - minus a cute little doggy - to terrorise for nine hours a day. My task was mind-numbingly simple and repetitive, just filling empty plastic bottles with car oil, via a spluttering, ancient machine that reminded me of *Bertha* from the kids TV programme of the same name. The machine would regularly jam which meant I had to ask help from Alan, an equally repulsive, 'Pom'-

hating cohort of Marilyn and Kathy's who would respond to my requests for help with so much foul-mouthed huffing and puffing, it wasn't clear whether he was having a coronary or would actually inflate and burst, like a child's balloon with the face of Jabba the Hutt painted on it. After several of Alan's temper tantrums of so-called help, I became too scared to ask for any more assistance and so soldiered on alone.

  I didn't have a single confidante there, relegated to eating my sandwiches alone in the shadow of the outside toilet whilst I listened to the shrieking merriment of Marilyn, Kathy and Alan all cruelly making fun of me from their out-of-bounds lunch room.

  Was this in fact Hell? The place where my twelve-year old self was convinced I would end up after watching *Tangerine Dream* eight years before? Had the so-called God passed judgement on my kiss with hot biker Jarrad three months before and now condemned me to the inside of Satan's spicy sphincter to spend eternity filling oil into bottles in the company of people that I wished I had enough dollars in my account to pay a hitman to assassinate? I wasn't meant to be *here*. This wasn't what Australia had promised me. In fact, a lot of Australia's promises were proving to be hollow. This clearly wasn't *Home and Away*. After just three days working there, I had to find a way out, which wasn't easy when I desperately needed to earn every dollar that I could. And so the only option open to me was to throw a sickie to be able to go to every job centre in Perth, in the hope of finding an alternative job that would be my saviour. I didn't find it. I had to return with my tail dangling between my legs to the chemical factory, to find I was to have a punishment meted out to me for daring to take a day off sick - which apparently was a crime worse than Marilyn's skin-tight floral jeggings. However, it was a chastisement that would lead to The Pink Rubber Glove Incident. Upon my reluctant return to the factory after my sickie day, I was immediately greeted by Marilyn and Kathy with an audience of Alan and half the factory watching behind them. Needless to say it wasn't quite a welcoming committee. Like a magician you would want to get a refund from, Marilyn magically produced a bottle of bleach, a brillo pad and a pair of Bright Pink Rubber Gloves and thrust them in my confused direction.

"*Got a new job for you today, sweetheart*" she informed me, hardly able to contain her glee and eliciting sycophantic titters from her army of flying monkeys - sorry - other factory workers - behind her. Before I had time to work out what the combination of these three cleaning tools would be entailing, I was unceremoniously marched through the factory, out through the back, across the yard and into the outside men's dunny where she finally stopped and jabbed her talons in the direction of the horribly stained and stench-ridden urinals. Obviously, my task was not for me to

take a piss in front of her whilst she watched but rather, as she so eloquently put it:
"Clean off the fucking piss you little homo. Then when you're done, do the fucking shitter". I was too stunned to say anything. Then she made me put on the pink rubber gloves as she watched, smiling, the lurid coloured gloves further branding me as the *"little homo"* before she departed and left me to my task. Despite her powers of assumption about my sexuality being spot on, no-one had called me a homo before to my face and certainly had not punished me for a day off sick by making me scrub stale urine and crusted flecks of faeces from the recesses of an outside toilet. As anger suddenly surged inside me, I decided I was not going to put up with this shit, in more ways than one. Suddenly consumed now with a boiling rage that would have sent the *Incredible Hulk* running for cover, I snatched up the cleaning products and marched out of the dunny and back into the factory. Such was the look of complete and utter ire on my face that workers took one look and actually downed tools to hurriedly follow me along my Path of Wrath, sensing something epic was about to happen. I found Marilyn and Kathy standing outside their little office, simultaneously smoking a cigarette each in perfect unison like less attractive versions of Marge Simpson's sisters Patty and Selma.
"You can't be finished already!" sneered Kathy.
"I'm not doing it" I snarled back at her.
"Don't think you're too big to clean the dunny. We all have to do it!" scowled Marilyn, joining in and putting her hands on her hips as if that would somehow intimidate me.
Yeah, like that was likely.
"Get fucked", I declared, adding *"That's if you can find a man willing to venture inside either of your hellholes."* nodding at their camel toes as I pulled the pink rubber gloves off my hands. *"Oh, and in case you're too stupid to realise, I quit so stick your fucking job."* And with that I threw the pink rubber gloves in their faces, as one got caught in one of Marilyn's satellite-sized earrings, eliciting shrieks from her and chortling from the factory workers assembled around us for the show. I marched past Kathy and Marilyn, the pink rubber glove still dangling from the latter's right ear and out of the factory, my head held high, victorious that Dorothy the Little Homo had melted both witches in a puddle of their own hatred. As I emerged from the factory back into the daylight after what had been the shortest working day of my life, I felt elated on the high of sudden strength that I had never known had lay dormant within me. It was the moment that the shy boy from Dagenham officially ceased to exist, to be replaced by this newer, braver (and at this second, still shaking with anger) model. I was ready to take on the world and any enemies that crossed my path.

*

It had been the trials of The Worst Job Ever that had helped forge a strong bond between Michelle and I. Drowning my sorrows nightly with her via the conduit of boxes of cheap white wine as she in turn sought solace from the The Dork's increasingly bizarre and possessive behaviour, our friendship grew closer in that I had now subliminally recruited her as my new 'beard', the adult successor to six-year old Fiona back in Leys Infants.

To the outside world we looked like a married couple minus the sex. It was the perfect platonic lavender union, hiding my true sexuality whilst I was hanging out by day on Swanbourne Beach, Perth's very own gay nudist spot and coming home to Michelle at night, feeling like a cheating husband. She was my best friend, I adored her - and yet I was still too afraid to confide in her about who I really was. And with good reason. Michelle had grown up with a homophobic father, who had indoctrinated her with his own prejudices. One night we went to the cinema to watch *Philadelphia*, a movie that Michelle had no idea was about a gay man - and one with AIDS at that. I was dismayed and disheartened by Michelle's anti-gay comments after the credits rolled. I knew then that I could never come out to her. I was terrified of losing her friendship if I revealed myself to be gay. Her mild homophobia was disconcerting but I knew it was through no fault of her own and I still loved her like the sister that I had always wished I had. Maybe all wasn't lost, maybe the help I was giving her with dealing with The Dork would score me some brownie points, enough stars for my merit chart that I could present as evidence of what a good friend I was, regardless of my sexuality, should she ever discover the truth. And The Get Rid of Dork Mission would score a veritable bonanza of brownie points.

Something had flipped inside of The Dork and she was devolving into full-on crazy. Already adhering to a vow of silence with only weird looks being a clue to what she was thinking about us, the only guess that Michelle and I could muster was that Angela was insanely jealous of our bond. It was a suspicion that was more than confirmed when one night, we persuaded Angela to join us for a drink at which point Angela got completely wasted and admitted she was a lesbian, one who was clearly in love with Michelle, owing to her trying to undress Michelle in the middle of a busy pub called Novaks where a singer nicknamed Baldy always played the same old songs. In this case, it turned out that Angela was playing the same song as me, the lyrics to hers tweaked slightly but the same ditty nonetheless. She, like I, was in the closet. But whilst I was still hiding at the back of mine, seven schooners of VB lager had oiled the hinges of Angela's, loosening the doors open and sending her tumbling out.

But now that Angela's secret was public knowledge, she did the only thing that comes natural to anyone with such a weight off their shoulders. She tried to gas us.

Yes, Michelle and I were about to find out that the most dangerous animal in Australia wasn't the redback spider I had found myself accidentally sitting next to on a park bench one afternoon. The poison from a redback was nothing compared to a quiet yet unhinged lesbian Mancunian with access to a gas cooker. Either mortified at her inadvertent coming out or furious that we hadn't asked how her day at work had been, a confession that was written in the diary that she left open, a tome full of childish scribblings that also labelled Michelle a 'stupid bimbo cow' and me an 'ignorant lad', something had now drop-kicked Angela into full-on Crazy Town. So as you do, you choose to gas the ignorant lad and the stupid bimbo cow.

Michelle did have a tendency to attract trouble, as did I, but neither of us had been prepared for the odour of gas to cancel out the scent of our respective perfume and aftershave. It took about a week to realise what was going on, waking up several mornings in a row to find that one of us must have left the gas running on the cooker, no doubt thanks to the consumption of just one too many boxes of cheap white wine. But after yet another day and another discovery of the gas running, I realised something far more sinister was going on, putting two and two together as I fathomed that the smell of gas would only appear minutes after Angela had left for work in the morning. I should have already been more suspicious that Angela had a temp office job that somehow required her to leave the flat at 5am when her start time was 9am and her workplace was only a ten minute walk away, whilst Michelle and I were still fast asleep and three hours away from rising ourselves.

On the fifth day, I secretly witnessed Angela's deed for myself, as she finished a cup of tea in the kitchen, and then deliberately turned on the gas on all the cooker rings before nonchalantly leaving for work. She was never seen again after that, apart from a couple of months later when I would randomly bump into her in a backpackers hostel in Bundaberg, Queensland, a meeting that was just equally surprising for both of us, and one that sent Angela scurrying away in fear to disappear yet again. And that really was the last I ever saw of her.

I should have been more sympathetic towards Angela but the psychopathic tendencies and morning gas inhalation put paid to that. I certainly had no intention of gassing anyone I might accidentally come out to. Michelle and I just shrugged off the incident, after all, it was par for the course now to encounter crazier than crazy characters on our travels.

*

Mine and Michelle's lavender 'marriage' went through a trial separation after Perth as Michelle wanted to take a break from Australia and go backpacking around South East Asia whilst I continued on around Australia, travelling up the West Coast, across the Northern Territory and down through Queensland and Northern New South Wales before finally returning to Sydney and re-uniting with Michelle there months later. I was more than surprised to find that Michelle had gone through a transformation in her attitudes towards gay people during her time away in South East Asia. Upon our reunion, she told me about the gay guys she had met in Bali and travelled with for a bit, adding how much fun they were and that maybe she had misjudged gay people in general. Now that's what I called progress. This should have been my moment to tell her that she had already been travelling with someone gay, that, murderous gas-loving lesbians aside, she'd already been having lots of fun with a gay guy from Essex who loved her like a sister. But I didn't. My reasoning was that I felt I needed to actually have sex with another man first, to officially consummate my homosexuality, to partake in the act of man-on-man or man-in-man action that would mean there was no going back. Until that would happen, I would keep up my facade. The irony was of course that the chances of getting to act on my gayness were slim to none when I was one half of what seemed to be a normal heterosexual couple travelling the world together. After a brief reunion with Sandra who still had Lisa the Liar clung to her side like a mollusc, Michelle and I left Australia as our year-long visas expired, to move on to a hitch hiking adventure around New Zealand.

*

Looking like a couple worked wonders when it came to hitchhiking through The Land of the Long White Cloud. We had already been informed on our arrival in Auckland that a boy/girl pairing was the best combination for getting drivers to stop and it was true, it worked wonders, as we never failed to get a lift to our next destination. Our 'couply' appearance was so convincing in fact that five times in a row we beat a rival shaggy-haired hitch-hiker who always turned up at the same roadside spot as us. Hitchhiking was without doubt the best way to experience New Zealand, getting up close and personal with the country from a local's point of view, as the drivers who gave us lifts ranged widely on the Normal - Outright Crazy scale. There was staunchly serious businessman Basil, whose name elicited such a burst of laughter from us both (as I thought of Basil Brush and Michelle thought of Basil Fawlty) that he unceremoniously ditched us in his offence. Then there was the fat man who called every woman driver a slut and laughed at every word that I said. When he said he was taking a detour to visit his Mum, I asked her how she was and he replied she was dead, to which I laughed, thinking it to be a joke when in actual fact he was visiting her grave. And then along came Ian, a creepy guy who gave us a place to stay for the night at his house in Blenheim, a house that sported severed pigs heads on the wall, a souvenir from his job that entailed making condoms out of pigs' guts for a living. He was up there with Jeffrey Dahmer and Fred West when it came to giving off a serial killer vibe but Michelle and I decided it was worth the risk as we desperately needed a place to stay, so that night we wedged the bed up against the door, just to be on the safe side. Less safe was the visit from Ian's preacher friend Mike who turned up unannounced before bedtime to join us for dinner, took one look at me and decided to launch into his views on homosexuality, adamant that gay men were *"trained to be queers"* and that *"they all have high pitched voices because the force of anal sex damages their windpipes"*. It was an excruciating dinner conversation, one in which I felt I should just keep quiet and not argue with his ridiculously bigoted views, dare I alert Michelle to the truth that I was one of these queers, albeit with my windpipe still intact and the pitch of my voice down at a safe gruff level.

When Ian dropped us off the next day, he shoved a damp toilet roll and some condoms made from the finest pigs guts into my hands with a knowing wink towards Michelle. It was a relief that he hadn't had a clue that I was gay, such as was his assumption of mine and Michelle's bedtime activities that in reality was just a case of platonic top and tailing. We were used to the sharing of a bed by now, a double bed being all that was ever offered to us each time we were given a place to stay for the night by various locals who had no idea we were actually a younger equivalent of Elton John and his one-time fake wife Renate. But then in Christchurch, we would meet a younger equivalent of *me*.

A travelling salesman had picked us up and as it was late into the night, he, like most others that offered us rides, also offered us a place to stay at his house. And so he dropped us off at his abode on the outskirts of Christchurch, and then promptly went out for the night, leaving us alone with just his fourteen year old son Justin for company. Despite Michelle and I feeling a tad uncomfortable that a man had just left two complete strangers alone with his young son, Justin seemed unfazed by it all. We ended up spending the evening with him watching *Coronation Street* and the Kiwi soap *Shortland Street*. It was something about the way that Justin was avidly watching the soaps, in particular his reaction to certain male characters on screen that clued me up straightaway. He was the Kiwi equivalent of my secretly gay fourteen year old self. I wondered if he did drag shows for his sick Grandma, had an Uncle who was *"funny"*, was in love with his male best friend, or if deep down he knew he was The Thing That Dare Not Speak Its Name. I wanted to tell him it will be okay to be gay, that it would be a long journey ahead of him, one that I was still on myself but at this moment in time I had a staunchly heterosexual 'relationship' to keep up the appearance of. For Michelle and I were getting like a married couple who had been in each other's company every minute of the day. We were trading little snipes with each other here and there, little bouts of mild bickering - and even had a big full-blown argument once over two minute noodles and the error I had made in not cooking her some when she was on her way home. We didn't speak to each other for half a day after that disagreement. We were becoming a platonic version of my Mum and Dad, arguing, as I ran the risk, like my Mum years earlier, of sporting noodles as a spontaneous hairpiece. I wasn't sure how much longer I could pretend to be such husband material, the pressure of my secret was clearly taking its toll on my close friendship with Michelle.

12 – THE FIJIAN NYMPHOMANIAC AND THE PING PONG BALL

1994 (aged 19)

After our adventures around New Zealand, Michelle and I headed to Fiji, where we had agreed, via a note pinned to a hostel notice board in Auckland, to rendezvous with Sandra (who had finally parted ways with Lisa) on the island of Nananu-i-Ra sitting just off the island's north coast. In the days before mobile phones, text messages and social media, our hopes of meeting up with Sandra were pinned on her receiving this flimsy piece of paper attached to a cork board with nothing but a small drawing pin.

Mine and Michelle's first impressions of Fiji weren't exactly favourable. It was grimy, rubbish-strewn with an inherent deforestation policy that had robbed most of the island of the lush green landscapes that we had expected. It wasn't quite the palm tree-and-coconuts island from the *Bounty* adverts that we thought we would find. Still, we had heard that Nananu-i-Ra was a little piece of paradise, where Michelle and I could spend a few days relaxing whilst we awaited Sandra's arrival. The boat to Nananu-i-Ra departed from the small town of Rakiraki where Michelle and I rocked up and found our way to Ellington Pier - pier being a loose sense of the word as it was in fact just a small stony outcrop with a few steps leading down to an even smaller wooden platform. Thanks to the phenomenon known as 'Fiji Time' the small speedboat that was to be our ride across to the island turned up over an hour late. But when it eventually rocked up, a big jostling fifty-something Fijian woman leapt out of the boat bounding around at a high force and loud volume like a newly charged Duracell bunny in a dirty sarong. She was Vani, the owner of the Kontiki Lodge, the only available accommodation on Nananu-i-Ra. We joined her in the boat, squashed up as she pointed out various islands privately owned by rich Japanese and Americans. She indicated one particular island to Michelle excitedly telling her that no less than five princes resided there all of which were *"fuckeen handsum!"* And she should go there and try her luck.

"Erm, excuse me, how do you know she's isn't my girlfriend?" I butted in, leaping in like a jealous fake husband.

"Oh pur-lease" cackled Vani, rolling her eyes knowingly at me. My heart filled with dread. She had me sussed already. I couldn't fathom why. Except that my gay aura maybe had the power to transcend oceans. For the rest of the journey, any glance at Vani would be met with a wry smile and tiny pursing of her cracked lips. Wow, she really was in need of some lip balm, I thought, realising of course that this was a very gay thought to have. Maybe I was more obvious than I realised but I was certain that Michelle still didn't have a clue as to my true proclivities.

A short while later, we waded ashore to find the island of Nananu-I-Ra was a lot more attractive than the mainland, with warm clear water, fringed by a golden beach and hammocks strung up between palm trees. It was a little tropical paradise. We were given a self-contained beach house right by the water to find we were sharing with three other guys, super-chatty Craig from Middlesbrough, a Japanese guy who could not speak a single word of English so opted to remain mute - and finally, Sebastian, a pony-tailed failed musician who had quit the music business on the brink of fame because the pressure was too much for him. I knew how he felt, burdened with the pressure of hiding my sexuality when people were starting to suss me out left, right, centre, up, down and across the middle. But I was not about to quit and return to a life of heterosexual 'normality', all I had to do was think back to The Pink Rubber Glove Incident in Perth a few months before to keep me re-focused towards my eventual coming out.

As soon as Vani left the beach house after checking Michelle and I in, Sebastian instantly pulled me aside and asked if Michelle and I were a couple. When I replied no, thinking that he maybe wanted to make a move on her, he warned me that we should *pretend* to be a couple - for my own safety.

"Safety from what?" I enquired, mildly perturbed at where this might be going.

"From Vani" stated Sebastian in the manner of someone telling you that your bunk mate with the odd square-shaped moustache was in fact Hitler. *"She'll pounce on you if she knows you are single."*

Apparently Vani was a highly charged sex maniac who relentlessly targeted every single man that came ashore the island as her newest toy of pleasure, blackmailing them that they wouldn't be able to leave the island until she had laid her eyes, preferably her hands, and ideally her mouth - on their penis. Sebastian's shudder at relating this and

his hollowed eyes indicated that his own appendage had already unwillingly been privy to various parts of Vani's sun-aged body. I confessed to Sebastian that I thought Vani had already worked out that Michelle and I weren't a couple, before adding:
"*Anyway, I think she already knows that I'm-*" I quickly stopped myself.
"*Am what?*" pressed Sebastian.
"*Way too young for her*" I blurted out, quickly thinking on my toes. Sebastian just gave me a look that combined sympathy, fear and the dreadful realisation on my part that she preferred her victims to be young and patted me on the shoulder as if I had just been sentenced to Death Row. I was left with a palpable sense of dread.

That evening, as all the residents of the beach house were just chilling out reading or brushing teeth and washing before the water supply was shut off at 9pm, the door swung inwards suddenly as if it was blown open by the Big Bad Wolf in *Three Little Pigs*. In marched Vani, the wolf in a sarong, clearly unannounced and certainly uninvited, accompanied by a younger Fijian girl that she dragged behind in her wake like a wide-eyed protégé to be imminently taught the skills of Fijian-style sex talk. Chewing incessantly on a piece of kava root, Vani pulled up a chair and immediately told us all to "*shut up and pay attention as I have come to talk about sex!*" which elicited a wondrous giggly-cum-gasp from her companion. Not missing a beat, Vani lurched towards me and snatched from my hands the Lonely Planet guide book to Fiji that I was reading.
"*Ah, Fiji! F-I-J-I. You know what those letters really stand for darling?*"
I shrugged as she leaned closer to me her teeth now chattering like a famished piranha.
"*Fucking Is Just Incredible!!!*"
She shrieked with a witch-like cackle as I immediately and instantly recoiled, glancing fearfully at Sebastian who just gave me a "*told you so*" look and shrug. Vani was indeed a sex maniac, a ruder, cruder, worse dressed and less hygienic version of Mrs Slocombe from *Are You Being Served?* It was only a matter of time before the conversation would be steered towards 'her pussy' in the same hopeful vein she had of trying to steer every male penis on the island towards it too. Bang on cue, she turned her attention to the silent Japanese guy whose name no-one knew. As the poor lad looked confused at Vani's sudden attention, Sebastian gallantly tried to intervene by saying to Vani:
"*Leave him alone. Whatever rude thing you say to him, he won't understand. He'll just smile sweetly and nod*"
"*Well now that's what I call fun, darling!*" retorted a defiant Vani as she sidled up to the Japanese guy's side and told him "*How about we go and check out my pussy in the bush, darling? Then I can give you a diving lesson!*"
Good God, Mrs Slocombe on heat was indeed in the room.

The Japanese guy just smiled sweetly and nodded at her.
But it didn't stop there. Vani then 'blushingly confessed' that she liked to watch the male guests masturbating in the shower. Upon demanding to know how she did this, she admitted that all the showers had spy holes through the back wall, where she would peer through and enjoy the show. She went on to snicker and state that she called wanking *"self employment"* and took a perverse pleasure in asking male guests the last time they were 'self employed', adding:

"I seen so many white dicks and the English men are so handsome. But..." she sighed, *"I reckon ninety-five percent of English men are poofters!"* her eyes suddenly darting over to me.

My eyes widened like two light bulbs cranked up to full blast by a dimmer switch. Craig butted in quickly.

"Is that because ninety-five percent of English men turn you down?"

Something about the way Craig leapt in here - and his lingering eye contact with me as he did - wasn't lost on me, alerting me to the fact that there was another gay man in this beach house. Craig's rebuttal had left Vani lost for words as Sebastian chimed in with a damning assessment of her motives.

"You flirt outrageously with men to scare them off because you are actually too scared of anyone getting close to you".

This obviously hit a raw nerve in Vani as she suddenly got up and marched out like a petulant child who hadn't got her way, pulling her companion behind her like a rag doll until the door slammed behind her and calm resumed.

She had left us in peace - but not for long. The daytime hours of the next day passed by relatively Vani-free and Sandra finally showed up, wading ashore from a speedboat as Michelle and I sunbathed on the beach. She had got the note in Auckland and here she was. It was great to have her rejoin us, *Charlie's Angels* had reformed, and in Sandra, I now had extra reinforcement in the Battle Against Vani's Sex Drive, support which I needed more than ever now as Sebastian had finally been able to leave the island that morning and had been replaced by two perpetually giggling Japanese girls called Yumi and Yuki. The male contingent of the guests was dwindling to drought-like proportions, with Craig and I - aka The Only Two Gays on the Island - the only mouth-watering drops of water left to quench the undulating thirst of Vani's very own Venus fly trap.

That evening, Vani tried a different method of seduction - to get us all wasted on Kava, a narcotic drink that tasted like *TCP* and could paralyse you if consumed in too vast a quantity. She gleefully reminisced at how the last bout of Kava-sipping had spawned a skinny dipping orgy with Penis-a-Plenty for her. Despite taking her claims with a pinch of salt, I still took the smallest sip possible each time. Thankfully I remained with full use of my limbs but Vani still came in for the kill as she cornered me behind the beach house as I tried to sneak back unnoticed.

"*Now that Sebastian has gone,*" she purred, "*you are the new object of my affection. I will tap on your window tonight. Be ready darling.*"

There was no way I was going to allow Vani to be tapping on *anything* that night. I had to get off the island. Luckily for me, everyone else had the same idea as I discovered that many other guests were desperate to escape. Within an hour, troops were rounded up, an audacious escape plan was drawn up and what will always forever be known as The Mass Exodus from Paradise took place, as every guest staying there rendezvoused in the dead of night to bribe the local speedboat owner to whisk us back to the mainland whilst Vani slept, blissfully unaware that the penis population had plummeted to zero.

Upon returning to the main island of Viti Levu, we all piled into a taxi and sped to the safety of the Hideaway Resort, on the southern side of the island. We holed up there for a few days, relaxing by day and enjoying the dubious evening entertainment by night of local Fijians impersonating American pop stars miming out of sync. It was bliss and not a single sex-crazed hostel owner in sight. But someone else was now out to seduce me.

Craig.

*

The chemical reaction of what happens when you set fire to a ping pong ball was to be the conduit of this particular seduction attempt. Credit where credit's due, Craig must have had it all planned ever since he saw my mortified reaction to Vani's assertion that a disproportionately large amount of English men were 'poofters'. He had laid in wait for the right moment, in this case whilst Michelle and Sandra were busy playing pool in the bar. As we watched the girls fit the balls into the triangle, making a joke that Vani alas had failed to secure a similar set-up, Craig suddenly asked me to come with him back to the dormitory where we were all residing in bunks, adding that he had something cool that he wanted to show me. Honestly curious, I followed him back to the dorm. Once inside, he closed the door behind us and reached into his pocket - to pull out a ping pong ball that he had pinched from the table tennis set in the main bar. Wondering for a moment whether he was intending to give Bangkok's best showgirls a run for their money, Craig then produced a cigarette lighter from his other pocket.

"*You ever seen what happens when you set light to a ping pong ball?*" he asked, in the overly-excitable manner of a small child that reminded me of my childhood on/off best friend Martin Schofield's own delight in crude insect dissection.

"*Can't say that I have*" I replied, wondering when in life - and why - someone would want to set fire to a ping pong ball.

"*Watch*" he commanded, as he clicked the lighter and ignited the small white sphere of plastic, causing it to fizz, crackle, then suddenly burst into a huge firework-like flame before fizzling out and dying again, leaving no trace at all of the ping pong ball.

"*Wow!*" I exclaimed, aiming for the Best Actor Academy Award for Feigned Excitement as I simultaneously wondered what the point of this whole exercise was.

Craig's eyes lit up, more than pleased with the reaction from his captive one-man audience.

And then he took all of his clothes off.

Ah, *there* was the point.

"*It's hot tonight. I need a shower*" he explained as he stepped towards me stark naked, the rising visible excitement of his penis now a match for my faked excitement at the ping pong pyrotechnics.

"*You should shower too*" he added, as I looked taken aback, then realised that he wasn't making comment on the dubious natural fragrance emanating from my armpits but was instead, extending an invitation in the same way his cock was now extending skyward. He proceeded to make his way very, very slowly to the shower, stopping with each step to look back to check my own state of undress and whether I was following him. Another small step, another sideways turn. It was like the childhood ritual of stepping along a pavement slowly trying not to step on the cracks. He looked back again as he reached the bathroom. My clothes remained adorned to my body. He disappeared into the bathroom and I heard the inviting sound of the shower being turned on. I sat on my bunk bed, torn over whether to join him or not. Craig was a nice guy but I didn't fancy him, not in the slightest. He was no *Home and Away* star or Jarrad the hot biker. But he was giving me an open invitation to finally act on my sexuality, to get intimate (albeit very wet too) with another man in the cramped environs of a Fiji backpacker hostel's shower cubicle. My heart was pounding. Fuck it, I thought, I can do this. I started to undress. Just as I was about to step out of my shorts, the annoying Canadian girl Jacinta who also slept in this dorm, suddenly burst in and decided this would be the right moment to repack her entire backpack from scratch, instantly killing, no murdering, the moment that hadn't even happened yet. Was it a sign that I wasn't supposed to partake just yet in intimacy with another man? Whether or not it was the work of divine intervention, I hurriedly re-dressed and sauntered past the Canadian Cock Blocker and out of the dorm, leaving poor Craig alone in the shower, wondering why I had turned him down.

It was awkward to say the least between Craig and I the next day and we never spoke of the incident in the dorm. Michelle, Sandra and I departed Fiji the day after, stopping for a couple of days in Raratonga before arriving in Los Angeles to complete our travels before returning to the UK a few weeks later, where we went our separate ways at Gatwick Airport to return to our respective home towns, Michelle back to Nuneaton, Sandra to Cambridge, and myself, back to Dagenham.

13 – THE CATALYST OF THE AUSTRALIAN VAGINA

1995 - 1996 (aged 21)

1995 was officially The Most Depressing Year Ever. I was back in Dagenham. I felt like Dorothy, returned to the boring black and white of Kansas, with her crazy adventures in Oz rendered as nothing but a dream. Sex-crazed Fijian nymphos, lesbians with murderous tendencies, glamorous transsexuals, even the Wicked Witches of the Perth chemical factory, they all now just seemed like a collection of crazy, colourful characters that had populated a mythical land that bore no resemblance at all to the reality I was now back in. Had I really been attempted to be picked up by and then chased a *Home and Away* star, been kissed by a hot biker, missed out on a ham-fisted seduction attempt with a ping pong ball?

Now, aged twenty and ensconced back in the confines of my childhood bedroom, with the view of the Fords car factory welcoming me back in a taunting *'I Told You So'* manner, it was if I had never been away. But inside my mind, I *had* been away, I had blossomed, I had grown up. I was different. I wasn't the same innocent boy that had left. I had still not acted on my homosexuality but I had come close so many times. I was still lurking in the closet but was nearly ready to come out. All I knew is that I didn't want to stay in Dagenham. I had to find a way to get back to Australia. It was my spiritual home. It was my Oz. It would take me well over a year to get back there.

*

Mum of course, was delighted to have me back in the family bosom as she quickly set about re-attaching the apron strings, this time with a much stronger fabric and fed me endlessly to *"fatten me up"*, probably as part of a sinister plan to make me so heavy that I would physically be unable to leave again.

I had surprised her with my arrival home at the end of my travels, choosing to just turn up unannounced when she thought I was still somewhere in America. As I entered the house and walked into the living room, Mum was in her armchair reading *The Sun* as always. She looked up and saw me at which point the reaction was as suitably emotionally dramatic as the morning I had left as Mum starting shrieking *"Am I dreaming?! Am I dreaming?",* before bursting into tears, thankfully this time of joy and not of distress. Dad then appeared in the living room wondering what all the commotion was about and upon seeing me standing there just muttered to my Mum, *"See, told you he'd be home".* I might have changed but my parents certainly hadn't. One thing that sadly had changed though was my friendships with Phil, Ant, Daz and Jo.

*

It was evident on my first night back that I had nothing in common anymore with the friends I had left behind in Dagenham the year before. Despite my jetlag, we had all met up and gone for dinner in Pizza Hut in Romford but it felt like a sponsored silence, minus the donations to charity. Their lives were exactly the same as when I had left. They asked me about mine. I just didn't know where I could possibly start, how I could talk about all my adventures without sounding slightly nuts or worse, ever so smug. The truth was, I had evolved and inadvertently outgrown the quartet of people that had been my best friends. Scooby Doo had been cancelled and wouldn't see another series of adventures. We had zero left in common. Our experimental homoerotic dalliances had been long forgotten and never talked about. Phil, Ant and Daz now all had girlfriends and living lives of staunch heterosexuality. The teenagers were now men. Michelle and Sandra were now my best friends but we all lived in different parts of the UK. It was a cheerless homecoming.

Even more depressing was the endless death that seemed to define 1995. I had already come home to the news that my friend Barry from ASDA had been killed a couple of months before I came back. He had followed his dream to join the Army but whilst on active duty in Bosnia, a fellow soldier stepped on a landmine which exploded, killing him and Barry instantly. He was, like me, only twenty years old. A few months later, gay Dean from ASDA hung himself after the death of his mother. Of the three teenagers that had staffed the ASDA Fruit and Veg Monday evening shift, I was the only one left alive at only twenty years old. I felt immense guilt that I never intervened in the fun that used to be poked at Dean for him being gay. It's so true that the most homophobic are actually gay themselves. By my inaction, I had been a case in point.

My Nan Shirley's dog Suki also died, the Welsh border collie that had been a fixture of the family since she arrived as a puppy in 1982.

Her death was then succeeded by about a dozen elderly neighbours popping their clogs one after the other, as if mirroring the current ridiculous Ebola-esque plague storyline in *Brookside*. Finally, to round off the death tally, gay 'Uncle' Billy died of liver failure from his alcoholism, an affliction that I now realised may have stemmed from having to grow up gay in an era when his sexuality was illegal. Whatever the reason had been, he had lived in Dagenham as an openly gay man. Which is more than what I was doing. But who could blame me. I was acutely aware of the homophobia all around me, which was horribly defined at my Grandad Bert's seventieth birthday party, a rather sedate affair compared to the usual extravaganzas that were thrown in the 1980s. Grandad had always maintained a fatalist belief that a human being should only live for *"three score years and ten"* and that, in his own words, he would *"have the needle"* when he reached seventy. We had always humoured him and as an extra birthday present, we gift-wrapped a fake syringe for his supposed euthanasia, to much hilarity.

Less humorous was the conversation afterwards around the buffet table, when the subject matter turned to my experiences in Australia and it was revealed that whilst I was out there, my Aunts had joked to my Mum that I would come back gay. To which my Aunt's new boyfriend replied that he would beat the shit out of me if I was. To say I was horrified would be an understatement. Dagenham homophobia was still thriving and now festering like a pus-filled yellowhead inside my own family and because of it, I retreated even further and deeper back into the closet, hiding in the box at the back that contained my 1980s shell suits and dungarees, which, like my true sexuality, must never see the light of day again. Dagenham had suddenly taken on a more sinister tone. I couldn't be gay in this town. Fiona's subliminal message to me aged six had finally got through. I still had the Football 1982 key ring as a reminder.

I had to get back to Australia. Somehow, I was going to make it happen.

*

It was now hard to watch *Neighbours* and especially *Home and Away* with all those hunks frolicking around in the sunshine, minus the one that had tried to pick me up at Lady Jane Bay, he having left the show by now. It was like the universe was having a horrible laugh at my expense, taunting me.

In the meantime, I tried instead to bring Australia to Dagenham when Auntie Carol decided she wanted a lodger and I suggested to her, no *manipulated* her into thinking that the best bet would be for me to put notices for her around various backpacker hostels in London, so that an Aussie, preferably, male, hot and gay with a penchant for Dagenham boys (in particular a getting chubbier by the day one) could sample the misleading delights of Dagenham for himself, and if I was lucky, squeeze me into his backpack and take me home with him when he left. Such a specimen was soon sourced in the shape of Calvin, a tousle-haired slab of prime Aussie beef from Melbourne who took up residence not only in Carol's spare room, but also straight at the top of my Lust List. Well, when I say list, there were no other candidates in Dagenham at the time so Calvin was the only one featured, making his throne at the top quite a lonely place for him. Luckily, Carol's new house was in the same street as mine, so I was able to see Calvin daily, making spurious excuses to visit Carol so that I could be in Calvin's presence. And then one day, Calvin invited me over to come watch a video with him. It was like Date Night for me, hoping that the choice of movie that Calvin had hired would give me a huge hint as to whether he was gay or not. He chose *Reservoir Dogs*, about as macho a film as there was in the video shop. I knew straightaway that he wasn't batting for my team, which was confirmed later that evening when there was a knock at Auntie Carol's door to enter Debbie, the sister of Carol's friend who Carol had set up with Calvin in a perverted twist on all the set-up with girls she had forced on me when I was younger. Talk about family loyalty! But at least this time, with Calvin and Debbie, her Cilla Black-like matchmaking had been a wild success, which was evident when Calvin hinted heavily that I go home so that he and Debbie could do their bit for Anglo-Aussie relations in the Argos-purchased bed in Carol's spare room.

*

During the course of the year, Sandra, Michelle and I would meet up for weekends as often as we could, where we would reminisce and generally miss our adventures in Oz. At the same time I felt a bit of a fraud as they still had no idea I was gay. We'd been friends for nearly two years now and still I was hiding my real self from them. We had talked about moving to Brighton together. I knew this was a town famous for its prominent gay population and the paranoid part of me wondered if Sandra and Michelle had only suggested this as a subliminal means of getting me to confess my homosexuality as they had in fact known the truth all along. This wasn't the case at all, as in reality, Michelle was just in the same boat as me, hating being back in her home town and also craving a return to Australia.

Michelle, Sandra and I did as many things Aussie-related as we possibly could, namely visiting and buying things from The Australia Shop, a surfeit of products that had been imported to remind London-residing Aussies of their homeland. And then out came the movies *Priscilla, Queen of the Desert* and *Muriel's Wedding* which only made us hanker for Oz even more. *Muriel's Wedding* in particular both enthralled and frightened me as I realised that I had been Muriel, ensconced in my bedroom in the early 90s listening to the *ABBA Gold* CD over and over again on my new hi-fi. But Muriel eventually grew out of it as her inner strength and self-confidence increased and made her bloom. It had to be my turn now. But my turn would have to wait, as first I had to deal with the dilemma of having found myself dating a woman.

Her name was Sally. She was seven years older than me at twenty-seven, an Australian from Sydney who was clearly not my type, as in she had boobs and a front bottom. The whole chain of events that somehow led to me dating her was eerily reminiscent of when Leanne Cresswell had badgered me to go out with Joanne Albright eight years previous in school. This time, it was the double whammy of Michelle and Sandra who would be doing the badgering.

The three of us had already been hanging out often in Aussie bar *Sheila's* in Covent Garden, Michelle and Sandra wanting to meet Aussie men and well, as did I, although of course the girls were hardly aware that actually all three of us wanted some Aussie cock. So instead I had to maintain the facade of chatting up Aussie women, or in this case, having them chatted up for me on my behalf, as I found myself being pushed into the company of Sally who was on a night out with her friend Genevieve.

I don't quite know how it happened but after one too many bottles of *Two Dogs* alcopops, I had somehow kissed Sally, given her my home number and arranged to go on a date with her. As I woke up the next morning with a killer hangover, the whole incident was proved not to be the dream that I hoped it had been when the home phone rang and chirpy, chipper yet strangely aggressive and bossy Sally demanded to know when our first date was going to occur. Whether it was a combination of a sore head or her cold-calling telephone sales technique of not hanging up until I had been verbally beaten into submission and agreed a place and time, I found myself unable to let her down or to admit it had all been some terrible-but-let's-laugh-about-it-anyway misunderstanding and so reluctantly arranged the date.

What the hell was I thinking? Was it the fear of having the shit beaten out of me by my Auntie's new boyfriend? Was it the need to make my Mum happy? Or was it the sudden and tempting realisation that Sally might provide me with a bona-fide way of getting back to Australia? But of course, despite her being now my third 'beard', there was no way I could go as far as to actually marry a woman. However, one hour into my first date with Sally, I already felt like we were married. I mean married in a way as being nagged at and bossed about to the point of either imminent divorce or preferably, a pre-arranged 'tragic accident'. All day long I was bombarded with instructions - being told to hold her hand, how quickly to finish my drink, how fast to walk, that another chocolate bar is not good for my waistline, even how to pronounce my th's even though I was from Essex and thus was physically impossible.

What would be more physically impossible would be the attempt at sex that night, demanded aggressively from Sally like a Mafia gangster who was threatening the harm of family members should my own member not take up residence in her vagina, post-dinner, no questions asked and no excuses whatsoever.

To say that the sex was disastrous would be like saying that the sinking of the Titanic was just a minor altercation with an ice cube. The trial - sorry, copulation - was to take place in the two bedroom house just off Edgware Road that she shared with approximately seventeen other Antipodeans. As a result, the location of our lovemaking was to be on a well-worn and badly-in-need-of-a-good-hoovering rug in the tiny living room, the psychedelic pattern on which was already giving me a headache, an ailment that I dare not complain about, in case of any threat to detonate an incendiary device in my Nan's kitchen.

Anyway, I didn't exactly have much time to contemplate how I was going to have sex with this woman, being just a tad nervous at the prospect of something akin to driving an articulated lorry down a cul-de-sac without asking for directions, as no sooner had we laid down on the migraine-inducing rug, then huge breasts suddenly bore down on me like a pair of apocalypse-inducing comets plummeting from the heavens and a frilly blur whizzed past my head which were her knickers being hurled across the room to rest on the electric fire, leaving me more concerned at the impending fire hazard she had created rather than the imminent copulation at hand.

"*Where do you wanna start?*", she purred, like a cross between Eartha Kitt and a cat coughing up a fur ball. Start? Start means the beginning which means there'll also be a middle and end. A journey. Just how long was she expecting this ordeal to last? I just had to get it over with. And so I reached out my hands, cracked my knuckles and cupped her breasts which felt like two large stress balls but if they were, they sure were not working, for my stress levels shot through the roof when she pushed my head down and instructed:

"*Lick me out and make me moist!*"

Do *what* now? What level of moistness was she hoping for here? That of my Nan's lemon drizzle sponge cake or something comparative to a soaking wet dishcloth being wrung out? Either way, I tried not to gag as I reluctantly slid southwards. And there it was, grazing against my nose like barbed wire, trying to entice me towards it. The first vagina I had seen since Stacey Waters' hairless Bermuda triangle of hair. It resembled the Sarlaac pit from *Return of the Jedi* minus the teeth. I hadn't a clue what to do with it as the scene from *Tangerine Dream* suddenly replayed in my mind. Re-enacting that might be a tad full-on for our first (and hopefully only) time together and I would rather she be left with her ovaries untangled and still intact. Instead, all I could do was to dart my tongue in and out of her fanny quickly like a lizard catching a fly. I felt ill. I thought back to the Kava sipping in Fiji when my tongue had gone a little numb. What *was* this taste? Had she forgot to wash in her haste to get down and dirty on the living room floor? Could she not see my distress here? Could she not realise I was Not Enjoying This At All? This might be a good time for her to reveal she was actually a mind-reader and could surmise that I was trying hard to imagine I was with a man whilst I was having sex with her, which was not in any way a realistic scenario because no man I would be having sex with would possess boobs the size of hers jiggling above my head. Except maybe the wrestler Giant Haystacks but I was sure he was dead. Or was that Big Daddy? Clearly, this random thought process of which wrestler had shuffled off to the big wrestling ring in the sky was not helping matters as Sally suddenly demanded that my oral cleansing of her vagina cease immediately so that my cock gets in on the action as she wrapped her legs around me like a Venus fly trap and kept pushing herself onto my penis, as if trying in the dark to fit a 50p piece in the meter slot to kick-start the electricity when the power had gone out. Which aptly described my level of excitement. Still I had to somehow get through this ordeal, well actually the only way was to imagine a succession of men's faces transposed over hers, as if you could in real life photoshop someone else's head on - in this case Sally's face was replaced with Jarrad the hot biker, the *Home and Away* hunk, even Craig and his aflame ping pong ball got a look in, each man I had come so close with and who was now starring in this home-made porno as I fucked him and kissed him and felt his ginormous boobs - and wait - boobs? The sex skidded to a halt quite quickly as Sally lay there with a look of disappointment on her face as if she had just unwrapped a tantalising gift that was revealed to be just one of my Mum's recycled bath sets.

And then she asked if I was gay. I feigned being utterly appalled. What made her suspect such a crime and make such a hurtful accusation? Of course I protested *"no, of course I'm not gay"* and put on my best hurt, offended face. She seemed so apologetic, said she was just checking. I wondered if the coming out of her boyfriends was a regular occurrence for her. Despite being tempted to tell her she might consider earning a good wage by becoming a professional fag hag, I felt guilty. Having attempted disastrous sex with this poor woman was the defining moment in my life when I had actually and finally admitted to myself that I was one-hundred percent gay and there was nothing I could do about it. In one sense, it was extremely momentous, in the other I knew I had to finish it with Sally and set her breasts and smelly vagina free into the wind where hopefully it would get some airing out.

We ended it over the telephone days later, the click at the other end of the line alerting me to the fact that Mum was listening in on the phone downstairs. She was like the Stasi, forever listening in on calls and 'accidentally' opening my mail. I understood the concept of apron strings but not when these also warranted what I suspected was a surveillance centre in the loft, an army of spies, bugs in the bedroom and secret cameras. I was twenty now, what exactly did my Mum suspect I was up to? I was not an enemy of the state or a terrorist. The only terrorising that had occurred was towards my penis courtesy of Sally's wildly overgrown bush.

I had decided that I didn't need Sally or any other Aussie love interest to be able to return to Australia. I would get back to Sydney my own way. But not before one more distraction...

*

Operation Return to Sydney was not going to be cheap. I was living at home but broke, working a variety of duller than dull temp jobs to try and save what I could, stocktaking machinery in a dairy and filing post in a post room amongst many others. I never regretted not going to University; my global adventures had been a much more defining education in my view. Just after I turned twenty-one years old and, just as on my eighteenth birthday three years before, was given another collection of plastic keys in nice presentation boxes that I always wondered what the hell anyone was supposed to do with, I landed a job as a security guard, placed at the International Bank of Japan in the shadow of St. Paul's Cathedral up in London. It was a job that required twelve hour shifts, a mixture of days and nights that would mess with my body clock, ruin my sleep pattern and kill any attempt at a social life but was a sure-fire way of saving money hard and fast.

Being a security guard was naturally not the most thrilling occupation to be had, my tasks just consisting mainly of routine patrols, manning the reception desk and checking for IRA bombs which apparently might be hidden in the hanging baskets and flowerbeds outside.

However the only thing exploding around this building were the insatiable sexual appetites of my ragtag band of fellow security guards. It was like an updated version of ASDA where this time it was the sheer boredom that was manifesting itself as endless sex talk. It was like being an extra in a sex comedy, *Carry on Securing*, starring cocky Pete who liked to announce his wanks, clearly his only action as his lurid tales of his sexual encounters with whoever was Office Slut of the Day were evidently more fictional than the Tory Party's election manifesto. Then there was elderly widower Joe who missed sex with his dead wife, talking about it as if he had been bonking her decaying corpse - and finally special guest star Carly in the post room opposite who would randomly and without prior warning or reasonable explanation, suddenly pull out her boobs as if breastfeeding an invisible baby, enabling Pete to announce yet another imminent wank.

As a result, I enjoyed the peace of my night shift patrols, wandering through the empty offices after dark, to see the clues on people's desks that alluded to who they were. Or in the case of one particular night, to come across a trader working very late who wanted to bribe me into helping him realise *"a fantasy of his"*. Alas that fantasy was to be 'accidentally' discovered bonking the office slut in the stationary cupboard, the ensuing mess of which would have done my old primary school teacher Mrs. Darby proud. I was to be the 'shocked' uncoverer of this sordid night time liaison in exchange for a bottle of Jack Daniels. I shrugged, agreed and we shook on it, later enabling a cross between Am Dram and *You've Been Framed*, an obvious set-up, the feigning of surprise as I 'accidentally discovered them', my torch light bouncing off his conquest's breasts and reverberating around the cupboard like a rotating glitter ball at a disco. She just lay there jolting epileptic-like as my torchlight illuminated his bare buttocks grinding between her legs as my sudden presence made him cum inside her within seconds. Oh well, I could take that as a compliment, feeling somewhat flattered that I could make a man cum just by walking into a stationary cupboard.

I hoped I might have the same effect on IBJ employee Dan, a handsome red-headed banker who seemed to be making any excuse to come to the security window and talk to me.

Now that, thanks to my horrendous sexual ordeal with Sally, I was finally accepting of my one-hundred percent gayness, I was suddenly acutely aware of the intricacies of the 'gay language', the body language, stolen glances, knowing smiles, undeniable yet very flustered sexual tension, all clear signs of someone being gay. It was like I had been wearing thick fogged-up spectacles for years and had now traded them in for Superman gay style vision. It was if the Wizard in Oz had pulled back his curtain just for me and exposed the true machinations of how being gay really worked. Somehow, gay auras were now visible to me all around and it was no wonder that mine had been as equally transparent in my time in Australia. It was a revelation.

Dan's gay aura positively radiated with a nuclear glow, and one that was projecting its warmth in my direction. Alas, I suspected that Dan was in the exactly the same boat as me, the newly gay nerve-wracking ramshackle ship, sailing the choppy waters of unspoken desire and feelings but too afraid to drop anchor and do anything about it. I was sure he could see my gay aura too, and I would do what I could to heavily hint without actually saying it that I fancied the pants off him. I would make sure I slowed down past his desk on my rounds, just so I could see him and smile as I passed. But it was useless. We were two peas in a pod, or more accurately, two homos in a dusty closet in desperate need of a good hoovering, both nervous gay virgins who clearly fancied each other but were both afraid to make the first move. If we ever ended up sharing the same lift, our conversation was nothing but a *"hi, hi"*, both trembling in each other's presence. Something had to explode sooner or later.

That explosion came courtesy of the IRA on the 9th February 1996. I was manning the front reception when the doors suddenly shook as if a bolt of thunder had rattled them. It was from a bomb exploding in Docklands. In a way, it was a catalyst to make me decide that it was time to leave the UK again. I had enough money but I was at a loss as to what to do about Dan. In the end, we had been pussyfooting around each other so much, that I decided not to act on anything with him, lest he give me a reason to stay in the UK. Unless I could persuade him to come with me. Which was even more unlikely.

Because Dan and I had never had a proper in-depth conversation, he had no idea I was leaving. On my last day at IBJ, as I manned the reception desk again, I said to my colleague Andy sitting next to me, that this was my last day, timing it so that it would be within earshot of Dan as he passed by, after finishing work for the day. Dan stopped in his tracks, looked at me. He looked devastated, in shock. There was a window of approximately three seconds where I could have leapt up from the desk, swept him in my arms, asked him to take a chance on me and come travelling with me. Instead, I just smiled as we engaged eye contact for a time which seemed to equal the length of the *EastEnders* omnibus. It was a smile that silently told him that I liked him but the timing was not right. For a moment it looked like Dan would say something - like he was having the kind of dream where you try to speak but no sound comes out, not unlike my childhood nightmares. As he stood there for an interminable few seconds opening and closing his mouth silently like a goldfish, he finally turned and carried on his way out of the building, continually looking back at me until he disappeared from view. I never saw him again. As I stared at the now empty corner where Dan had just vanished around, I still had another chance, as part of me still had wanted to leap up and run after him, like the end of a cheesy movie where there is always a race to the airport to tell someone you love them before they get on the plane. Which, by the way, I never understood the point of; they could always catch a later flight and catch up with them. But I just sat there, lamenting what might have been. Meanwhile Andy was squeezing my leg and hinting heavily that *he* was gay. Clearly, the

National Grid-like electricity he had just witnessed between Dan and I was more than enough to clue him up to my true sexual orientation. He squeezed my thigh again. I was too shocked to say anything as I realised that the bank not only was full of horny security guards, wide boy traders and office sluts, it was also full of closeted gays.

Three days later I had left the UK again and was on a plane to Moscow.

14 – THE FIRST TIME

1996 (aged 21)

I remember the lyrics well. *'First time, first love, oh what feeling is this, electricity flows, with the very first kiss...'*

Now I knew that Robin Beck was leaving just a few minor details out. Where was the verse warbling on about the fear, the terror, the wondering in what to do with another man's erect penis when it suddenly appears in your close line of vision? And what about the pain, Robin? What about the pain?! Yeah, thanks love, stick a college hunk of the cover of your single but fail to confess that he had been nothing but a cock-tease.

Mind you, it wasn't just Robin that had been misleading me, I had been a bit deluded myself in the hopes of experiencing the romantic, earth-shattering way - complete with full orchestra and a chorus line of dancers - that I would finally lose my gay virginity by having sex with another man.

For the reality was quite different, the ground-breaking love scene that I had envisaged in my mind was to be replaced by a much cheaper version suffering from budget cuts, dodgy lighting, unconvincing props and cheesy dialogue, to result in something that was more experimental student film rather than epic awards-baiting blockbuster. And I was the starring actor who hadn't properly rehearsed his lines, leaving a scene so awkward and cringe-inducing that it would be better off left on the cutting room floor, until it inevitably surfaces to be featured as an outtake on Denis Norden's *It'll Be Alright On The Night*, renamed *Oh Well, It'll Just Have to Do*. But do it did and The Deed happened on 14th September 1996 at approximately 3.30pm, in a location that should now be more than familiar. But let's just rewind a few weeks first...

*

I had finally arrived back in Sydney in June 1996 after a four month adventure that took me through Russia, China, Hong Kong and South East Asia, an epic traversing of the globe that spawned many a crazy incident. Starting with a week-long trip across Siberia on the Trans Siberian Express and ending in Bali before returning to Sydney, I was blacking out on vodka, table dancing with Russian dinner ladies, being rescued unconscious from a toilet by a trainee Korean monk, held at gunpoint by Chinese police over a missing pillowcase that had been used as a wank rag, got terribly sick after unknowingly eating a dog in Thailand and been the victim of a con man who had impersonated me and drained my bank account in Singapore. I felt like I had been the guest star in an outlandish bonus season of *Dynasty*. Sydney seemed rather dull in comparison once I finally made my long-awaited return there and took up residence in a dorm room in the Travellers Rest hostel in Kings Cross. It was here, that as I got down to the last fifty dollars in my pocket and seriously considered giving up, fate would take an upwards swing again, via a job given to me by a man whose marital problems would indirectly lead me to finally losing my gay virginity.

*

I moved out of the Travellers Rest after a couple of months and into an apartment in Potts Point with three fellow English backpackers, Ned, Kate and Gaby. The apartment/English ghetto was swanky with a view of Sydney Harbour and the city skyline, the skyscrapers of which were marginally less high than the levels of testosterone within the apartment's four walls, emitted by ladies man Ned who was forever boasting about the power of his hard drive (his laptop that in 1996, was approximately the size of a breeze block). Soon after moving in, I found myself to be caught up in the collateral damage of a love triangle between Ned, Kate and Gaby as Ned and Kate embarked on a torrid affair to much histrionic jealousy from Gaby, a Brummie drama queen who wore the world's noisiest flip flops and who had a penchant for sudden tearful meltdowns that were brought on by such traumatic events such as running out of loo roll or a biscuit collapsing soggily into her cup of tea because of a woefully underestimated dunking time. Now full on hysteria from her was the order of every day now that Ned and Kate had dared to fall in love with each other. And apparently, it was all my fault that such a love had bloomed as I had been the one to oil the heterosexual love machine by graciously offering to sleep in the lounge three nights a week so that the bedroom I shared with Ned could be freed up for the regular at-it-like-rabbits consummation of his and Kate's desire for each other. With Gaby's temper tantrums and subsequent soundtrack of stomping around in her irritating flip-flops that I wanted to steal whilst she was sleeping and throw into the harbour, it was no wonder that I kept away from the apartment as much as I possibly could.

Decreased dwelling time in the apartment was easy by day as, despite not having a work visa, I had a job as a handyman, a job which I had completely blagged my way into. After getting down to my last fifty dollars and seriously considering giving up and returning to the UK, I came across an advert pinned to a hostel notice board to help renovate old houses for local estate agent Drew Bloom. A hour later I was being interviewed by Drew and his wife Sharon, bigging up my skills in all things DIY that in reality was one occasion where I had helped my Dad paint a wall, but in this desperate need for months of cash-in-hand work, a simple paint job had been exaggerated to a skill-set of finely-honed proficiencies that upon request of my expertise-level, were met with a *"yes, I can do that"* bare-faced lie. Can you plaster a wall? Yes, I can do that! Can you lay a patio? Yes, I can do that! Can you lust after the incredibly hot male cop in enticingly tight shorts who works in the cop shop opposite our office? Hell, yes I can *definitely* do that! How much saliva would you like me to paint the walls with for that last request?

Anyway, somehow I got the job and started the next day, hoping I could just continue to blag it as I went along, anything to get me out of the apartment and away from the murder-inducing noise of Gaby's fucking flip flops.

*

The fact that I was working in Australia illegally was one that Drew was well aware of and one that was silently agreed would never be discussed - in exchange for me helping him keep up the high values of his properties via a miscellaneous collection of not-quite-by-the book assignments. The particular 'highlight' of these tasks was the time we staked out the house next door to one of his properties, it containing a rather large tree that was devaluing Drew's property - and which had to be dealt with. Enter me. As soon as the house's occupants had left work for the day, Drew hoisted me over the back fence, armed with an axe, to chop the tree down and leave its remains in a neat pile whilst Drew manned the getaway car. I could hardly protest to him that I wasn't quite comfortable with this line of work, any work I was doing after all was illegal in the eyes of Australian immigration, an illegality that Drew was using for his own benefit in a kind of unspoken blackmail. And it was a deal with the Devil that would also require me to help Drew keep up his extra-marital affairs. The 'Don't Ask Don't Tell' nature of my visa issue was being returned with an identical sideline in helping keep Drew's myriad of mistresses serviced and renovated in the same way as his property portfolio. Somehow, in my home and my work life, I had become the willing facilitator of heterosexual sex lives, helping Ned and

Kate fall in love whilst simultaneously assisting Drew get his end away by lying to his wife for him and helping him organise illicit encounters. I didn't want to be complicit in so much deceit. Especially as Sharon seemed so genuinely lovely. Could she really be that blind to her husband's relentless philandering? So many times, at moments when Drew was infuriating me, I wanted to tell Sharon the truth, to make her realise that she was a woman worth so much more than being shackled to a cheating estate agent. I was getting angry with myself for my absolute lack of courage but this anger was also self-projected. For I was as deceitful as Drew, still hiding my true self. Dorothy was now the cowardly lion, as I had taken on strumpet Kelly Owen's role from the school play in 1985, metaphorically jumping screaming if a scarecrow - in this case any gay man - dared smiled that knowing smile at me. Enough was enough. I was nearly twenty-two years old. It was time to lose my gay virginity.

*

It was Saturday 14th September 1996, a gloriously sunny day and I had an unplanned afternoon off from work, thanks to Drew's infidelity finally being rumbled, the dramatic uncovering and punishment of his latest extra-marital affair that would ironically lead me to partake in *my* first Actual Sexual Exploit with another man.

I was working on a house in Paddington with Drew on site, he rewiring a bathroom light whilst I sanded the main staircase. Suddenly the front door slammed open as Sharon stood in the doorway, her face contorted with anger and tears as she flew into the house, shrieking and screaming for Drew to come face her, interspersed with howls in my direction that asked of me:
"You won't believe what that fucker's been up to!"
I didn't dare respond that unfortunately I knew all too well that it wasn't a case of what Drew had been up *to* but rather who he'd been *in*. Before I could think of a suitable response for Sharon, Drew appeared, trying to placate her like she had only discovered his minor crime of leaving the toilet seat up, which ironically he might have wished he hadn't, for Sharon, suddenly possessed with a wild brute force, threw a jar of Bolognese sauce all over him, pulled him by his tie into the bathroom and slammed the door behind her. I was dumbstruck for a second then quickly followed where all I was able to hear through the locked bathroom door was Sharon yelling a string of profanity-laden questions and statements such as *"Tell me the fucking bitch's name!"*, *"You cheating cunt!"* *"I'll kill you and that fucking slut!"*. And each dramatic declaration was being peppered with the sounds of Drew's muffled protestations getting drowned out - quite literally - by the flushing of the toilet. It was clear to me what was happening here. The cheating estate agent was getting his

head flushed down the bog. I wondered for a moment whether Drew's dad had ever told him that was supposed to happen at senior school. Not quite knowing what I should do next, I tapped on the bathroom door and gingerly enquired:

"Is everything okay in there?", which, when met only with another *"tell me the whore's name - but I - FLUSH!"* sequence of overheard conversation, I backed away, slipped out of the house to leave them to it and took the afternoon off. To end up at Lady Jane Bay.

*

It was weird to be back at Lady Jane Bay, nearly three years having passed since my near miss with the *Home and Away* star. The place hadn't changed at all, with the random men circulating along the path and vanishing into the bushes, or sitting on the rocks 'admiring the view', the latter of which I was doing right now, albeit having ventured closer than ever before to the nudist beach below. I had found a smooth rocky outcrop directly above the beach with a bird's eye view looking down, happy to chill and be the voyeur until I was brave enough to actually chance it down there. I stripped to my shorts and lay on the stone, enjoying the feel of the sun on my skin as I wondered if Drew had survived the head-down-the-loo wrath of his wronged wife.

It was when reaching for my sun cream that I saw it. It was unmistakable. A huge, erect penis peeking out from the bushes directly opposite. It looked like a lighthouse amongst the foliage, the light bouncing off it, like a homing beacon to the suddenly nervous, trembling, skinny Essex Boy on the rocks just a dozen or so yards away.

I looked away. Then I looked back. Then looked away again. Then looked back. And repeat. My head would have spun loose from its axis and tumbled down onto the gay nudist beach below had I continued this *Exorcist* style spinning of it for much longer. I looked again. This time the man that the penis was attached to was actually beckoning me over. He wanted me to join him. Which meant he also wanted me to... I gulped so strongly that it could have been mistaken for a unexpected clap of thunder on this blue sky day. Fuck it, I thought, sucking in the deepest breath of courage that I could possibly muster. And I homed in to the bushes.

I had of course, completely forgotten about the sheer *Krypton Factor* assault course-style challenge that defined any attempt to actually clamber through the branches and foliage. A feat so hazardous that by the time I finally arrived at my potential conquest's side, I resembled, not *Stig of the Dump* this time, but instead an eighties soap star with huge hair that had been inadvertently back-combed by the combined force of various tree branches and a tumble over a large boulder. Nonetheless, I was just pleasantly relieved to see that he still had an erection which had inexplicably not withered in the long time it took me to actually get to it.

His penis still glinting like a skyscraper in the sunlight, he beckoned for me to take a seat on the ground next to him, as if this was a job interview with a practical test as part of it. I felt the sudden need to make small talk, not unlike the times in which I would get cornered by some obscure Auntie at a family party with whom I had no choice but to find something appropriate to say to when she remarked on *"how I had grown"*. Well, if I ever saw her again, I could now regale her with the tale of something else that had grown.

I asked what his name was. He looked at me blankly. I wondered for a second whether he had amnesia. But in fact, what I had just asked violated some strict rule in the Outdoor Cruising Code of Conduct. It would take me a long time to learn that swapping names was not appropriate in these types of encounters. As was asking for their phone numbers.

His eyes looked at me, then at my right hand, then at his penis. I realised he wanted me to touch it. Sure, okay, why not? I flexed my arms, cracked my knuckles as if preparing for a military exercise then reached out... and grabbed hold of it. This was it, the first time I had ever touched another man's penis. I suddenly felt like I was in the outtakes of the world's most awkward gay porn movie. I suddenly blurted out that this was the first time I had ever been with a man. This blushing confession made his eyes light up as if he'd successfully hoisted a soft toy in one of those claw machines you find in amusement arcades and he instantly whipped a small video camera out of his rucksack. Shit, he wanted to film us. Despite being somewhat impressed at the speed of his impromptu movie making, I wasn't sure if I wanted my first time with another man, the long-held fantasy of mine, something so scary and yet so wanted for many years to be committed to celluloid. Could I really adhere to the request to play up to the camera whilst commands were being barked at me to shout words of appreciation that contradicted my discomfort? Luckily for me, the camera was out of battery.

It wasn't quite the romantic moment that I had been wishing for but it was still life-changing nevertheless. As we finally got dressed, I asked for his phone number, got a good laugh in response with a side dish of eye-rolling and was told to always remember my few minutes with him whenever I had a wank. And that was that.

My head was swimming on the bus back to the apartment. I had finally done it with another man; or rather he had technically done it to me, as my participation level was akin to being one of those 'Annie' dolls used in First Aid training, lying there occasionally jolting. But gay sex was gay sex. A mix of pain and pleasure that was entwined with the branches that had just about shielded such an act from public view. I realised that I was no longer a gay virgin, a relief that came with a side dish of mild catatonic shock at what I had just done. That my virginity had been lost to a complete stranger instead of a boyfriend, outdoors in the middle of some bushes, with zero romance and no declarations of love, only demands to *"tell me that you like it!"* by someone whose name I never knew and will never know. It was like a childhood Christmas again with the anticipation of what is inside the enticingly wrapped package under the tree being revealed as something which will require the thanks of *"well, it's the thought that counts."* But still, I couldn't deny the momentum of the entire fifteen minute experience, no matter how sore I felt or how afraid I suddenly felt in the shower later that I had somehow broken my bum.

 Back at the apartment, I picked up a message from Drew that it was safe to come back to work tomorrow then Ned and Kate came home and asked how my day had been, to which I replied *"just normal"* instead of telling them that I had witnessed my boss's head get flushed down the toilet by his vengeful wife then absconded from the potential murder scene to go have gay sex for the first time in the bushes overlooking a nudist beach. Somehow I didn't think that their own day quite matched up.

 So now, I had finally confirmed my one hundred percent gayness by losing my gay virginity al-fresco to A Man without A Name. As I come to terms with this life-changing event, I wanted to shout it from the rooftops, for the world to finally hear what I had been hiding about my true self all these years. But my shouting would not even be a whisper; it wouldn't even be sign language. For I was still too scared to tell anyone, my fear of rejection perversely ever stronger now that I had finally consummated my homosexuality.

 A few days later at work, I was tasked with using a sandblaster to strip off ancient layers of exterior paint from a house in Paddington. The inhalation of decades old chemicals caused me that night to trip out as if I'd consumed a whole field of magic mushrooms. Ned had to restrain me as I hallucinated snakes in my bed and hands coming out of the wall, trying to grab me. I thought I was going crazy, that either the Monster of Abnormality was now real and that he was out to punish me for having had sex with a man or the pressure of hiding in the closet was finally getting to me. I really was going all Jack Nicholson in *The Shining* this time. After that, I started standing up to Drew, refusing to partake in the ever more dangerous odd jobs he was assigning me.

 Dangerous in a different kind of way was the fact that, now I had come to terms with gay sex, I realised that I rather enjoyed it. As my sexual confidence and bravado increased I kept going back to Lady Jane Bay for more. And more. And more. Until one day when I was out grocery shopping with Ned, Kate and Gaby - and came face-to-face with an American jock that I had sex with the previous day. I instantly panicked, went dark red and gasped so suddenly and loudly, that my friends thought I had an undetected peanut allergy. But the American didn't even recognise me. That brush with being outed though still didn't deter me from going back for even more. I was the obedient puppy now let off its leash to run wild and do the human gay version of sniffing other doggy's bums. However, the increase in quantity of my sexual adventures were met with a parallel decrease in the quality of men I was 'adventuring' with, culminating in meeting a guy and having sex that was so weird on his part, it made me look like a pro.

As always, I had encountered him at Lady Jane Bay, where he came over to chat me up, asking for my name. I sniggered as I was now clued up to this cruise-and-pick-up faux-pax so gave him a false one. After being tempted to use an outlandish pseudonym such as Tarquin or Horatio, I settled on Stuart as homage to my unrequited teenage love. In turn he told me his name was Dave. Wow, even years later, salt was still being rubbed in my teenage wounds. However what was being forcibly restricted inside his tight red trunks was more than enticing so we got the bus back to his flat in Woollahra after he decreed that he needed the comfort of his own bed. Fair enough, I thought, after all I was getting a tad tired of the post-sex removal of soil, twigs, stones and grass stains.

Arriving in his bedroom a short while later, he asked for a few minutes whilst he *"got prepared"*, directing me to peruse his photo books of Jason Donovan who he was adamant was gay. I wasn't sure what Dave was preparing exactly - the extraction of his tight red trunks from his legs might be a good start - as long as it wasn't something that would involve my imminent demise and the disposal of my body parts all over Sydney. I had after all, taken the risk of going back to a complete stranger's flat. Well, the 'preparation' that had needed to occur before the removal of clothes and the ensuing act of sex was the putting on of Olivia Newton John's *Xanadu* seven inch single onto his hi-fi, because in Dave's own words, he could *"only stay hard and cum if Xanadu is playing"*. Okay, not quite the response I was expecting but I was willing to give him the benefit of the doubt and see this through.

Of course, it didn't help that *Xanadu* was only three minutes and twenty-seven seconds long so every three minutes and twenty-seven seconds, Dave had to stop to put the record back on again so that Olivia could continue the backing soundtrack to our clumsy sex. Never before had I wished I had brought my mix tapes with me, not imagining for one second that Olivia could be someone's oral stimulant, a musical pre-cursor to Viagra for a man in Sydney whose penis would instantly deflate as Olivia stopped singing or just paused to take a breath. Meanwhile I was so bored, I just gazed at Jason Donovan on the floor, wondering if it was really true that he was gay and if so, had that picture of him and Kylie in Bali from 1988 been nothing but an elaborate set-up?

Once *Xanadu*-sex was finally over, Dave gave me his number, but knowing that I would never get to hear the rest of Olivia Newton John's back catalogue, I discarded it in the nearest bin upon leaving.

*

My newly-acquired confidence as a gay man didn't come without its drawbacks, the most prevalent of which was my paranoia that now I had Done the Deed, the 40 watt light bulb illuminating my gay aura had been swapped out for a 100 watt replacement. I was convinced that everyone knew what I was getting up to; even innocent enquiries from my flatmates were met with paranoid defensive responses. But they were none the wiser. However, someone else was clued up to my gayness...

For whilst I had obtained the confidence of a sexually active gay man, I had also gained something else - in the form of my very own transsexual prostitute stalker.

Carmella was one of the many prostitutes that touted for business by lining the steep incline of William Street all the way up to Kings Cross, which was my usual route back to Potts Point from the city. These were less-than-desirable hookers that resembled shop mannequins that had been dressed by someone in a coma. It was therefore surprising how many clients they were able to attract. Carmella, however, always seemed to be the one not getting any tricks. Standing alone in the same spot every night whilst her rivals negotiated the price of hand jobs, blow jobs and if they were lucky; makeover jobs, Carmella would greet me with her 'come hither' smile which was always returned by my 'no thanks' smile. Another night, another smile. I admired her persistence, even when she added the mention of her name to one of her still-not-tempting grins. She seemed smitten with me. It was an unrequited affection that would in fact lead her to start following me everywhere, to the supermarket, to the local bar, even to my apartment building. Several times, she actually got inside the environs of my abode, where I would find her in the hall, down by the indoor pool and jacuzzi, never saying a single word, just smiling creepily at me. One day, taking a poolside shower after relaxing in the jacuzzi, I emerged to find her sniffing my damp trunks in the changing room. Detective Carmella hot on the trail of gay scent. Eau de Crack mixed with heavy chlorine. I said she could keep them. I should have told her about the video of My First Time that nearly got made; if the battery had been fully juiced I could have offered a kind gesture in return for her unrequited stalking of me and pre-ordered the popcorn for her. But alas, after taking my trunks with her, I never found myself on the receiving end of her attentions again.

*

I was getting to the point now where the coming out of the closet was inevitable. I didn't want to hide anymore, I had found the Real Me and he needed to make himself known. I was given a confidence boost when the British film *Beautiful Thing* was released in a local Arthouse cinema. I went to see it alone one evening and found the story of the two council-estate boys who fell in love so heart-warming and life-affirming that I went back to see it for a second and third time, singing *The Mamas and Papas* on my walk home where I would pass Carmella and get no response to my cheerful wave to her. I even mimicked the character of Jamie in *Beautiful Thing* by going to a newsagent and buying (not shoplifting) an imported copy of the magazine *Gay Times* where I read an article on the current gay love story between the characters of Simon and Tony in *EastEnders*, episodes of which were watched by myself and fellow backpackers in a local bar courtesy of video tapes that someone's Mum was sending over. Simon and Tony were the 90s version of Colin and Barry. And this time, they got to have an Actual Kiss. This *EastEnders* storyline coupled with *Beautiful Thing* only heightened my feeling of being liberated but at the same time, I felt frustrated with myself for still not being out and proud. I needed to tell my family and friends that I was gay, so that I could forge ahead with finding true happiness, free from restraint and the allergy-inducing dust of the closet. I had three choices, tell them over the phone, write a letter or go home and announce my gayness in person. There was only one clear winner, really. I had to go home and come out to everyone – and weather their reactions - face-to-face.

15 – COMING OUT

1997 (aged 22)

It was 1997. A year that would see multiple tragic deaths - that of a Princess, a saintly nun, a fashion icon - and the most shocking demise of all - that of my time in the closet.
For it happened on 20th May that year. In a tiny store room with terrible fluorescent lighting located in the back of a posh supermarket in London's Chelsea. Twenty-two and a half years of confused feelings, of same sex attraction, of unrequited love, of missed opportunities, disastrous sex with a woman and then man-on-man encounters of varying quality, had led to this defining moment in my life. It was the moment that I first told someone that I was gay.

I was still in Sydney at the dawn of the year, which did not get off to a good start as I welcomed in its first minutes whilst lying blind drunk on the pavement outside McDonalds at Circular Quay thanks to downing the white wine decanted inside an empty lemonade bottle, which had been consumed all by myself as a result of losing all my friends in the New Year's Eve crowds, a loss that I was convinced would be re-enacted voluntarily should I admit to them that I was a gay man. Alone in a sea of people and barely able to put one foot in front of the other, I somehow managed to walk home, escorted by two Canadian girls who came to my aid and in return asked for a threesome, a task which I clearly would have been unable to perform, even if I wasn't gay. Instead, all I could offer them was a cup of tea and a biscuit as if I had suddenly morphed into Thora Hird, incontinent and lacking a working appendage. They left after less than a minute.

Aside from the ill-effects of too much white wine, I also strangely started to feel homesick, not for Dagenham but for England. For the first time, I actually surprised myself as I realised that I wanted to go home. Australia had lost its allure for me thanks to a combination of several factors. I was already fed up with working for Drew by now, who despite his reconciliation with Sharon, had become the Boss from Hell. We clashed over trivial matters, namely my ire at the tone of his commands to me, which culminated in a stand-up argument in a posh Vaucluse mansion that I was decorating, where he sped off in his car and I burst into tears and threw a can of paint over the balcony in anger where it landed in the back garden of Tom Cruise and Nicole Kidman's Sydney residence next door. I decided against climbing over to retrieve it, dare I cause a scandal of a gay boy found wandering around Tom Cruise's back entrance. Clearly the pressure of still being in that damn closet was getting to me. The nearer I was getting to coming out, the higher my stress levels were climbing. These were compounded by the added factor that Australian immigration were now after me, thanks to me getting tipsy with an Irish painter and slipping up that I was working illegally, a fact that the Irishman promptly reported to the immigration authorities to claim the cash reward offered for information on illegal workers. Luckily for me, a couple of things saved me from deportation. Namely that the Irishman never knew my surname and also the bad timing on Immigration's part when they turned up to arrest me at a house where I had finished working on just the day before, only to bump into Drew who denied all knowledge of my existence. When Drew told me about the near miss, I burst into tears in his car. He had saved me. Maybe deep down, he was a nicer guy than I gave him credit for. I felt a tad guilty that maybe I could have saved him from his head flushing a few months before.

However, my brush with potential deportation was telling me that it was time to go home. My paranoia at people finding out I was gay was now being kept company by my equal level of paranoia that Australian Immigration would turn up at any second to throw me out of the country, which would result in a ban from me returning for at least five years. I just couldn't spend another day constantly looking over my shoulder, nor could I keep up the double pretence of being a skilled handyman and being robustly heterosexual. I knew my time in Australia was up, it was telling me I had to go home and face up to the Real Me. To bring him back to the UK to be revealed in all his glory. To come home to come out. And so, on Valentine's Day 1997 I left Sydney and flew back to the UK.

*

I didn't surprise my parents this time with my arrival home, as they picked me up from Gatwick Airport and drove me back to the family home in Dagenham where along the way, we passed the 'Lego flats' where Stuart Pincer was still residing after all these years. I thought about trying to make contact with old school friends and also Phil, Ant,

Daz and Jo but decided that the past was the past. And anyway, I had a new life in London to forge for myself as I couldn't bear to be back in Dagenham again for a second time. And so I promptly moved up to London proper where I rented a bedsit in Kensal Rise, the only area that I could afford and one which was defined by all manner of nefarious behaviour including a couple of drive-by shootings. But still, it was my own place and more importantly, I had my independence, something that I desperately needed in order to be able to find the strength to finally tell my family and friends that I was gay.

Another reason I had to move up to London was so that I could be closer to my new job as Senior Sales Assistant at brand new posh Chelsea supermarket Bluebird AKA The Gayest Place Ever to Work. My confidence was resurrected in living in the bright lights of London and working at Bluebird, a workplace that was a little gay bubble, with nearly seventy percent of the staff being gay, the surrounding of which could only help ease me out of my closet. But even though I was now encircled by other gays, I had still not officially let any of them know that in me, they had another member that was bolstering their numbers.

This all changed because of my manager David Mills, the thirty-six year old openly gay man who had interviewed me and given me the job. He was unofficially 'married' to a Moroccan immigrant for visa purposes who lived in Luton for some unexplained reason but more crucially, thanks to his eyes being expertly fine tuned into seeing gay auras, he could sense something was playing on my mind. And he knew full well what it was. He just needed to hear me say it out loud.

On the morning of 20th May, David found me staring into space and asked me if everything was okay with me. I found myself replying that I was scared, confiding in him that I needed to tell my parents and friends something about me but wasn't sure I was brave enough to actually be able to say the words.

"Want to tell me?" David said warmly.

I just nodded. Five minutes later, we had found a quiet spot in a small store cupboard that was being used as a makeshift office. And that's where I told David the two words that I hadn't yet ever uttered to a single soul.

"I'm gay."

"Yeah, I know. So am I" he said.

"Yeah, I already knew that" came back my reply.

Of course I already knew that David was gay. This was thanks to Ricky Locke from the Cheese Counter, the self-appointed Chief Gossip Queen who would corner me daily in the fridges, in the cloakroom, in the staff canteen, on the shop floor and each time whisper *"I know, but I'm not telling!"* into my ear. What did he know and thus was not telling? That I, like him, was gay? And if so, how did he know? Was it my puffer jacket from *Next*? Could he see me salivating over Federico the Italian Stallion on the Charcuterie Counter, who I swear was getting his uniform altered so that it clung to his chest more tightly. Whatever it was, Ricky *knew* and of that I had no doubt. And he was not telling. That - I wasn't so sure about. I decided the best way to deal with the threat of Ricky was to embrace it - and so I befriended him and before long we were cackling together in the corner of the staff canteen like younger versions of *Coronation Street's* Ena Sharples and Minnie Caldwell in the Rovers Return snug. And it was here, during the munching of a ham and cheese toastie, that Ricky told me that David Mills was gay.

My coming out to David was momentous. Why hadn't I realised before that it would be a lot easier than I thought to say those two magical words?
"I'm gay."
That's all I ever had to say. All these years. Just two simple words. I was pissed off with myself for having left it until I was twenty-two years old to actually utter that incredibly short sentence to anyone.

David suggested that we go for a drink in Soho after work so that we could talk properly. A drink that turned into several which combined with the flirting between us, resulted in a passionate kiss which then culminated in me spending the night at his flat which in turn ignited a short but thrilling affair between us for several weeks. Ricky Locke was going to have a field day with this turn of events. But strangely this was one piece of scandalous gossip that never came to light, so good were David and I at keeping our affair a secret.

I was loving working at Bluebird, now having come out as gay now to all my colleagues and friends there, witnessing the swift sacking of a new manager whose homophobia was clearly no match for The Power of the Gays he was insulting and best of all, getting to meet the endless celebrities that shopped there, most of which had featured strongly in my childhood at some point in time. Our customers were TV and movie stars, former heart-throbs either ageing well, badly or disgracefully, even Joan Collins and Kylie Minogue showed up, the latter of who apologised profusely to me when she bumped her shopping basket into my leg. She expressed her regret three times to the point whether I wondered if it was my growing bruise she was sorry for or her subliminal recruitment of me as her gay follower nine years earlier. Regardless, it was as if all the gay icons from my childhood were now popping in to check on my progress and see how gay I was getting. The answer to which would be that I was shagging my boss David whilst also developing feelings of love for another David - my colleague and new buddy David Compton, a gay hunky Welshman working alongside me on the Fruit and Veg stall. Yes, thanks for asking but clearly I'm getting very gay, more evidence of which might be my recent shop floor argument with Elle McPherson over the availability of red potatoes or my altercation with Gail Tilsley from *Coronation Street* who had a meltdown because I couldn't sell her a smaller bunch of mint than what was on sale. Both Elle and 'Gail' quickly learnt never to cross paths and get shouty with a gay man who was now out and proud and thus could easily deal with stroppy supermodels and histrionic soap stars. Well, only in my work life as in my home life I still had one foot firmly in the closet.

*

Michelle had since joined me in the Kensal Rise bedsit, having returned to the UK from her own travels in New Zealand. Also unable to bear returning to her home town of Nuneaton once again, she hot-footed it down to London as I let her platonically share my bed once more. I was glad to have Michelle as company, as life in the bedsit was being tested to the limit thanks to the noisy neighbours next door who would party all night long, causing a deafening ruckus that even rendered my earplugs useless and which was a lot worse than my shouty subconscious bellowing at me to *"FUCKING COME OUT ALREADY!!!"*

Soon after, Michelle and I decided to move to Raynes Park in South London, renting a five bedroom house in which we sub-letted three of the rooms out at market rates so that mine and Michelle's monthly rent each was a grand total of £20. Our new flatmates were Frank the Scottish Stud, odd-but-we-hope-not-in-a-serial-killer-kind-of-way Michael and finally Tracey, a blonde Kiwi who was always resplendent in a pair of purple knickers, the power of which lured men nightly to her bed where she shagged the living daylights out of them and then discarded them on the sofa downstairs for us to find and kick out in the morning. Maybe I was just jealous that she was getting more cock action than I was, something that could easily be remedied if I could just come out and thus have a place to bring men back to.

*

As of July 1997, the two Davids - Mills and Compton - knew I was gay. As did Ricky Locke and countless others at Bluebird. But my best friend Michelle didn't. And neither did my family, despite me giving them a heavy hint when I got completely drunk at my Auntie Janet's 40th birthday party and danced suggestively to *Young Hearts Run Free*, miming in an eyebrow-raising way to each line of *"my Man and me"* as family members looked on with expressions of concern that I had possibly developed a crack habit.

Michelle had to be first to know The Truth. Maybe the revelation that her best friend was gay - and always had been through all our adventures around the world together - would be the enlightening education that would finally throw off the shackles of her father's bigotry that had been forced onto her. And maybe attending Gay Pride on Clapham Common would be that exact kind of education.

I should note that I hadn't been the one that suggested we go along to Pride and *"hang out with the gays because they're fun"*. These were Tracey's exact words whilst her, Michelle and I sat bored in the house that Saturday afternoon, sharing the remaining leftover Pimms from the housewarming BBQ a few weeks previous. Michelle's reaction was hardly one laced with enthusiasm, even less lukewarm than the Pimms we were imbibing, but I had sensed an opportunity here. *"Sure, why not?"* I said in a perky yet not at all suspicious kind of tone. *"I have no problem with the gays, I work with lots of them and they're a right laugh"*. I swear Michelle elevated an eyebrow of mistrust at me as I said this, but nevertheless, an hour later we were at Clapham Common being swallowed up by a whole field of gayness - and Dannii Minogue sporting long blonde hair as she mimed *All I Wanna Do* on the main stage. It was the last time that Pride would be a free event so I got in there just in time. The whole gay world that had forever existed, waiting for me to join their ranks was now all around me. Men kissing, holding hands, unafraid to show - and to be - who they really were. It was intoxicating. Michelle and Tracey were less impressed, I think Tracey was expecting a sordid orgy of inequity in the hope of luring a gay man with the power of her purple knickers, (unbeknownst to us, that was indeed occurring behind some nearby foliage) whilst Michelle looked a tad uncomfortable at the sight of the undulating exchange of male saliva taking up residence in every corner of her field of vision. After half an hour, both Michelle and Tracey announced that they wanted to go home. My heart sank. I wasn't ready to vacate the glitter-soaked premises just yet. But I equally wasn't sure if I was ready to be left alone here either. Then I remembered that Ricky Locke and more of my gay colleagues from Bluebird had mentioned about going to Pride. If only I could find them in the crowd somehow. And so this was my excuse for wanting to stay behind when Michelle and Tracey announced their exit. Michelle's eyebrow hoisting now reached a James Bond level of height at my insistence on not coming home just yet. Tracey just emitted a knowing smirk. Clearly, her purple knickers imbued her with the power of deduction as well as seduction. As I watched Michelle and Tracey disappear towards the exit, I was suddenly overcome with the monumental realisation that I was a gay man surrounded completely by other gay men. I thought back to the times I was too afraid to enter gay pubs in Sydney, but now I was inside the biggest open-air gay pub of all. I didn't know what to do with myself. I felt suddenly lonely. Everyone around me was in couples or groups, circulating around me as I stood rigid like a human statue, completely unsure of what to do next. Suddenly the painfully shy boy that I once was, burst out of me again like the creature from John Hurt's belly in *Alien*. I looked away at every smile or eye contact made in my direction. I didn't dare talk to anyone, let alone try and chat someone up. My intoxication had downgraded rapidly to complete helplessness and insecurity. I decided to try and locate my colleagues, the other 'Bluebird Gays'. This was of course in the days when none of us possessed a mobile phone so all I could do in my efforts to track them down was to repeatedly circulate through the crowds, hoping in vain to spot Ricky Locke or maybe I could catch sight of Mark from the cheese counter's equally cheese-coloured peroxide blonde hair, an impossible task when nearly every other head sported exactly the same look.

After an hour of searching, my enthusiasm for Pride had waned and so I left to return home. When I got back to the house, I found Michelle still up, waiting like an anxious mother. I realised there and then that it was time to tell her the truth about me, to finally clamber out of my Narnia-like closet and reveal that I was a man's man. It would be a moment more than worthy of a doof doof cliffhanger in *EastEnders*.

There was still an hour until closing time at the local pub, the Raynes Park Tavern, so I suggested we go there for a couple of night caps before the proverbial bell tolled. The pub was only a two minute walk away but now it seemed further away than Australia, as I mulled over in my mind exactly how I was going to spill the beans. We arrived at the pub and found a quiet table in the corner. Michelle wanted a lager shandy and I wanted a Bacardi Breezer but opted instead to order a pint of lager, probably in a subconscious effort to butch up the imminent explosion of gayness that was about to turn the Raynes Park Tavern's dubious flock wallpaper a more colourful shade of pink.

Michelle and I exchanged chit-chit for a few minutes whilst the nervous trembling of my leg underneath the table was causing seismic activity across the whole of South West London. Finally, I blurted out:
"I have something to tell you... about me."
I was convinced Michelle must have known what was coming next to append to that declaration. Those magical two words again.
"I'm gay."
She stared at me dumbfounded for what seemed like the length of the last Ice Age. And then she promptly burst into tears, spilling them waterfall-like into her lager shandy and watering down its already weak strength even more. My own strength was equally plummeting, as for a few horrified seconds, as I watched Michelle sob, I wondered if I had just lost my best friend in the world.
"Please don't cry" was all I could muster.
Michelle wiped her tears and finally engaged my stare.

"I'm not crying because you are gay" she said quietly. *"I'm crying because you're my best friend and it hurts me to think that there are people out there who will now hate you even though they don't know you, just because you're different to them."*
And with that, I burst into tears too. In part because of Michelle's overwhelming acceptance of me and in part because of the realisation that I would indeed now have invisible enemies. But the joy of being out and embraced, far outweighed the petty prejudices of people that had never met me.

As Michelle and I continued our mutual cry-fest, we were now attracting the attention of the other pub patrons, no doubt wondering as to the cause of our Biblical-like flood of tears, or maybe they were trying to decide which one of us had dumped the other, what with the appearance we always gave of being a hetero couple when in fact we were now officially Gay Man and his best Fag Hag.

Michelle and I left the pub to the still-bemused looks from others and ended up walking the streets on this warm summer night until we found a park bench to call home. We chatted for the next four hours, hardly pausing for breath. I cried, she cried again. She apologised for any anti-gay comments that she had made over the past four years of our friendship. Various light bulbs fizzed and exploded over her head as all the pieces fell into place. I confessed everything, my furtive encounters and loss of my gay virginity at Lady Jane Bay, the truth about meeting the *Home and Away* star, abortive gay sex to *Xanadu*, my affair with David Mills and my love for David Compton. I even shared my memories of pre-pubescent and teenage unrequited love for James the Boy in the Green Parka and Stuart Pincer the Teenage Gigolo respectively. We hugged and laughed and cried more. Michelle's acceptance and support was nothing short of stellar. If it was one of those typical feel-good Hollywood movies, a crowd of people would have suddenly appeared and burst into spontaneous applause. But then came a reality check.
"You have to tell your parents" Michelle stated.
She was right, and if there was any time to tell them, it would be now, riding off the coat tails of this euphoric wave of acceptance that I had just been showered with from my best friend.
"I'll tell them tomorrow", I promised. There was no going back now.

I kept my word. The next morning I was up early, despite not getting to bed until after 5am. I was on a high of determination to finish what I had started the night before, to declare to the world who the Real Me was. Once Mum and Dad had been ticked off the Coming Out List, there would be no stopping me.

I took the train and then the tube to Dagenham, a journey of nearly two hours, enough time to possibly talk myself out of it. But each flash of doubt that crossed my mind was exterminated Dalek-style by the happiness I now felt at Michelle's unwavering vote of confidence in me.

As I turned the key in the front door of Mum and Dad's house, the four brick walls that had encased many of my secretly gay feelings over the past years, I took a step inside, knowing this would be the last time I would enter this house as a closeted gay man and would emerge again as the out and proud counterpart, maybe accompanied with a bellowing smoke machine, flashing lights and drum roll, not unlike the transformations on *Stars in their Eyes*, when some dowdy checkout girl would disappear behind a screen and inexplicably re-emerge as Shirley Bassey. I entered the living room to find my Mum occupying her usual position, in her armchair by the door, immersed in that day's tawdry copy of *The Sun*. I suddenly remembered its front page furore of disgust a decade before at the gay kiss in *EastEnders*.

I kissed Mum hello and sat on the settee. My Dad was out at work. Maybe it was for the best; maybe it would easier to approach this one parent at a time.

"Done anything nice this weekend?" Mum asked me.

"Actually, yes. Yesterday I went to Pride. On Clapham Common."

Silence from my Mum. She actually folded *The Sun* shut, a very rare occurrence.

"Pride?" She looked at me puzzled and concerned. *"I saw that on the news. That's a thing for funny people".*

There it was again, her ubiquitous use of the word funny to mean gay.

"You mean gay people" I corrected her.

"Fine, those then."

"Then what do you think I am trying to tell you?" I suddenly exclaimed cryptically.

Maybe trying to turn this into a quiz, as if Mum was a contestant on her favourite show *Catchphrase* was the best approach here. Maybe she could also have a buzzer that would reveal square-by-square an image of her son with another man. But she still wouldn't get it.

"What, that you're funny?" she asked, obviously thinking/hoping that I was joking.

"No, that I'm gay."

"No, you're not."

"Yes, I am. I'm gay and have been for as long as I can remember, even if I didn't really know it at the time. But I am. Gay. Completely gay. I don't like women. I like men. I fancy men."

Okay, I was clearly over-egging the point now, getting carried away in my determination to get through to her. I would like to say that Mum then leapt up from her armchair and threw her arms around me, hugging me tight as she re-iterated that I was still her son and she loved me regardless, and maybe knew of a hot eligible bachelor she could fit me up with. But that was only happening in some alternate universe that I was not privy to have a starring role in. Maybe that was the turn of events that my doppelganger in the Blue Mountains had instead experienced.

Instead the next few minutes were horrific. I'm talking pure horror along the lines of the end of *Raiders of the Lost Ark* when the Nazi's face melts off (which gave me nightmares for weeks afterwards by the way).

"No son of mine is a fucking poofter!", Mum suddenly screamed. I suddenly yearned for the now-preferable word of *"funny"* instead.

"What are you?! A rent boy?! A transvestite?! Do you own a handbag?! Wear women's clothes?! Oh my God, do you have AIDS?!" she continued to yell, the unrelenting clichés continuing to spew forth from her now foaming mouth, as she clutched her head and paced around the room like she either desperately needed a wee or was looking for a weapon, the nearest thing being a tacky flamenco dancer lamp brought back as a gift from Spain. Luckily, Mum didn't resort to bashing some sense into me with a frilly dancing Spaniard whose undergarments strangely radiated out bright light and warmth but I was still completely aghast. This wasn't at all the reaction I had been expecting, nor anticipated as a worst case scenario. Michelle's warm acceptance had been a trap, to lull me into a false sense of confidence, only to be now confronted with this woman that I thought was my Mum, but had been replaced by some lunatic, firing out all manner of swear words like the girl in *The Exorcist* with unrelenting Tourettes. It was akin to the shock that Luke Skywalker felt when finding out that his father was Darth Vader. My whole existence had now been pulled into question.

    I started crying, trying to explain that I possessed neither any women's apparel or accessory nor the AIDS virus. And I was far too skinny to be a rent boy. I was gay but I was still her son, her first born. I couldn't help being the way I was, I never had a choice in the matter. I pleaded, I begged, I tried unwaveringly to make her see sense. It was a conversation that was the inevitable sequel to the one in 1989 when she had asked me if I was gay as a result of 'PincerGate'.

    Finally, Mum fell quiet and slumped back into her armchair. The tornado had passed through the room, the trail of destruction wreaked but now an eerie calm had settled. I really thought I had made some headway, that the much-needed Mum Hug was now coming. Mum leaned forward in her chair.

"So tell me," she said. *"What do you and these blokes do with each other? SUCK EACH OTHER OFF?!"*

    The tape had been rewound and my face was melting off in horror again. This time my tears evolved into anger, as I ordered Mum to tell Dad and stormed out of the house. On the way out, I stamped on

Mum's copy of *The Sun*, hating it for every homophobic thought and idea it had brainwashed my Mum - and indeed the general English population - with over the years. I cried all the way home on the tube and train back to Raynes Park.

16 – THE EVIL FIRST BOYFRIEND

1998 - 2000 (aged 23 - 25)

Despite Mum's reaction, I had done it. I was OUT, albeit having to learn to live with the disappointment of Mum not being able to accept my sexuality. Meanwhile, my Dad had no discernible opinion on the matter, either because of his never discussing anything personal or because his brother, my Uncle Jimmy, was gay and it was thus something that he was used to within the family. I was content not to talk details of my sexuality with him; happy to just have it silently acknowledged and hopefully accepted. But whilst Mum and Dad now knew who the Real Me was, no-one else in my family did. Mum had put paid to that by telling me that my being gay was a shameful family secret, one that, should my Nan Shirley ever find out about, would cause her to die of a heart attack thus etching her death forever on my conscience. Was this my super-power? A God-like ability to finish off elderly women with just a simple homosexual revelation? I didn't like this cruel side of my Mum. I loved her dearly but my heart was breaking at her steadfast refusal to accept me for who I really was. It was a heartbreak that was compounded when my Grandad Bert died two weeks after I came out, a couple of days before his 72nd birthday, dying at an age just a year older than the *"three score years and ten"* he had wished he would expire at. The last time I had ever seen him alive was when I borrowed a lawnmower from him to tackle the unwieldy lawn in my back garden at Raynes Park in preparation for a summer barbeque. I never got a chance to return it to him personally as three days later, whilst watching horse racing on the TV from his favourite armchair, he suffered a massive fatal heart attack, whilst my Nan cooked his lunch in the kitchen, oblivious until she went into the living room to find her husband of fifty-two years dead.

Grandad's funeral was the first one I had ever attended and over the coming years, it wouldn't be the last. As I watched the curtains encroach around Grandad's coffin at the crematorium, I wished I had been given the chance to let him know the truth about me - but Mum would tell me in no uncertain terms that Grandad would never have accepted me as gay. I knew she was right. He had been truly 'old school', of 'that different generation' that would never have understood having a grandson who preferred men to women. But whether he would have reacted badly or not, I still missed him and his dark humour. 'Three score years and eleven' seemed a pitiful amount of time for a life to end at. Life was indeed cruelly short. It had to be lived.

*

    But I had a long way to go. I had to forge ahead regardless with or without the acceptance of my family. I now had to join the ranks of Gay World, to throw myself at the mercy of the most preened, pouted, moisturised, eye-gelled, self-critical, fitted, kitted and spun-dry gym bunnies on the block. I mean, even the mingers knew that Clinique wasn't French for hospital.

    My baggy ill-fitting T shirts were replaced by tight sleeves that accentuated my arms that were in turn more defined from working out, my hair was cut stylishly, my confidence as an Out Gay Man was skyrocketing upwards.

    At first I decided to join a gay social group, the existence of which I had sourced from an advert in the back of *Gay Times*. The group was in Hammersmith in West London and I was offered a ride there by the leader of the group, an elderly gentleman who kindly came to Raynes Park to pick me up in his car to drive me over the river, where he promptly took a short detour to park up down a deserted side street and reassure me that I would have fun, a promise that was demonstrated with the reassuring touch of his hand on my thigh. I was already suspecting that maybe this social group would not be to my taste, a suspicion that was confirmed when I arrived and thought I was back at school again, as I was surrounded by camp sixteen year olds. I felt like the Grandad of the group at twenty-two. Maybe I was just envious of them. These guys were out and proud in their teenage years. They had actively disassembled their own closets as easy as a flimsy flat-pack IKEA wardrobe. Why did I leave it so late? To now be of an age where I didn't want to join in with their Spice Girls dance routines? Aged ten I would have fitted right in but that little boy doing drag shows for his sick Granny had long since evolved. And more uncomfortable was the fact that these teenagers were presided over by a somewhat creepy older man that led me to suspect that my thighs were not the only ones to have received the healing power of his veiny grasp. I sat alone in the corner, like being the awkward DJ again at a family party, looking for the right moment to escape, eventually hightailing it out of there when everyone was distracted perfecting the exact moves to *Spice Up Your Life*.

I realised that I was too old to be joining gay support groups aimed at teenagers so instead I decided to bravely work my way around the gay bars of London. My affair with David Mills had fizzled out and he had left Bluebird to take a new job at wine emporium Vinopolis. David Compton had also quit and much like The Boy in the Green Parka eighteen years earlier, had also vanished without trace. With both Davids no longer on the scene, I did what I felt was the natural next step for me and decided to see what the famed Gay Scene had in store for me.

*

At first I plucked up the courage to venture into Charing Cross gay bar Kudos alone, where I hid behind a thick Sunday newspaper reading about the death of Michael Hutchence in Sydney where I had been just a few months before, whilst I simultaneously tried to work out the exact nature of who was making eye contact with who, a copious amount of eyeball-shifting that resulted in me taking a Swedish guy home to my bed where he refused to cum because ejaculation was *"too messy"*. Which was ironic considering that his penis emitted so much frothy pre-cum it was as if his cock had rabies. I promptly went all Purple Knickers Tracey on him and despatched him to the sofa downstairs so that I could get a good night's sleep - until the next night when hopefully another - and keener to ejaculate - man would find himself the guest star in my bed.

Now that I was gay, out and on the scene, London felt like one big sweet shop to me, it having a gay bar in nearly every suburb as well as the concentration of them in Soho that were more tightly-packed than all the men's pants that were being whipped off. And I was working my way around them all, visiting each and every one, refusing to let my Mum's non-acceptance of my sexuality deter me, ignoring her attempts to still pair me off with any girl who did so much as mention my name.
"Oh, I saw Jo/Claire/Natalie/Sharon at ASDA the other day, she asked after you. You and her would make such a lovely couple."
It was nice to know that countless members of the female species were *"asking after me"*. I could have called them to regale them with the sordid details of how I was getting more confident as a gay man, how the sex was great, how I was having plenty of it, but most of all, how I was going to find love. True love with another man. But within a year, my impressive progress would all be undone in spectacular fashion by just one man.

*

It was astounding at how quickly the new-found freedom and excitement of being an out gay man was destroyed. It was now March 1998 and I had been out now for eight months, my closet left well and truly behind as just a receding, shrinking image in a rear-view mirror. I had been enjoying my singledom and all the fun that came with it but I was ready for an actual boyfriend. I wanted to know what it would feel like to be a fifty percent share of a gay couple, to have a 'other half', to be able to say *"we"* like the Queen instead of *"I"*. But as yet, I had no luck in finding anyone who was remotely anything near potential boyfriend material, with my love life being nothing more than a series of drunken one night stands. Maybe London just didn't provide suitable candidates for a boyfriend.

And then along came Sam.

It was a Monday; the start of another working week when I noticed that the Bluebird flower stall had a new recruit. I hadn't even known they were hiring so I was more than surprised to suddenly find this new thirty-something 'muscle mary' in a blue apron stringing together a hand-tied bouquet of flowers. I was instantly mesmerised. I had a thing for older men, attested to by my affair with David Mills. I had to find out who this strapping new florist was. I could already tell he was gay. My ability to pick out another gay man had been finely tuned now in the months since my coming out and I was more than adept at sussing one out, just by the eye contact, body language - or in this case - by the muscle-hugging tight T-shirt, shaved head and very slight mincing way that this particular specimen strutted over to the flower buckets.

I made up some random excuse to go over and talk to Chris, the also-gay Florist Manager with the intention of dropping something 'very gay' into the conversation to clue the mysterious new florist instantly up that I was 'on the same team' as him. What I hadn't expected was to find him serving Joan Collins at the moment I decided to saunter over. Seriously, was the universe taking the piss once again by having Alexis Carrington-Colby-Dexter-Rowan cock-blocking me? Suddenly flustered after Ms. Collins had finally sashayed away, all I could think of on the spot was to talk to Chris about the very mild weather we were having today then randomly mention the awful one-night stand I had just had *"WITH A GUY"*. Even Chris, a seasoned gay of nearly forty, was taken aback by the sudden conversation switcheroo that was slightly less startling than if his mother had suddenly started waxing lyrical about her new vibrator in the middle of a discussion about the rising price of Bingo. Regardless it did the trick, the new florist introduced himself as Sam, his interest in me was peaked and within days we were chatting animatedly which culminated in Sam asking me out for a drink, then another, then another. Two weeks later we were officially boyfriends. I was ecstatic that I finally had my first proper boyfriend, a real-life Action Man, complete with muscles, good looks, a full set of teeth and thankfully an actual penis.

My exciting new relationship evolved quickly, as, three weeks into it, Sam asked me to move in with him. Even though only attention-seeking celebrities with something to promote move this fast in fresh couplings, it still took me all of five seconds to say yes. The house in Raynes Park had never been the same since Michelle had moved out to set up home with her new boyfriend, so I felt it was only right that I should follow suit. Or in this case follow the Muscle Mary to East Dulwich in South London where he owned a converted school house. It wasn't exactly the Carrington Mansion. More like the Bates Motel. His house was in a mild state of disrepair and many rooms only half decorated which Sam announced I could now help him finish, what with the combination of me living on site as well as my decorating and DIY skills that I had acquired during my illegal tenure in Sydney. Despite having a niggling suspicion that Sam had only moved me in for my skill in handling a paintbrush rather than a penis, I brushed away the doubts with a coat of magnolia emulsion and was happily satisfied that at twenty-three years old, I had already set up home with another man. It was all I had ever wanted - to have a boyfriend, a loving relationship, a home together. The sleeping around had been fun, there was no doubt about that, but now, with Sam, I had something far more fulfilling. Or so I thought.

*

Sam and I were not alone living in this house. Sam had a lodger, a Spanish gay Goth called Emi, a strange creature who lived a vampire-like existence in the second lounge which had been turned into his bedroom, with all traces of daylight blocked out via thick black curtains on the windows. Emi would only surface at night, sporadically appearing without warning to shuffle silently through the lounge to the kitchen, not a semblance of any eye contact made, to take a single beetroot from the fridge back to his room for his dinner, the munching of which only heightened his Dracula-like aura. His fingers and lips were permanently stained purple/red which clearly highlighted that his inability to wash was on a par with his aversion to daylight. Emi's existence should have been the first clue that I had just moved into the Hammer House of Horrors. I dreaded to imagine what other monsters might be lurking in the basement or loft, when in fact, I would soon come to realise that the only real monster in this house was Sam. I was about to find out that I had entered into a union with the dark monster from my childhood nightmares, the Monster of Abnormality, only in this case, the abnormality in question referred to my relationship. But it was too late, I was already trapped in the nightmare.

*

Sam started to show his true colours very soon after I moved in with him. At first it was belittling remarks here and there, then constant undermining that soon evolved into outright bullying. Just a couple of months into our relationship, as my self-confidence started to plummet downwards, I realised with horror that Sam was in actual fact the real-life equivalent of the aliens from the TV series *V* that I had loved as a child in the 80s. Sam was lizard queen Diana, with the friendly human face now peeled off to reveal a fork-tongued evil reptilian underneath. But I was his helpless pawn, as he exerted mind-control manipulation over me, moulding and controlling me, pushing me away from my friends so that I barely saw them, leaving me completely at his mercy. I had been brainwashed, just in the same way that Diana in *V* brainwashed scientist rebel Juliet. But Juliet had fought it whereas I had been weakened too much to resist it. It was just me and him now. Emi had finally moved out, no doubt to suck on the blood of innocents in the dead of night. So now I was alone in a creepy house with a power-hungry boyfriend who had moulded me into his subservient plaything. It would only get worse.

*

One evening, in the late summer of 1998, I was sitting watching TV when I heard Sam come down the stairs, grab his jacket and go to head out of the front door, not even saying one word to me. This was by now a common practice of his, regularly giving me the silent treatment for no apparent reason so that my paranoia increased exponentially as to what I could have possibly done wrong to upset him. Sometimes, if I was lucky, I would get an explanation for The Things I Had Done Wrong, which would range from not arranging the cheeses in the fridge properly, closing the bedroom door a quarter of a decibel too loudly, not making the yolk runny enough in a fried egg, and worse of all, daring to phone a friend as if I was a stupid contestant on *Who Wants to Be a Millionaire* or in this case *Who Wants to Have an Abusive Boyfriend*.

But on this evening in particular, I really had no clue as to the cause of Sam vacating the house in silence so when I innocently enquired as to where he was going, I was told matter-of-factly that he was going *"to a gay sauna in Battersea for a shag"*. Or several if it was busy. In no uncertain terms he coldly warned me to get a grip, to wake up and smell the foul smelling coffee that there was no such thing as monogamy, that this is how gay relationships worked and that he was entitled to go out and have random sex whenever he felt like it and with no explanation needed. And with that he slammed the door behind him and went off. I was heartbroken but at this point, I had been so brainwashed by him that I began to believe his 'words of wisdom' as I lay awake all night waiting for him to come home. Even the next day, I listened intently as Sam cuddled me and reassured me in how own soothing way that he was the best I was ever going to get and if I dared try to leave him, I would be condemning myself to a life spent alone as no-one else would want me. The rose-coloured glasses through which I viewed my dreams of love and happiness whilst growing up gay, were now well and truly shattered. But my mind was not my own anymore, it was his, and like a slavishly deluded member of a cult, I believed every word that my leader was telling me. That I was indeed nothing, that I was useless, that only he could be my saviour. I was nothing but a losing playing piece in a twisted game of Snakes and Ladders, slipping back down the rungs of gay confidence to languish at the starting square again. I was the free bird recaptured and shoved back into a cage. It couldn't have got any worse. But it did.

*

The first bout of violence towards me occurred in November 1998. Sam was now the trio of seven year old bullies all rolled into one, but he didn't have sharpened lolly sticks, he had fists. I had imagined that as a gay man, I run a risk of encountering violence towards me at some point in my life, but I never dreamed for one second that it would come from my boyfriend.

It was my wish to see Michelle before she emigrated to New Zealand that resulted in me finding out the quickest way to descend a flight of stairs. Being pushed down the stairs was the natural next step, a sequel to the prelude a week previous when Sam boiled over at me for for accidentally breaking a vase, a crime which resulted in him smashing his fists through the bedroom window. As broken glass rained down on the street below, I genuinely feared for my life and tried to run, only for Sam to grab me at the top of the stairs. It would be another week before he actually went as far as throwing me down them.

I had been quietly devastated to learn that Michelle was emigrating permanently to the other side of the world. But I had barely seen her or Sandra for months now, because of becoming the bad friend that Sam had manipulated me into becoming. But I couldn't let Michelle leave the country without seeing her. She had called me, asking me to come to her leaving drinks in Wimbledon. I wanted to go, to be able to say a proper goodbye to my friend who had supported me in my coming out - and who had also had the premonition of people maybe wanting to hurt me. She had no idea that I was being hurt on a regular basis - and maybe it was this potential revelation that Sam feared, should I get a chance to see her. As I begged him to let me see Michelle, getting as far as putting my coat on, my wish to leave was met with a forced tumble down the stairs as if we were recreating a scene from *Whatever Happened to Baby Jane?* Or in Michelle's case, it would be *Whatever Happened to my Gay Best Friend?*

As I lay on the middle landing looking at the stairs going up and the stairs going down, I couldn't help but lament at how Sam couldn't see the irony in banishing me from seeing the very woman that was so instrumental in my coming out and thus led to him meeting me. Of course, as I lay here seeing stars I guessed that Sam wished he had never met me. How else could I explain me getting an up close and personal view of the skirting boards lining the stairs? They were dirty. Sam's fastidious cleaning skills were not as precise as he liked to make me believe. Meanwhile, Michelle left for New Zealand thinking I was happy, so happy in fact that I had become one of those people that never sees their friends anymore once they become one half of a couple. And in this case, I was a friend who apparently could not be bothered to even come and say goodbye before she departed the country for good.

I couldn't reach out to anyone. Certainly not my Mum and Dad, fearing the *"I Told You So"*. In the rare occasions I was allowed to see any friends, Sam would always accompany me, putting on a smiley and friendly act of being The Best Boyfriend Ever. A few times, I tried to convince myself to leave him; all I had to do was pack a bag and run. But my free will had been so destroyed that I really believed that I would never meet anyone better, that I was worthless and that this was as good as it got. Until one day, when Sam was yet again giving me a week's worth of silent treatment for another undisclosed 'crime', something inside me clicked. I had finally had enough. I still wasn't brave or strong enough to end the relationship so instead I decided to play him at his own game. Whilst he was on the sofa, still completely ignoring me, I went upstairs, packed a bag, put my jacket on and walked out of the front door, not saying a single word to him and definitely not giving him an explanation as to where I was going. It was time for *him* to get paranoid in mulling over The Things That *He* Had Done Wrong. I took a bus to Clapham Junction then caught a train to Brighton where I checked myself into a small bed and breakfast near the seafront in Kemp Town. It was a cold and blustery January. For a whole week, I wandered the streets, ate alone in restaurants, enviously observing happy couples and families and spent hours just sitting in my room, watching TV and wondering where the hell I went wrong and why my life had taken such a dramatic wrong turn. I was again Dorothy at the fork in the yellow brick road, but I hadn't taken the path to the Emerald City, I had taken the other trail to a place that didn't glitter or sparkle in the slightest, a route that was overgrown with so many weeds of loneliness and despair.

I returned to London a week later to find Sam on the sofa. He had assumed I had gone home to Mum and Dad but when my Mum had phoned the house one day leaving me a message, Sam realised that I wasn't where he thought I was and he had no idea as to my whereabouts. He had written me a letter, he was sorry for all the things that he had done, he admitted he was completely fucked up due to an even more fucked up relationship with his father. Great, let's blame this all on daddy issues. In his own words he told me that *"the ice was melting"* and he *"would try and become a better person because of me."* Being the fool that I was, I gave him another chance, wanting to believe there was some good lurking inside him somewhere.

And things did improve for a few months until one evening in August 1999, when I was home alone watching *Ally McBeal* on the television. Sam come home and whilst unpacking groceries into the fridge, proceeded to inform me that he had contracted HIV, related to me in the nonchalant manner of telling someone that broccoli was out of stock in the local supermarket. He had never stopped going to saunas for sex, clearly unsafe sex, as I was now learning. I could never watch *Ally McBeal* again after that, it just stopped being funny.

I had a HIV test and luckily had not been infected but that didn't diminish my anger towards Sam for putting me at risk in the first place. However, I was torn between staying with Sam and supporting him through this or to get the hell away from him as fast as I could. I chose to stay and support him, even though life with him was as miserable as ever as I still lived on a knife edge, waiting to say or do the something wrong that would make Sam's fists rear their knuckles towards me yet again.

*

Meanwhile, Bluebird was no longer a fun place to be. All the gays had left and a new regime had taken over headed up by an arrogant power-hungry Australian chef who relentlessly interfered in the running of the food store. I decided to quit my job there to get an IT qualification so that I could change to a better paid career, one that could earn me a decent enough salary to be able to save money for the day when I would somehow escape from Sam. Then one day in September, I popped back to Bluebird to attend Florist Manager Chris's leaving drinks. Sam was working and as I came up to him he pulled me aside and said he had some bad news. David Mills had been found dead in his flat. He had been out on a date with a new man which he cut short after complaining of a headache. The next morning he was dead from meningitis, found alone in the bed that he and I had spent many a night in during the height of our affair. He was thirty-eight years old. I was numb at the news. I also felt sick at the irony that it had to be Sam to be the one to tell me of David's death. Sam had no idea of the history that David and I had shared, how he had been so instrumental in giving me the courage to come out, how we had enjoyed a short but wonderful love affair. But now he was dead. Happy and healthy one day, dead the next. Just like that. It didn't make any sense.

The last time I had saw David was earlier that year in a pub in Chelsea for another Bluebird leaving drinks do. As I was leaving, he followed me outside and asked if I was happy. I lied that I was. He hugged me. There was still something there between us. A vision of what might have been. I would never have thought for one second that this would be the last time I would ever see him alive. At Chris's leaving drinks, shortly after learning of David's death, I tried hard to hide my pain, unable to let on exactly what David had meant to me. My friend and ex-Bluebird colleague Claire, a close friend of David's, took me to a quiet corner and told me that she knew about David and I, that I had meant the world to him and that he had been very worried about me being with Sam. I broke down and sobbed in Claire's arms. I cried for David. I cried for the death of my gay progress. I cried for help. That night I accidentally called out David's name in my sleep which infuriated Sam, a fury which resulted in him banning me from David's memorial service. And thus I never got the chance to thank David for all of his help in me coming to terms with my sexuality.

After David's death, I was more determined than ever to formulate my escape plan for getting away from Sam. But it was a plan that ultimately I didn't require, as fate intervened in early 2000 when Sam's father died. Sam had always claimed that he hated his father and it was clear that he had many issues towards him, but this paternal loss still resulted in Sam deciding to sell his house and move home to the Midlands to look after his mother, an act of caring that completely contradicted the monster I had been in a relationship with for the past two years. Sam wanted me to move up to the Midlands with him. I said no, using my new IT job as an excuse to stay in London. I instead moved in with Sandra, as at first Sam and I maintained a relationship in which we would see each other only at weekends, an arrangement that unfortunately for Sam, meant that the time I was able to spend away from him was a period when I could begin to blossom again and regain my strength. And it was this new-found strength that enabled me to finally finish it with Sam, during a telephone argument when I successfully called his bluff on his threat to end it with me, condemning him to a life back in the Midlands whilst a couple of hundred miles away, I healed one bruise at a time thanks to Sandra's friendship and unwavering support. I had emerged strong again, in fact stronger than ever. My new gay life since coming out had hardly been the fulfilling adventure I had expected but I was going to push forward, to pick up where I left off. And I swore to myself that no man, no bully, would ever send me hurtling backwards again.

17 – COMING OUT (AGAIN)

2002 (aged 27)

In March 2000, I had moved in with Sandra into her shared house in Tooting, sharing with her and another flatmate Franny, a Cornish primary school teacher who was somewhat of a challenge to live with, due to her two annoying habits. The first being that she liked to stand outside my bedroom door, demanding to know at any given hour every detail of what I was doing, which was trumped by her second habit – a penchant for flashing her minge at every possible opportunity, preferably whilst on the phone in the hallway so that the first thing I would see upon entering through the front door was Franny's Fanny as she deliberately uncrossed her legs as if she was Sharon Stone in *Basic Instinct*. My basic instinct was to run and hide in my room, where of course she would station herself outside asking what I was doing, like a vicious circle of irritation. Franny also loved vodka as much as her exhibitionism, so much so that she would down entire bottles to the point where Sandra and I would find her passed out in her room so spectacularly that on more than one occasion we really thought she was dead.

Thanks to vodka-swilling and fanny-flashing Franny, Sandra was spurred on to buy her own place and in June 2000, she bought a house in Leyton, East London where I joined her as her lodger. Leyton was an area of dubious character, defined by a fake fishmonger at the bottom of the street that was in reality a crack den and a regular ice cream van that seemed to only attract the custom of shifty-looking adults. It was long before any Olympics would come along and gentrify the area to the point of unaffordability. Still, I was free of Sam and happily single again, lodging with my great friend of seven years standing. And little did I know that someone very familiar was living just a ten minute walk away in Stratford.

It was in the entrance to the local Safeway supermarket where, after three years, David Compton walked back into my life. The blonde Welsh Wonder who I had loved in 1997 when we worked together at Bluebird and who had vanished without trace after quitting, had now returned, in the flesh, giving me that winning smile that had always made me go giddy. We hugged and chatted until David suggested we go for a drink that night in Soho to catch up properly which meant the only news I had to tell him was that I spent a couple of years trapped inside a violent relationship.

Anyway, David and I rendezvoused that night in Kudos, the very first gay bar I had ventured into three years previous. I told him about Sam whilst David told me that he and his Italian boyfriend had broken up, as we got steadily more drunk until David suddenly kissed me. I was more than taken aback, even more so when David went on to inform me that he had always had strong feelings for me, feelings so intense in fact, that this was the reason he had quit Bluebird and disappeared, afraid of acting on his feelings for me when he was already in a relationship. He kissed me again. This time, I kissed him back. From that night on, just for a few weeks, we became Best Friends With Benefits, having drunken nights out that would always end with torrid sex or sudden 'intimate moments' in the most random of places, even having sex once behind the wheelie bins at a friend's wedding reception. We were that classy. It was seedy, I knew that. But I was addicted to him. Unfortunately, David had another addiction. For Class A drugs. His reliance on narcotics was just one of two secrets that he kept from me. The other being that he and his boyfriend had never broken up and were still very much together, rendering me as not just the best mate providing benefits but also 'the other woman'. Sadly, it became clear to me that David was on a self-destruct mission which would end with his drug problem becoming so bad that it would bring about the end of our friendship and his disappearance again just two and a half years later.

*

Perversely, unwittingly being David's secret lover had boosted my confidence. After I ended our affair, that same confidence was soon being helped by a miraculous, exciting new discovery. It was a website on the internet called *Gaydar*, named after the phenomenon of how a gay man is able to recognise a fellow gay man. It was nice to finally have a name for the thing I had always referred to as 'seeing someone's gay aura'. Anyway, *Gaydar* was the website that every gay man in the UK seemed to be on, a place to find friendship, sex, even love. Whilst David Compton was addicted to cocaine and heroin, I was addicted to *Gaydar*, giving myself the profile name 'CockneyBlueEyes' and spending hours upon hours messaging guys and arranging hook-ups, logging on as soon as I was home each day from my new job as IT Support Officer for Estee Lauder, practically wetting myself with excitement each time the snazzy sci-fi sound effect alerted me to receiving a new message. You could say that I carnally made the most of my *Gaydar* membership. After all, I had a lot of lost time to make up for thanks to Sam. But deep down I still held out hope for a proper relationship, although I was not sure whether I was really ready to take a risk on another one. But my dream guy had to be out there somewhere, the one man who would give me my Happy Ever After. Who was I kidding, I was hardly a fairytale princess what with all my bed-hopping that would have put even the most athletic horny frog to shame. And Prince Charming was hardly going to be found lurking amongst the many headless torsos now proliferating within the cyberspace of *Gaydar*, talking body parts that delivered such romantic openers such as *"Top or bottom?"*, *"Stats?"* Or *"Do you fuck?"* a particular chat-up line that meant the spirit of Stuart Pincer ironically lived on in the spirit of certain gay men. Regardless, there had to be someone like me amongst them all, a guy who equally didn't want to run the risk of ending up an old spinster who would eventually be found dead in their armchair with cats pissing on their lifeless knees and a Pot Noodle still spinning in the microwave.

And that's when I met Will, a handsome dark-haired twenty-nine year-old freelance IT consultant. He messaged me, I messaged him back, we exchanged more virtual get-to-know-you's and then met for a first date in the real life that we forgot existed, in The Yard bar in Soho. I instantly liked Will, he was kind, sweet, gentle, funny - he was as far opposite to Sam as you could possibly get. Our dates quickly escalated into a relationship and just a few weeks later, we had already moved in together, at first in Will's tiny rented bachelor pad in Rotherhithe, before together renting a new, bigger flat across the Thames in Limehouse. It was my living with Will in a one bedroom flat of domestic bliss that would lead to my Second Coming Out, like I was a gay Jesus Christ too impatient to wait until The End of Days.

*

It was summer 2002. I had been on my monthly visit to my parents, where my Mum, although glad I had traded in *"that effeminate Sam geezer"* for this mystery new man, still wasn't one hundred percent comfortable with my sexuality, which still meant that Nan and no-else in my family knew that I was now on my second boyfriend five years after coming out, a fact that still might bring on Nan's supposed fatal heart attack. My Auntie Carol has also been visiting that day and offered me a lift back to Limehouse, which I considered slightly odd but didn't think anything of it, so graciously accepted.

Carol's ulterior motive soon made its grand entrance when we pulled up outside my apartment building where she turned off the engine and said that she wanted to ask me something personal, revealing that she had been snooping on the new website *Friends Reunited* and found my profile on there. Okay, I thought, where is she going with this? It was true that I did have a profile on *Friends Reunited* and through it, Fiona my infant 'beard' had found me where we had exchanged chit-chat and I told her I was gay, which she didn't seem at all surprised to hear. Carol went on to say that on my profile, it mentioned that I was *'living with my partner in Docklands'*. Oh shit. My face went crimson as I realised that I had indeed added such a revealing line of text to my profile. *"I just want to ask..."* continued Carol, *"This friend that you live with... is he a friend or a FRIEND?"* How many times did she need to use the word friend to get her point across? I knew what kind of 'friend' she wanted me to reveal that Will was, not one that played with your *Star Wars* figures or Stickle Bricks but rather one that preferred to play with your penis and your arse and put them together like a jigsaw that really wasn't that complicated to complete as it only had two pieces.

I told her the truth. Everything in fact. That not only was Will my boyfriend and we had been together for nearly a year but also that I came out to my Mum five years previous but had a vow of silence slapped on me, like a family fatwa as if I was the Essex Salman Rushdie, authoring *The Satanic Perverses*. Carol's response left me gobsmacked. Not only did she say she didn't care I was gay, she also offered to telephone every single member of our family that evening and tell them the news, doing the coming out for me in a series of phone calls that would qualify her to take part in one of those TV charity telethons. In this case, the charity that needed support was her gay nephew about to announce his gayness by proxy of his Aunt.

Carol kept her word and later that night, I received phone call after phone call from various members of my family stating a myriad of things ranging from that they didn't mind, that they always suspected, that they wanted me to be happy, that they loved me regardless - and - *"have I told my Nan yet?"* Gulp. Yes, Nan Shirley now knew. So far I hadn't heard from her, nor had I heard about the fatal heart attack that was supposed to befall her. I got the call from her the next morning. She *"wanted to see me"* ASAP. I had been summoned. Having your company forcibly requested by Nan Shirley was serious business.

Now seventy-four years old, she still ruled the roost from the comfort of her reclining armchair and accompanying army of cigarettes. Nan's potential disapproval equalled metaphorical banishment, in the same vein as Alexis Colby putting her sister inside a crate and shipping her off to Caracas. Regardless, I had no choice but to face her and so went over to her house the very next day. Due to Nan's mobility issues thanks to a bad knee, I, like other members of my family, had a key to her house as letting yourself in was far easier than waiting the eight minutes or so it took for Nan to stub out her latest cigarette, put her armchair back into the upright position, rise out of it, locate her walking stick, totter at a glacial pace to the front door and open it to let you in. I took a deep breath and entered Nan's hallway. I was physically trembling, my gulps of fear as loud as thunderclaps. I wasn't sure I was ready for a repeat of the coming out to my Mum five years previous. Would I get the same accusations of a penchant for women's clothing and a sideline in male prostitution? Well I was in Nan's hallway now and there was only one way to find out. There was no going back plus clearly she already knew that I was gay. It was just her judgement on it that was outstanding.

Her house was empty, Uncle Roger was out and no-one else was around, as if all the minions had scattered and hidden in terror at the verdict about to be passed. Even the spiders were hiding. The door to the living room was closed. All I could hear was the sounds of a daytime chat show emanating from the television set. I peeked through the frosted glass and could sense the ghost of Grandad sitting in what used to be his own armchair, still facing the television at the perfect angle. I pushed open the door. Of course, with the One Woman National Chain Smoking Championships taking place inside the living room, I was immediately engulfed by a pea souper nicotine fog. Fighting my way through the mist, I finally could make out the figure of Nan in her armchair.

"Hi, Nan" I stuttered.

The fog magically parted and Nan just looked at me with the kind of emotionless yet fierce stare that I had often seen in action when a newsagent had short-changed her or Grandad had forgot to buy the Viennetta ice cream on the weekly shop.

"Take a seat" she ordered, motioning for me to sit on the settee next to her huge pile of *Take a Break, Chat* and other inane magazines in which she was addicted to solving the word puzzles and crosswords found inside, in the vain hope of winning desirable prizes ranging from a top of the range watering can, a year's supply of hair lacquer or for the most complex puzzles, a weekend trip to Skegness. I was always roped in by Nan to finish completing these puzzles for her, my monthly visits to her consisting of hours on this very settee, correcting Nan's often hilariously wrong or misspelt answers or the way she would try and make a five letter word fit in the boxes for an eight letter word. I fondly remember the time during our first holiday to Spain, when during a pub quiz, a question was asked as to the name of the slave in the TV series *Roots*.

"*CUNTY CUNTY!!!*" had shouted Nan as her arm shot into the air, to the sounds of shocked squeals, embarrassed laughter and a small burst of rapturous applause from two drunk men in the corner.

Now, as I was sat on Nan's settee beside the evidence of all the quizzes I had helped her with, I wondered if they could be used as leverage. Maybe my gayness could be balanced out by the fact that the knowledge I had festooned into these puzzles, had once helped her win a tea towel.

"*So*" said Nan, finally stubbing out her cigarette, "*I believe we have something to discuss.*"

Yes, Nan, four down, a fruit with eight letters is mandarin not grandson, I was tempted to reply in an effort to pre-diffuse the coming apocalypse with ill-timed humour. Of course I didn't though, all I could reply was:

"*So, Carol told you about me then?*"

Nan's eyes narrowed. "*Yes, she did.*"

Gulp.

"*And there's only one thing I want to say*" she continued.

She leaned forward now, the proximity of her head to mine not dissimilar to the alien's and Sigourney Weaver's in the first *Alien* movie.

"*I don't give a flying shit that you're gay, all I care about is how big your boyfriend's willy is.*"

My mouth dropped open in shock and hit the floor with a thud as I turned a shade of red that would elicit jealousy from a post box.

"*Well?*" she insistently probed, "*How big is it, then?*"

"*Quite sizeable actually*", I found myself replying.

"*Fabulous!*" she exclaimed, "*Now can you help with me the big crossword in this week's Take a Break? I'm completely baffled.*"

She was not the only one. That was the entire coming out to my Nan done and dusted, just like that, with a declaration of my boyfriend's penis size and the solving of a jumbo crossword puzzle in *Take a Break*. I did go on to tell Nan that according to my Mum for the past five years, my coming out was supposed to result in her death from cardiac arrest. Nan declared that she would "*deal with*" my Mum, two words which for the troublesome pikey family at the end of the street meant a threatening gesture with a garden rake but for my Mum - her first born daughter - would mean an education which would result in Mum's admittance of how silly she had been all these years. Her talking-to from Nan worked wonders and from then on, Mum magically morphed into a woman truly accepting of her son's sexuality, going so far as to wishing I could meet the right man, sensing maybe that Will might not really be the one for me. But if he wasn't, then who was? A holiday to Key West, Florida that coming Christmas would present me with the answer. Or so I thought.

18 – NEVER FALL IN LOVE WITH A DALLAS COWBOY

2002 - 2003 (aged 28 - 29)

My relationship with Will was already hitting the proverbial rocks when we embarked on a fateful two week holiday to Key West in Florida for Christmas 2002. We had been together for nearly a year and a half now and I thought I loved him, I really did. But my experiences of love so far in my life had amounted only to that of the unrequited kiddie and teenage kind, as well as the delusional love of the 'gay virgin syndrome' and violence that had been disguised as love. Now, aged twenty-eight, hindsight was an unwanted gift on a level with Mum's traditional recycled Christmas bath sets. But it showed me the niggling truth that my relationship with Will had maybe been a rebound of sorts, the hasty jumping into a union with a kind, gentle man so soon after enduring the mind control and fisticuffs from Sam. I had re-grown stronger than I had anticipated as Sam had killed off the last traces of the naive, nerdy boy from Dagenham. Maybe I was too strong for Will. I was never again going to settle for anything that truly didn't make me happy. And the truth was that I wasn't sure if Will made me feel sunny inside anymore.
And that's when Patrick Ferrara walked into my life and changed everything so spectacularly.

*

Meeting Patrick was all thanks to having a go-go boy's crotch in my face, a close encounter of the awkward kind that probably kick-started many a love affair in Key West. It was the second night of our holiday and Will and I were propping up the bar in the Bourbon Street Pub, a raucously gay venue featuring strong cocktails served by muscular shirtless barmen, potent drinks that loosened morals as well as underwear, handed to you between the legs of the go-go boys that were parading all over the bar counter doing unenthusiastic dance moves that made my cousin Kim's need-a-wee shuffle seem like a J-Lo dance spectacular. This dubious entertainment could be cranked up a notch by handing the go-go boys dollar bills, albeit with a puzzlement of where to put them as the choices were clearly quite limited due to their lack of attire. It was whilst debating where to stuff a dollar bill when I first clocked the impossibly handsome man with the sexy Latin looks, sitting on the opposite side of the bar with a companion, as together they ingeniously managed to donate their own dollar bills to a rival go-go boy in a manner that was going to prove a tad uncomfortable on his next trip to the bathroom.

It was when Will disappeared to this very bathroom that a particularly aggressive go-go boy, looking slightly of the age where he blatantly needed a rest, marched over and gyrated his clearly-stuffed package in my face, my appreciation of which was of the level which prompted Mr. Gyrator to ask me why the English always had to *"look so fucking miserable."* I retorted that being happy did not mean having to sit there sporting an inane grin like a demented clown to which he snapped that:

"You do realise that I am go-go boy of the year?"
"Which year?", I snapped back, sending the now-offended go-go 'boy' stomping off across the bar and nearly slipping on some spilt beer, as I heard an appreciative giggle at my go-go boy dispensing skills and turned to find that the handsome Latino man and his older companion had somehow teleported to my side of the bar and were now sitting next to me.

"See, told you he'd be English" said the Latino, revealing a Texan drawl as he and his buddy exchanged a curious look between them. I introduced myself as they in turn unveiled their identities as Patrick (31) and Sean (40), a couple from Dallas (of all places!) who had been together for ten years, a fact that was mentioned no less than eleven times, as was Patrick's repeated question of where I was from, his drunkenness translating into a short-term memory loss that made him think he was in the film *Memento*. And it was after the thirteenth time of me reminding him that I was from a place called Dagenham, when, out of nowhere, Patrick suddenly kissed me - no, *snogged* me - on the lips. As he pulled away, leaving me with the same open mouthed sex-doll look that had adorned Donna Baker's face at The Postman Knock Kissing Debacle, I had no time to react as equally suddenly, Sean snogged me too. Then Patrick did again. Then Sean did again. It was like being inside a Pinball Wizard machine with Texan tongues instead of tiny silver balls. Meanwhile, Will was *still* in the bathroom.

"I... I have a boyfriend" I finally stuttered, quickly adding *"He's in the bathroom"* in a desperate way that someone would vehemently try to prove the existence of Big Foot.

"You guys in an open relationship?" was the response from Sean. *"Patrick and I are"*

I knew the definition of what an open relationship was. It meant that whilst you are quite happy tucking into your Smart Price cupcake from ASDA, you also want to sample the Waitrose gateaux, the Tesco muffin, the Sainsbury's iced bun. But even with all those delicious treats that you can't stop having, you still want to cling on to the safe comfort of the ASDA cupcake.

"No. We're not" I finally answered.

Undeterred, Patrick and Sean went on to dictate *"The Rules"* that the two of them adhered to in order to successfully maintain a relationship whose door was so wide open that it rendered the heating inside pointless. These rules basically consisted of a trio of commandments:

1) Thou Shall Only Play Together And Never Apart.
2) Thou Shall Not Sleep With The Same Guy More Than Once.
3) Thou Shall Not Keep In Touch With Any Guy We Have Sex With.

I just nodded, delighted to be made aware of the somewhat brief *Open Relationship Instruction Manual*, a tome that *War and Peace* didn't have to worry about competing against in terms of length. Sensing my apparent nonchalance, Sean then dragged Patrick away, over to another go-go boy who was already crouching in anticipation of some dollar bill inserting. But Patrick was discreetly looking back at me. Maybe he, like I, had realised the presence of the electricity that occurred between us. I checked to make sure my hair wasn't standing on end just as Will finally returned from the bathroom - and to my honest confession that the two men currently playing jam the dollar bill inside the go-go boy had come over and kissed me.

"What, both of them?" said an incredulous Will, as if it was surprising that even one man had locked lips with me, let alone two at once. I looked over at Patrick again, who smiled at me in a way that somehow ignited an unexpected fire within my belly. Sensing the danger, I suggested to Will that we should find a different bar to drink in the next night.

*

If only it had been that easy. The next night, Will and I went drinking at the Atlantic Shores resort instead, away from the concentrated gay nightlife on Duval Street. I was still thinking about That Kiss with Patrick, but not so much about the companion-piece kiss with Sean. And that's when Patrick and Sean showed up, Patrick looking somewhat happy that they had tracked down the fugitive that was I. There was no escape from the spark between Patrick and I, more than evident as the four of us got to know each other over endless cocktails that ended with Patrick and Sean's sudden suggestion of a foursome back in their hotel room. I surprised myself with how the idea of getting intimate with Patrick suddenly appealed to me. But this was something more than just sex, for I had strange feelings towards Patrick that told me I wanted something much more. And then I remembered Patrick and Sean's rules, in particular Rule Number Three of *'Thou Shall Not Keep In Touch With Any Guy We Have Sex With'*. I realised that I didn't want sex with Patrick if it meant never seeing him again. For somehow, even from afar, I wanted him in my life. Luckily the foursome never materialised as Will got so blind drunk that I had to escort him back to our hotel, which resulted in an emotional argument that culminated in Will telling me that he wanted us to try an open relationship, to, in his own words, *"be more like Patrick and Sean"*.

Will had apparently decided that if it could work for them then it could for us, despite my suspicions that Patrick was far from happy with his own arrangement of sexual freedom with his boyfriend. This was confirmed at another night back at Bourbon Street Pub where Patrick confessed to me whilst Will and Sean were dancing, that he was deeply unhappy, that Sean had broken the rules once before and had an actual affair. Patrick got tearful as he told me how morally and emotionally bankrupt he was. He needed a way out. We held hands under the table.

*

Meanwhile, I had now reluctantly agreed with Will that we *"would try"* a threesome. Will needed no more encouragement as the next night, he brought a young English guy back to our room in a version of domestic bliss that was not *"Hi honey, I brought home the shopping"* but *"Hi honey I brought home a horny twink"*. He was a pale, mildly attractive specimen who joined us in our bed but whose idea of foreplay was to continually spit down my throat. It was like having sex with the puppet *Spit the Dog* but I was adamant that I was not going to be his puppeteer Bob Carolgees and put a hand up his arse.

Needless to say, this wasn't what I had expected from a relationship. And it certainly wasn't what I wanted. For I realised that I wanted Patrick.

*

The holiday ended and Will and I returned to the UK. I tried to put Patrick to the back of my mind but because of not falling victim to Rule Number Three, the four of us were keeping in touch, well it was more Patrick and I that were exchanging the e-mails, all very friendly and innocent but with a subtext that maybe only Patrick and I could sense was lurking unspoken there between each line.

Meanwhile, against my better judgement, Will and I had pushed forward with our own open relationship, adopting the same 'Rules' as Patrick and Sean, my deep down reasoning being that I wanted to prove that such an arrangement could never work. I refused to let Sam's claim be corroborated, that gay men, despite being in a relationship, were still free to go around and have sex with whomever they wanted, whenever they wanted. I wanted a solid, loving relationship with another man, steadfastly not wanting to believe that its chances of existence were slightly less than Elvis Presley being found alive on the moon. Maybe I did still possess a leftover smidgen of naivety after all.

*

Will and I continued the openness of our relationship by going on holiday to Sydney that Spring, which for me was a strange experience to be "doing all the gay stuff" again in my old stomping ground - this time with a boyfriend. It was strange even to be on the nude beach again at Lady Jane Bay where I could see my younger self from seven years before, lying terrified and nervous on the rocky ledge above, or sitting admiring the view whilst a *Home and Away* star tried to pick him up. I wondered now if Mr. *Home and Away* had been in an open relationship himself.

On Oxford Street, Will and I were in and out of all the gay bars without even a moment's hesitation at the door. It was free, easy; I had a boyfriend, how far I had come since my last time in Australia. But yet something was wrong. Very wrong.

At the end of the holiday we picked up a guy in a bar and brought him back to our holiday apartment. I had to go to the bathroom during the ensuing threesome and when I came back to the bedroom, I just stopped in my tracks and stood silently in the doorway, watching my boyfriend fuck another man. I left them to it and slept on the sofa. I realised there and then that this was never going to work for me. And thoughts of Patrick still lingered, notions that still gave me butterflies in my belly. And then, upon our return home, there was an e-mail waiting in my inbox from Patrick and Sean, inviting Will and I over to Texas to visit them. We booked our flights the very next day.

*

The Texas holiday that August would be one that would start off well but soon devolve into a disaster scene, as two open relationships collided, exploded and threw out the shrapnel of hurt and confused emotions.

As soon as I laid eyes on Patrick again at Dallas airport, all the feelings for him that I had been fighting against in Key West erupted volcano-like to the surface again. There was a deep connection between us, one that Sean and Will were now not blind to. Within days of staying at their house and taking a road trip to Austin and San Antonio, arguments had boiled up respectively between Will and I and Patrick and Sean as jealously simmered like a potent home brew.

And then one evening, back at Patrick and Sean's house towards the end of the holiday, something happened that clued me up straightaway that Patrick maybe had the same feelings for me as I did for him. We were all in front of the TV together, along with Patrick's best friend Woody, watching *Queer Eye for the Straight Guy*, which could have been a commentary on all my years spent in the closet. Will and Sean were sent out to get more beers from the local liquor store and once they had gone, Patrick immediately got up and headed into the kitchen, giving me a look that in no uncertain terms was instructing me to follow him. Leaving Woody alone on the sofa, I took the hint and followed Patrick into the kitchen, where he stood waiting for me. He asked me if there was something on my mind, if there was anything we needed address or to talk about. It was as if his eyes were imploring me to just Say The Words. I knew what those words were. I had fallen utterly in love with him, the kind of love that was defined by longing and pain. I now knew what it felt like to properly be In Love. It was nothing like I had ever experienced before. I was madly in love with this man who not only lived thousands of miles way from me, he also had a partner of ten years, who was currently down the liquor store with my own partner. I had realised the enormity of this in the hotel in San Antonio a few days before, where I had cried into my pillow, a sequel of tears to the last time I soaked a polyester pillowcase when my Mum had accused my fourteen year old self of being *"funny"*. The hurt of that didn't compare to the sheer pain of now being in love with a man that I couldn't be with. And yet, I strongly suspected that maybe Patrick wanted to be with me too. I knew this because we had held hands as we shared a taxi to a dance party, we had stolen an illicit kiss behind a palm tree in an outdoor bar, a kiss that Patrick told me he had been wanting to exchange with me from the moment he met me, until I reminded him that he actually did kiss me the moment he met me. This new kiss however was crushed minutes later when Sean presented Patrick with their latest threesome participant and he was whisked away, throwing a look back at me that screamed that not only did he not want to be doing this anymore, he also wanted me to save him from it.

But the unspoken feelings we had for each other were wrong. Wrong. So many levels of wrong. Like taking an elevator ride up all one hundred and thirty six floors of Wrong Inc and emerging at each and every level to be greeted by a stern receptionist screaming *"WRONG!"*.

But here I was, alone with Patrick at last in his kitchen, Sean and Will due back any minute. It was now or never to tell him how I felt. I was just about to blurt out that I loved him when Woody bounded into the kitchen as The Divine Angel of Intervention, an intervening that was clearly deliberate, judging by the look that he gave us both – and the incredibly long time it took him to remove a beer from the fridge. The moment had passed.

The next day, Will and I left Texas, the flight back to the UK thick with a silent tension between us. The day after returning to our flat in Limehouse, I received an e-mail from Patrick saying that he had a letter that he wanted to send me, asking for my parent's address, stating that it would be 'safer' to be delivered there. When it arrived, I couldn't get to my parents fast enough to retrieve it, hurriedly opening it to read what he had written inside. I could hardly believe my eyes as I read the ten pages of hot Texan handwriting, the fevered scribbling of someone who clearly had a lot to say. Patrick poured out all his feelings, everything he had thought or felt towards me since we met in the Bourbon Street Pub at the end of the previous year. And he said he loved me. He was *in love* with me. He loved me so much that he wanted to shout it from the rooftops. It was there, written in his own words. I don't know how I restrained myself from turning into Julie Andrews and dancing gleefully along the street whilst bursting into song.

Straightaway, I wrote a letter back to Patrick, delivered to his own parents address, telling him that I loved him too. We went on to exchange several letters, in which we agreed that I would end things with Will and he would end things with Sean. We could both close the unwanted wide open doors of our current relationships and move into another room together where the door would stay closed. We would somehow find a way to be together.

*

Will was halfway through eating the steak I had cooked for him when I told him. Okay, my timing could have been a bit better, I could at least let him have his dessert first but he asked me if something was wrong between mouthfuls and I just blurted it out. I wanted us to break up, to put an end to our relationship of nearly two and a half years.

To this day, it's the worst thing I have ever had to do to someone. The pain of breaking someone else's heart is far worse than breaking your own. But, despite our ups and downs and deterioration of our relationship, it still came as a total shock to Will. He cried. I cried. It was a lot worse than when I made six year-old Fiona cry when I kissed another girl. For now a grown man was crying because his boyfriend loved another man. I didn't want to hurt someone like this but I felt it wasn't fair for Will to be with someone who no longer loved him and so I needed to set him free. What a cliché, it's not as if he was trapped under the floorboards in Fred and Rose West's house. But the fact of the matter was that I was completely in love with someone else several thousand miles away in Dallas and him and I were on the verge of starting a new life together. Or so I thought.

The upshot was that Patrick never came through for me. At first his e-mails to me became less frequent and of lessening length, a sudden silencing that would result in me trying to find reasons to e-mail him, only to get short, punctuated, suddenly business-like replies in return.

After my break-up with Will, I went on holiday to California where Patrick promised he would rendezvous with me in San Francisco as he was on a business trip in nearby Oakland. He never turned up. The last e-mail I got from him was to tell me that he had decided that he wasn't brave enough and that he was staying with Sean. The kick in the teeth was that for him, I had been the catalyst needed to make them work things out. I was devastated. Until, when I thought it through, I realised that he had also been the catalyst for me too. A propellant for me to understand that I would never settle again for anything less than happiness.

And so I picked myself up and dusted myself off, determined that my search for my perfect man would continue unabated. He had to be out there somewhere. At least I now knew what being in love really felt like. I just hoped that one day I would get to feel it again with someone who would truly reciprocate it.

19 – PINK VOMIT IN THE USA

2004 (aged 29)

The luminously bright coloured puke of a naked New Yorker more than summed up my next series of disastrous entanglements with American men. I don't quite know why I had suddenly become fixated on the idea of moving to the USA. More than likely it was because of the dream that Patrick had peddled to me, that future of a life with a hunky American partner that had been briefly and tantalisingly dangled before my eyes. Although the credibility of such a product was like a knock-off bag from Romford Market that looks like the real thing but falls apart on its first journey outside of the house. All I knew was that I was starting to seriously wonder if I had truly fucked up. Because it hadn't been right and I wasn't happy, that what I had to keep reminding myself. And yet, now, at the start of 2004, my long-held dream of the perfect love-filled life as a gay man had unravelled spectacularly to the point now where I was broke and back living at home with my parents in Dagenham. I was back in my childhood bedroom for the first time since before leaving for Moscow in February 1996. Dagenham had played its cruel trump card, its black hole-like pull sucking me back in at the lowest points in my life, in this case, whilst I was licking my wounds from two failed relationships and a broken heart from falling in love with someone that I couldn't be with. Dagenham was as much a shadow of its former self as I was, with most local shops having long since disappeared or now boarded up. This wasn't how I envisaged my life to be a few months shy of turning thirty. I needed change. I needed love.
I couldn't afford a place of my own, so decided to work, work, work, taking on an extra part-time evening job working at the gay sauna Chariots in Shoreditch, just manning the reception as I took customers' payments and handed them towels and a locker key. It was this job that truly opened my eyes to a different, darker side of gay life. There was something just so unappealing about seeing men sitting in dark cabins for hours, waiting for the right guy to knock on their wide open door,

trapped inside a windowless environment like the residents of tiny bedsits with glory holes the nearest thing to a glimpse of the outside world. Were these the men that had tried and failed to find love and instead had to make do with finding random cock? A lot of them were 'straight' and married, that's for sure, the removal of wedding rings a commonplace sight in the changing rooms before venturing up to a twelve man steam room. Were these the still-closeted men that had decided to stay hidden and go the whole hog of marrying their 'beards' and living a life of lies? Then there was the elderly man in biker leathers, a possible older incarnation of Jarrad from Bega who had given up on love and would spend all day, every day in a cabin, from opening time until closing time, just sitting, waiting, ignored by the young, sneered at by the old and completely blanked by the other men that were so lost in a haze of hard drugs that they thought a communal shower obviously resembled a toilet and therefore an appropriate place to defecate with an unyielding splatter reminiscent of my infant Fairy Liquid paint exercises. Except it wasn't Nanette Newman endorsed washing up liquid that was being inhaled up the noses around here - it was GHB - a drug meant for sedating horses, which warranted weekly calling of ambulances to despatch the latest victim to hospital. Needless to say, it wasn't a nice place to work and was in fact putting me off gay life in general. Meanwhile, every move of the staff was watched and eavesdropped on by our bosses via CCTV and hidden microphones which meant that they were snooping on the flirting transpiring between myself and Polish cleaner Radek, a young innocent of just twenty years old who proclaimed his love for me after I agreed to accompany him to Gay Pride at Finsbury Park. I was flattered but could only see my younger self in Radek, the naive innocence of youth, and the folly of the 'gay virgin syndrome'. I told him it would never work between us, not alluding to my real thoughts that maybe Sam had been right all along, that gay relationships were a waste of time and arguably a life spent seeking casual sex inside grotty saunas was the best it was ever going to get. I was getting more cynical and I didn't like it. I was actually turning *into* Sam, now even sporting the same shaved-head look that he had. But of course, I didn't possess the violent tendencies.

    And then one evening, as if to witness my devolution for himself, Sam actually showed up at the sauna. I hadn't laid eyes on him for nearly four years. As I saw him in the queue, shuffling nearer and nearer to reception - and thus to me - it was as if the muscle memory of my body kicked in and starting aching, remembering the bruises from those years before. I wasn't sure what I would say to him, how I would react, or how I would deal with his inevitable smugness at the downturn of events that saw me now working in a gay sauna, the haunts of his that had rendered me alone crying in our bedroom night after night during our relationship.

    As Sam finally reached the reception desk, my palpitations were replaced by shock as I was taken aback at Sam's appearance. His right arm was jutting out at an awkward, twisted angle. He looked, for want of a better word, mangled. He seemed just as shocked to see me as I was to see him. He explained the cause of his disability, in that he had been training to be a circus acrobat and had suffered an accident which had completely shattered the bone in his right arm, now leaving it permanently sticking out as if forever wanting to shake your hand. I didn't know what to say, as Sam just took his towel and key and shuffled off into the darkness of the sauna, like a monster relegated to hiding back in the shadows where he came from. Part of me decided it was karma for his abuse of me - but another part of me felt intensely sorry for him. I would never see him again after that evening. Regardless, encountering Sam was the kick I needed to remind me not to hurtle at breakneck speed down the Highway of Cynicism but to dust myself off and go forth once again in trying to find True Love.

*

    It was in August of that year when the man of my dreams strutted into my life. Okay, he was clearly far off from deserving such an accolade as this was the third night in a row that he had visited Chariots. So I knew right off the bat that he wasn't husband material but hey, it was a steamy and sultry summer, I was perpetually horny and this guy was hot. Smoking, impossibly attractive, six-packed body-to-die-for *hot*. His name was Greg. Gorgeous Greg. He was an American psychiatrist visiting London from New York, his analytical skills only outdone by his masterful expertise in flirting. For somehow, this hot hunk was into *me*. Needless to say, I was more than flattered to be the object of his attentions and in receiving his flirtations, I was happy to be as shallow as the only end of a swimming pool that I could venture into. A swimming pool that I wished to be filled with carbon copies of Gorgeous Greg. I was a bit obsessed with Americans at the moment, maybe it was the failed love for Patrick that was spurring me on to find a replacement for him, a newer, more reliable model whose instruction manual didn't include three pages of text on how to deal with his boyfriend of ten years. But this time, my lust was realistic, as I knew that Gorgeous Greg would only be someone that at some point would require full use of his warranty. After four evenings of flirting and teasing, Greg announced he was returning to New York. I never expected to see him again, he having been a fun distraction for me, boosting my self confidence again, but as he departed Chariots for the last time, he gave me his number and told me to look him up if I ever came to New York. The thing was, I *was* coming to New York. Just two weeks later in fact.

*

When Sting was warbling on about being an Englishman in New York, I'm sure he must have missed the verse that involved said Englishman having to contend with a naked, comatose, pink vomit covered Manhattan psychiatrist in a tiny single hotel room in Chelsea. This incident of thwarted sex and the mopping up of pink vomit would be the pinnacle of this particular Transatlantic adventure, a holiday that had materialised when some friends from Los Angeles who I had met in Key West and stayed in touch with since, invited me to join them in New York to celebrate a fortieth birthday. I didn't need to be asked twice. And so I headed across the Atlantic again, armed with two pieces of information that reflected both my past and future dealings with Hot American Men. One was Gorgeous Greg's phone number. And the other was an e-mail from Patrick, telling me that coincidentally, he was going to be in New York on business at the same time that I would be there visiting. And he wanted to see me. I wasn't sure how I felt about the idea of coming face-to-face with him again, especially just one-on-one for the first time since we had met nearly two years previous. But hey, the past had already re-surfaced this year in the now disabled form of Sam so I might as well tackle another returning visitor to my life.

I agreed to meet up with Patrick on my first full day in Manhattan and, unlike his promised rendezvous in San Francisco, this time Patrick actually showed up, convening with me as agreed beside the Bethesda Fountain in Central Park. I could almost feel the cherubic stone angels above my head tutting their disapproval at me as I waited for the Man Who Stole Then Broke My Heart. When Patrick finally arrived, we greeted each other like two business colleagues, with a handshake and inane chit chat that made no mention of anything that had previously transpired between us. We went out for dinner and it was upon dividing the bill that Patrick asked to come back to my hotel room for a private chat. I was more than a little taken aback - and nervous at the idea of Patrick and I alone together in a location that in another place and time would have seen us making mad passionate love in. But not now, not after everything that had happened - or to be more precise - *hadn't* happened - between us. Instead, as he perched on the edge of my bed, Patrick broke down crying in my arms, barely able to get his words out between sobs as he grabbed my face and kissed me, telling me tearfully that he still wanted to be with me. He admitted that he had fucked up by sticking with his sorrowful relationship, that it had been *"easier to be unhappy than to be brave"*. He begged me for another chance, asking me to wait for him whilst he made things right and left Sean.

I said no.

    This wasn't a no that could be misconstrued as was the case with my no to the *Home and Away* hunk when asked if I frequented any Sydney gay bars, this was a no that meant NO, its negative message stoic and unwavering. I explained to Patrick the fact that I had even surprised myself in realising - that I had finally got him out of my system and was not going to spend my life waiting for someone who wasn't brave enough. I told him that he had to find happiness in whichever form worked for him - but it wasn't going to be with me. He looked stunned. I walked him out of the hotel onto the street where we said a final goodbye. I watched him walk away until he disappeared out of view - and there would be no feelgood 'race to the airport' as my love for Patrick was well and truly over. I never saw or heard from him again. I felt strangely liberated, possessing a sudden euphoria that I had taken charge of my life in this way. But as one American left my life forever, another swiftly arrived to very briefly try and take his place. Yes, I called Gorgeous Greg.

*

    With Patrick now consigned to my personal history book, I wasted no time in dialling Gorgeous Greg's number, reaching him instantly as he in turn wasted no time in suggesting that he come to my hotel room that afternoon so we could finally act on all the flirting that we had traded a couple of weeks before in the less glamorous surroundings of a grimy London gay sauna. As I was due to leave for dinner with my friends at 6pm, it would involve some very tight scheduling, a tightness that in fact was on a par with Gorgeous Greg's bum so I wasn't going to let the fact that we only had a spare half hour get in the way of anything. Dashing back to my hotel, I quickly tidied the room and checked my appearance. However, any concern at jetlag making me look slightly zombified was superseded by Greg's own visage when he turned up at my door fifteen minutes later. His eyes were already glassy when he staggered into the room, taking his clothes off with each step, as he admitted that he had taken a hit of GHB on the way over, the full effect of I was just about to witness, as he proceeded to pass out on my bed at the precise moment he removed his underwear. So much for foreplay. I know we were on limited time here but the transition from stripping out of your clothes to post-coital passing out should really constitute some actual sex in-between. I just stood there, unsure of what to do as Gorgeous Greg had been replaced by Sleeping Booty, lying prone - and more worrying - completely motionless on my bed. I tried to prod him awake. No response. He was practically comatose, reminding me of Franny from Tooting in her vodka-coma, having to gingerly check for evidence of actual breathing. Regardless, dead or alive, it was clear that sex was not going to happen now and I had to dress for dinner soon, my appetite for which suddenly waned when Greg suddenly gurgled and spewed lurid pink vomit down his waxed chest as if regurgitating Pepto-Bismol. I tried hard not to take offence to this mildly unflattering reaction to the sight of me naked but I couldn't just leave him there.

I suddenly realised the absurdity of this situation I was in. Here I was, due to meet my friends for dinner in a matter of minutes and instead I was stuck in a ridiculously tiny hotel room in Manhattan, horny as hell, whilst a naked hunk (clearly now rescinding his right to be a hunk) was lying in a GHB-induced coma on my bed, with the elongated dribble of pink vomit that had made its show-stopping debut from his mouth now cutting a swathe through his nicely-trimmed pubes and encircling his limp, shrivelled penis.

After the disaster that was my failed love for Patrick Ferrara, I finally flipped.

I slapped Greg. Hard. In fact the only thing now hard in this room was the intensity of my slaps around Greg's chops. I slapped him again. And again. It was like that scene in *Airplane* when all the passengers form a queue to bitch slap the hysterical woman. But there was no queue here, and certainly no comedy either as I just wanted this waster out of my room asap. I started to panic, fearing that I would have no choice but to leave him there and go out for dinner, only to return later to find him choked to death on his own luminous vomit which would inevitably result in me being banged up for assisting in the accidental death of a complete tosser.

I was going to wake this bastard up come hell, high water or now dried puke. So I continued to slap Now-Not-So-Gorgeous Greg, smacking, shaking, and thumping him. I was like a demented bitch on heat exacting revenge on that Action Man figure that had been revealed to have no penis upon undressing it. Aged six, I was disappointed. Aged twenty-nine I was fucking furious. I surprised myself at my sudden feistiness. Long gone was that innocent, shy young boy from Dagenham.

After several rounds of slapping Greg, leaving his cheeks surpassing the pinkness of his vomit and reaching a stage of beetroot red, Greg finally woke up, looked bleary-eyed at me and just shrugged as he said:
"*Sorry 'bout that dude.*"
"*Sorry? Is that it?!*" I grabbed his clothes, threw them out into the corridor, pushed him out of the door and slammed said door in his face.
Then I waited, for what seemed like an age, listening to what sounded like a barely re-animated zombie trying to redress himself outside my bedroom door. Finally I heard his footsteps stumbling down the stairs and out onto the street outside. Peeking from the window and making

sure he had finally gone, I tutted at the remnants of pink vomit on my bed sheets, took a deep breath and got dressed for dinner.

You would think that after getting my heart broken by Patrick, and my bizarre liaison with Gorgeous Greg, that I would have learnt my lesson about the False Promises of Hot American Men. But no. I went back for more. Because a year later I had moved to Los Angeles, where my dating exploits with the local gay men there would quickly shoot up the scale of pure insanity.

20 – THE LA GAY MAN'S BIBLE OF EXCUSES TO MAKE WHEN YOU ARE AFRAID TO COMMIT

2005 (aged 30 - 31)

Where could I possibly start? I had never lived in a place before whose entire gay male population were crazier than the patients in an insane asylum and flakier than the rare snow of an English winter. The city of course, was Los Angeles.

By now, I had ventured into writing screenplays as a hobby and lucked out when my first one won a screenwriting contest in Hollywood and was being optioned by a film producer there. It was just the cue I needed to try and reset my life in a new locale and so, in early October 2005, I moved to Los Angeles for a three month trial period. Screenwriting aspirations aside, the 'City of Angels' also provided another alluring possibility - that of meeting the still-elusive Man of My Dreams, for which a sun-kissed Californian would more than fit the bill. Texas had already let me down thanks to Patrick and New York was firmly crossed off the roster due to Gorgeous Greg. And in the first half of 2005, I had also added North Carolina to the Do Not Date Men from Here list, after a disastrous and inexplicable long-distance relationship with Jason, a hairdresser from Charlotte. Our transatlantic romance only lasted six months, beginning outside a shopping mall in downtown Charlotte and ending in the North Terminal at Gatwick Airport. For a long distance relationship, six months was pretty good going. Until I realised that in those six months, we spent only a total of twenty actual days together. So essentially it was really just a three week relationship. And that was three weeks too long. One of those weeks was spent in France and Italy, a trip I had arranged for Jason's first visit to my side of the pond, a trip that also included the presence of his fag hag Kat, a spiky-haired and multiple-pierced punk whose eternal whingeing could drive even the most happiest of people to thoughts of imminent suicide. Her relentless moaning was on a par with Jason's as together they managed to extract the negative stupidity out of any given situation. My alarm bells should have started ringing on the train to Gatwick Airport when Jason and Kat happened to mention how great it was that their airfare from Charlotte to London also included the cost of all their accommodation, transport, food and spending money throughout France and Italy. Realising after a few seconds of my hysterical laughter that they were not joking, my mouth fell open in disbelief. So this was why seventy percent of Americans did not own a passport. As I gently explained like a primary school teacher to two very naive young children that the $300 they paid for their plane ticket to London did not cover every other possible expense they would incur, they started freaking out like two schizophrenic patients given the wrong medication, with Kat going into sheer meltdown, stopping just short of pulling the train's emergency alarm as she screamed hysterically that she had to call her Mom and get money wired as this was all so unexpected! And no, the cost of the call to her Mom was not included in her airfare! We hadn't even reached the airport yet.

  The holiday just lurched from bad to worse once we actually arrived in France as we had to spend our evenings walking the streets for hours as Jason and Kat refused to spend more than five Euros on any meal, which resulted in endless hungry meandering which in turn only made worse the fact that Jason was sporting a small colostomy bag on one side of his stomach that was catching the leaking fluid left over from his recent liposuction procedure, despite already having a twenty-eight inch waist. I wasn't sure exactly how thin Jason wanted to be, I dared not point out that no-one should ever sleep with a man that you can lose in the sheets. Regardless, Jason's vanity was only surpassed by his and Kat's insatiable need for ice-cold air conditioning inside every ancient ruin in Rome which meant that a visit to the silent majesty of the Pantheon was to be drowned out by repetitive Southern American accented cries of *"Where's the air con?! Why is there no air con?!"* It was the worst holiday I had ever endured, stuck with another Hot American Man who I had zero in common with.

  Jason was already hard to sustain in-depth conversation with, so during the previous months of our relationship, I would prepare for each phone call with him, by making a list of topics to chat about just so that I would be able to keep the conversation going. If I'd made a list of all the reasons why we were unsuitable, we could have talked for days. The European trip of 'unexpected' travel costs and lack of air-con was the final nail in the coffin for Jason and I and we ended it at Gatwick Airport just before he boarded his flight back to North Carolina. We never saw each other again.

*

Maybe I would have better luck with American men in California. And that good luck seemed to arrive early when my move to Los Angeles occurred at a time when I had somehow acquired a boyfriend who was waiting for me there.

His name was Torrey and he was a lawyer on sabbatical in London during the summer of 2005. I thought I couldn't go wrong with a hot American lawyer, after all, Harry Hamlin in the TV series *LA Law* had featured quite regularly in my teenage wank bank. And now his real-life counterpart was wooing me in my home city, declaring his passion for me and making plans for us to build a relationship and life together as soon as he returned to Los Angeles, with me following just a week after. I was besotted. Of course I checked first that Torrey did not have an addiction to chemicals that were intended to send horses to sleep and that any potential vomit of his was a normal shade of puce rather than pink. He seemed normal. For the first time since Patrick, I was genuinely excited at the idea of having a Hot American Boyfriend.

A boyfriend in fact who would turn out to be just the first in a whole string of Los Angeles gay men whose combined flakiness was on a such a mammoth scale that it could have caused blizzards in the Californian sun. Yes, you guessed it; it all went horribly and bizarrely wrong.

As soon as I touched down at LAX and switched on my mobile phone, it buzzed endlessly with text messages from Torrey telling me how he was counting the minutes until seeing me and he wanted to come over straightaway to the condo in Pasadena where I would be staying. I was the excited child again on my first day at a new school, eager to make use of the shiny new pencils, in this case, a long piece of American wood possessing a slightly off-kilter curve.

My abode belonged to my friend Bernie, a single travelling salesman in his mid-forties who was away on business on my first night in Los Angeles and had left me his key, which meant that the whole condo was free for mine and Torrey's first night together, which arrived no sooner had I unpacked and showered as Torrey turned up at the door sporting a huge bunch of flowers. Keen *and* romantic! This was off to more than a good start! Within minutes we were making mad, passionate love on the living room floor during which he told me that he loved me. I was astounded. Had I really lucked out and already found My Man with such a serious lack of effort in sourcing him? Within only three days, I would get my answer...

Torrey and I had agreed to meet up the next evening after he had finished work for the day but at lunchtime I got a text message from him to say that he had to work late and so was unable to meet me.

I was disappointed but no problem, I thought, I can go one day without seeing the man that had just told me that he loved me. We arranged to instead see each other the next evening but yet again, another text message came though from Torrey to inform me that this time he had come down with a bad stomach after eating seafood for lunch and could we postpone again until the next evening? Reluctantly, I agreed but the lunch time déjà vu once again reared its uninvited head the next day when the now obligatory text of postponement arrived from Torrey, this time asking me to call him that evening as he had *"terrible news"*. Like a diligent, concerned lover, I made the call. Asking Torrey what was wrong; he cut straight to the chase and told me that he could no longer see me.

"Did I do something wrong?" I asked, trying to hide my upset.

"It's not you", replied Torrey, *"The thing is... is... is... is..."*

Okay, was he rapping now or stuck on repeat?

"The thing is what?" I enquired, now desperately bored of the word 'is'. And with that I heard the sound of what seemed to be Torrey bursting into hysterical sobbing.

"The thing is... I've just suddenly remembered that I was abused by my father when I was a child and because of it, I can now never get close to a man."

Huh?

"What do you mean you suddenly remembered? When?" was all I could respond with, my head swimming with confusion at such an unexpected and outlandish revelation.

"After we had sex" came his reply.

I wasn't sure whether I should be offended. Was he telling me that sex with me was a dubious experience that summoned up the repressed memories of being kiddy-fiddled? I'm sure Australian Sally would have agreed. But I'd had plenty of gay sex by now and felt I wasn't that bad at it. Or was it just a genuine coincidence that the memory of such a traumatic event surfaced at the exact moment my penis entered his mouth? Could Torrey's distress really be real?

"Let me help you." I said, not sure how to respond. *"We can get through this together. After all, you said you love me and-"*

I realised he had hung up.

I confided in Bernie about the way that I had just been dumped by Torrey. He just rolled his eyes back in his head like one of those creepy dolls cousin Kim had when we were kids, patted my shoulder sympathetically and told me:

"Honey, you just got excuse number 24 in the LA Gay Man's Bible of Excuses to Make When You Are Afraid to Commit."

It wasn't an actual book, just a metaphorical one, but I wished I could find an actual real copy in the local bookstore, for it would have saved me a lot of wasted time. I refused to believe Bernie, unable to fathom that a man who, from the twisted recesses of his mind, would squirrel up some bizarre lie about being abused as a child rather than just say he didn't want to date anymore.

"But he said he loved me", I sighed.

More doll-like eye rolling and sympathetic shoulder patting from Bernie.

"Before or after sex?"

"During."

That was all Bernie needed to know. Apparently everyone blurts out *"I love you"* during sex. It's like sexual Tourettes. 'Yeah, just there. I love you. Slide down a bit. I love you. Watch the teeth. I love you. Squeeze, squeeze. I FUCKING LOVE YOU!' Bernie went on to tell me that apparently, his friend had once got the *exact* same excuse from someone he had been briefly dating.

"Welcome to LA, honey" said Bernie, as a final footnote to my first experience with a gay Angeleno. I didn't want to give credence to the theory that all gay men in LA could be this fucked up. Oh, how wrong could I be? For I was about to find out every one of the first twenty-three excuses in *The LA Gay Man's Bible of Excuses to Make When You Are Afraid to Commit.*

*

The aforementioned mythical tome was not just a bible; it was a whole fucking catalogue, reams of the hot men from the underwear section of the *Kays* catalogue, now climbing out of the flimsy, glossy pages into a real life that was far more feeble than it was glossy.

Charlie the Gardener was my first post-Torrey date, a blond slightly over-confident jock who I spent my 31st birthday with in a cabana in West Hollywood gay bar The Abbey. Drunk on mojitos and stuffed with burritos, I was then being whisked back to his Hollywood Hills mansion bang next door to Paris Hilton's for a spot of post-dinner sex. However we only got half way through the actual copulation as Charlie decided to blushingly confess that it wasn't really his house and we were in actual fact inside his ex-boyfriend's palatial home, into which he had broken and entered in the same way he was attempting a similar exercise with me right now. Charlie didn't require a second date as he just needed to barricade him and me inside, turning the whole place into one big - and admittedly very opulent - panic room with me as a bargaining chip of potential jealousy in the breakdown - and hopeful mending - of his relationship. I just rolled my eyes Bernie-style, grabbed my clothes and left, running the gauntlet of the paparazzi outside Paris Hilton's house as I felt tempted to give them better dirt on the intricacies of the domestic bliss of Paris's gay neighbour.

Next up to bag a short but memorable guest appearance in my Adventures in LA Gay Dating was the Abercrombie and Fitch model who turned out to be a Mexican dwarf. Let me explain.

I had been out drinking in The Abbey again, this time with Bernie and other friends, as usual cranking up my British accent which was a sure-fire way to get the attention of various Americans, their *"Wow, where are you from?"* or *"Oh my, I love your accent!"* being the perfect start to a conversation that I always hoped would end in post-coital pillow talk. On this occasion, my best Dick Van Dyke meets Jamie Oliver impersonation had somehow drawn in a crowd of unrealistically good looking beefcakes, a shallow collective of perfect white teeth, chiselled abs and perfect pecs. It was like a toy factory production line of Ken Dolls had ended up in The Abbey, despatching the latest models into an environment where Barbie was well out of sight and coked off her tits in the bathroom. And they were all hanging on my heavily English-accented every word. It turned out that they were out to celebrate the birthday of one of their friends, who was a model from Abercrombie and Fitch, the exact kind whose face adorns their bags with the sole intention of making you cum in your pants before you set foot through the door of one of their stores. And it was Birthday Boy himself who was at this moment chatting me up. Besides being mildly intoxicated, I still had to pinch myself that Mr. Abercrombie was actually flirting with *me*. Promising myself that I would never, ever lose my English accent, my wonder was replaced by sheer awe when Mr. Abercrombie asked for my number, saying that he'd like to go on a date with me the next afternoon, his phone quickly emerging out of his trousers like a horny ferret as he asked me to dictate my number to him. I quickly obliged, watching with excitement as he punched every digit of my number into his phone's keypad. He then had to go but promised me he would text me the next morning to arrange that coffee date.

The next morning came and bang on cue, so did Mr. Abercrombie's promised text, requesting that we meet at a coffee shop on Santa Monica Boulevard in West Hollywood. I was going on a date with an Abercrombie and Fitch model, I could hardly believe it. Just like my homework sleepover with Stuart Pincer sixteen years previous, I arrived a full fifteen minutes early, taking up residence on a stool by the window so I could keep watch for Mr. Abercrombie's grand entrance. As the time approached our agreed meet time, there was still no sign of him. Then bang on time, I heard a voice:
"Over here. I'm over here!"
I looked around. I could not see Mr. Abercrombie at all. He must have been excellent at being able to project his voice like a ventriloquist. If

so, I was more than happy to be his puppet and have him put his hand wherever he wanted.

"No, over here! Just here!" came the voice again, as I suddenly realised that it seemed to be coming from somewhere down near my legs.

I looked down. Standing in front of me, his head barely reaching my waist, was a Mexican midget, a real-life Latino munchkin that looked like he had just come from a casting for the telenovela remake of *The Wizard of Oz*.

"Can I help you?" I asked.

"It's me", he said, smiling excitedly and introducing himself as Ricardo. *"I'm so glad you got my text and still wanted to meet"*.

Still wanted to meet? I hadn't remembered wanting to meet at all. Don't get me wrong, I wasn't 'dwarfist' at all, but I was at any second about to commence a date with Mr. Abercrombie that would be hotter than the double mocha cappuccino with extra cream that I was currently sipping in anticipation of his arrival. It was then that the crushing realisation coincided exactly with mini Ricky Martin's confession. The text to arrange this date had come from *him*, not Mr. Abercrombie. I was more than a tad confused. Had Mr. Abercrombie had drastic plastic surgery overnight that rendered him half the size and of a completely different ethnicity? Of course he hadn't.

The truth was that Ricardo had been standing with the circle of hunks in The Abbey the night before, had taken a liking to me himself and had thus eavesdropped on me giving my number to Mr. Abercrombie and had noted it for himself. I had a hazy flashback and suddenly pictured him standing nearby. In my line of vision at the time, I thought he was a pot plant. It was clear that Mr. Abercrombie had not followed through with his promise of a date. Instead, a Mexican dwarf was my consolation prize. But credit where credit was due. I admired Ricardo's sheer audacity and bravery and agreed to a coffee with him, making it clear that we would never work out, a fact brought home by me stepping down from my stool to find Ricardo's face still only reached the level of my crotch. Which might prove useful for a blow job for two men of wildly differing heights - but not for a long-term match. And so after coffee, I sent Ricardo on his way. I never heard anything at all from Mr. Abercrombie.

*

So now, my experiences with LA gay men had so far amounted to fictionally kiddy-fiddled lawyers, cock-tease Abercrombie and Fitch models and accidental coffees with eavesdropping Mexican midgets. It didn't get any better, in fact not improving one iota, as I found myself in even more bizarre situations and flaky encounters, ranging from an actor whose morning parting gift to me was his resume and headshot, hoping that by having sex with a writer he could sleep his way into a movie, from a teacher who turfed me out of his bed at 4am in the morning because his boyfriend was due back from San Diego at any minute, to a waiter who took me back to his house, refused to turn the light on and asked me to have sex on his bed but to ignore the big lump beside us that was his sleeping boyfriend.

And all these disastrous dates were taking place whilst I was temporarily living in the supposed gay centre of Los Angeles - West Hollywood, or to use its abbreviated term - WeHo, which I realised was just a R away from Whore.

I had been asked to apartment-sit for a friend of Bernie's - a hairdresser called Robert, who offered me a free residency in his apartment in the heart of WeHo. But this living arrangement came with a caveat - I also had to house-sit Robert's pet dog. She was a scary-looking pit-bull named Charanna whose fearsome looks belied the sad fact that she suffered from separation anxiety and so had to be dragged into and locked inside the bathroom every time I left the apartment, even if it was just for a few seconds, otherwise she would tear the place apart in her distress.

Robert's apartment wasn't quite the WeHo pad that I had been expecting, in reality being a depressing daylight-starved box inside a rundown block which resembled a collection of Bates Motel clones all around a grim sun-free courtyard. Robert had also told me to help myself to any food and drink in the house, the only tempting thing being a box of *Ferrero Rocher* chocolates in the cupboard that seemed to move as I approached them, which wasn't a vision problem of mine but was in actual fact because of the hordes of maggots emerging from inside them, a sight that would have cleared the Ambassador's Ball within seconds. Meanwhile, a loony guy in a yellow raincoat would try and follow me home each night from the local Seven Eleven, the hours of which were also being adhered to for the incredibly loud domestic quarrels of the neighbours. I instantly regretted agreeing to apartment-sit this hovel but I had to uphold my promise to Robert to look after poor Charanna.

I identified with Charanna's separation anxiety. She was lonely, I was lonely. I had more in common with a crazy pit-bull than I had with any gay man in Los Angeles. Still, there was one benefit to my dog-sitting that I would quickly discover - in that taking Charanna on her walks was a sure-fire way to cruise the streets and exchange flirty smiles with the other gay dog owners living in the neighbourhood. Only problem was that Charanna was so uncontrollable, I'd get pulled along at high speed and not even get a chance to see what any of these hot men looked like, their faces nothing but a blur as I was dragged past at high speed. And the one and only time I got to actually talk to a sexy dog owner, ended with me being chased out of the neighbourhood because I forgot to bring the poo bags when Charanna decided to unload a humongous sized shit on his immaculately manicured front lawn. And of course this would be the one time that Charanna doesn't pull me away in a blur like *Road Runner* but decides to sit down and take a chilled out rest. If dogs could pour a cocktail, kick back in shades and say *"honey relax"*, this is what she was doing now.

Still being in the middle of West Hollywood meant that it was an easy walking distance to the gay bars nearby where I would seek solace and still hope to find that elusive guy who possessed something mildly resembling sanity. And then one night, I thought for a second that I may have found him as I got chatted up by Gary, a Hollywood movie producer. We arranged a proper date for the next day, which I expected might involve me taking an excursion up to his Hollywood Hills mansion but instead Gary insisted that he come down to spend the evening with me inside my temporary apartment. I like to tell myself that it was the sight of my abode that put him off as soon as he had arrived, as whilst we were cosying up on the sofa together, Gary suddenly announced that he just wanted to cuddle because on the way over in the car he had decided that he preferred women at the moment. I just got up, opened the door and told him to get out. As I stepped into the courtyard for just a few seconds to check he had driven away, I realised I hadn't locked Charanna in the bathroom and so came back in to find the dining area trashed, a cushion torn to shreds and the curtain rails yanked off the wall, leaving gaping holes in the plaster.

Enough was enough. Ill-timed dog shit, maggots inside posh chocolates and holes in the wall kinda summed up my one and only brief attempt at living in West Hollywood, if not Los Angeles itself. I was never going to meet The Man of My Dreams here. Now I realised why Bernie and his friends were eternally single. I decided there and then to end my trial run of living in this city and the day after Boxing Day I returned home to London.

21 – TOO MANY DATES MAKE YOU INCONTINENT

2006 - 2007 (aged 31 - 32)

True connection is what everyone wants, right? Many couples are indeed lucky to find it - that special magic which screams 'we are destined to be together forever'. Ken and Deirdre... Richard and Judy... Ant and Dec. Even Fred and Rose West found a special connection. Can't be easy re-laying all those floorboards on your own. Now that's what you call soul mates. Why was it so hard though to find a soul mate of my very own?

Upon my return from Los Angeles and back living with Sandra as 2006 dawned, I realised that if I was to find my own magic connection, I now had to embrace the one place where getting connected was de-rigueur. The internet.

It had been five years since my sojourn into *Gaydar* which had led me into my relationship with Will, but now *Gaydar* was not the only kid on the block peddling their own cyberspace 'happy ever afters'. There were now a whole myriad of competitors, not only the gay-focused ones but also others that gave tick box choices upon signing up whether you were looking for heterosexuals, homosexuals, bisexuals, trisexuals, asexuals, pansexuals, polysexuals, metrosexuals or give-me-sexuals. Or more simply, whether you were a man looking for a woman, a woman looking for a man, a woman looking for a woman, or in my case a man looking for a man. What about a man looking for a man who wasn't a nutter or a wanker or an annoying combination of both? Where was that option in the drop down list of choices in order to selectively cobble together your own fairy tale? I clearly wasn't convinced that fairy tales could be created from a world of headless men and talking body parts where Snow White would have to pay for the month's trial before she could attempt to match the face to the penis and work out how far away Horny the eighth dwarf lives. Even she would be reticent about her love life becoming a cycle of log on, click, message, log off, climb on, climb off, take a shower, done, log on, next.

Needless to say, I was clearly dubious about embracing the world of internet dating, but still, the men to be found on there couldn't be worse than the rogues' gallery that I would usually meet in bars. I just had to develop the right techniques to successfully sell myself in the internet dating age. With so much competition out there, it was technological Darwinism and only the mentally and physically fittest would survive. And the message being peddled was that internet dating was not just about getting physical. You could find love too. Really? I wanted to find the kind of love that didn't depend on my broadband connection, the lifelong commitment that would prevent me from a possible fate of ending up old and alone in the blink of an eye and wondering why the Earth couldn't have just spun a little bit bloody slower.

Problem was I was now into my thirties which meant in gay years I was a re-animated corpse. Even I had wised up to the rules that your twenties are for shagging, your thirties for choosing and your forties for marrying. But it was difficult to engage in thirties-era choosing when being in your actual thirties immediately rendered half the gay population uninterested in you.

Upon re-activating my 'cockneyblueeyes' *Gaydar* profile, I was tempted to do as others do and lie about my real age, maybe stating that I was twenty-nine, until I realised that guys would naturally assume I was thirty anyway and just knocking a year off. Maybe I should go lower? Then again, maybe not, as I needed to give off at least a whiff of experience in the bedroom. Higher? Well that was out of the question as I didn't want to get blocked before I'd even sent a message. And I certainly didn't want to come across as desperate to settle down, sending messages that between the lines were enquiring about potential wedding attire and advance registration at the local nursery. That would be a profile for www.calmthefuckdown.com.

In the end I decided to honour the truth of my age. I liked being thirty-one; it felt like a good age to be. Unfortunately, it didn't feel as good to be back on *Gaydar* again. It had clearly lost its magic, a sad reality heightened by the fact that I recognised many men from my previous stint five years ago - and they were still lurking on there, their happy endings clearly still eluding them. Instead, like I, they were cast adrift in an unrelenting virtual orgy of waxed abs, talking nipples and headless torsos saying *"hi"*. My Nan Shirley would have called the police. But this was the way that love was now supposed to happen, the quickest way to meet someone special, a method two decades too late for Julia Roberts' *Pretty Woman* wanting to meet her Richard Gere. Which in the case of what was to be found on *Gaydar*, reminded me that no matter how much it was spun, Julia Roberts was not a lost, misunderstood woman looking to embark on a long lasting journey with her soul mate but was still a hooker. Not unlike the online behaviour of advertising intimate body parts and flogging them to strangers. Oh look, a fourth picture of your penis from a different angle. Really? I'm sure it hasn't changed that much in the last two minutes. Oh it seems it has. And then the corkers of chat-up lines such as *"Hey sweetie, can you accommodate?"* Am I listed as a B&B? And what's with that little emoticon of a little smiley face with red cheeks? I don't even know what that means! Are you blushing at what I asked or are you having a hot flush? Where is the little face to mean I'm feeling bloody beyond frustrated at the narcissistic body fanatics who have seemingly interrupted their bicep curls in the gym to take a photo of themselves in the mirror? Or the endless photos of shirtless men holding up phones in front of their faces like under-dressed assistants from *Carphone Warehouse*.

Nevertheless, I still decided to dive in head first, taking the viewpoint of the old adage that if you throw enough shit at a wall, eventually some of it will stick. And so I arranged dates. Many of them. Date after date after date. Even to the point where I arranged three dates for the same evening and had to use expert prowess and excuse-making to be able to service all three without any of them suspecting, like being a contestant on *Supermarket Sweep*, adding as much meat into my basket as I could in a limited amount of time. Unfortunately and yet predictably, most of this prime cut beef was well past its sell-by date, products that not only had been woefully mislabelled but should have been removed from the shelves full stop. For I was to discover that the flakiness of LA gay men had blown across the Atlantic to also infect London.

It was the new dating website *My Single Friend* that became my new playground, a new venture from property guru Sarah Beeny who should have instead utilised her renovating skills on guys' profiles that promised the human relationship equivalent of a 'compact, designer bijou pied-a-Terre in South Chelsea' which in reality was actually a windowless broom cupboard with dubious carpet stains in Battersea. There was the *"fun-loving HR executive"* who in real life was so boring, it was hard to sustain anything remotely resembling a conversation for more than three seconds, owing mainly to the fact that he could not go for more than those three seconds without snorting endless lines of cocaine. It was a drug habit that was so unrelenting that even whilst being trapped with him for a whole weekend on a tiny boat moored off the coast of the Isle of Wight, he refused to let choppy waters deter him from his intense nose-powdering as he tried dismally to hoover up rows of coke as the rough motion of the boat lurched him from side to side to give a whole new interpretation to 'line dancing'.

Then there was the *"hot Irish architect"* who actually preferred it cold, very cold in fact, as he only wanted sex if I was covered in chunky chocolate chip *Haagen Daaz* ice cream, unable to comprehend the fact of the erection-diminishing effects of the low temperature of said ice cream.

Next up was the *"nomadic boy-next-door"* who, upon our first date, revealed that he was actually a homeless vagrant, a fact which I was ready to deal with, had he not with his next breath, cruelly rejected me for my lack of having a six pack. And to top off the list of Desperately Disappointing Dates, finally there was *"Milton Keynes' answer to Jean Claude Van Damme"* who somehow on the train journey down to London had shape-shifted into the love child of John Inman and Julie Andrews, a camp parody of camp who danced dementedly along the street like he was Maria Von Trapp overdosed on Prozac and kept trying to reach for my hand as he exclaimed how excited he was at the connection we had - a connection which I unplugged as soon as I delivered him back to Euston station.

Clearly, for me anyway, *My Single Friend* was hopeless. I wanted to be settled down by now but relationship material was never going to be found on here amongst the coke-snorters and *Sound of Music* auditionees, not forgetting to include those with profile photos taken at weird camera angles that made them look like they had a tiny head on a huge body, like one of the playing pieces from *Cluedo*.

Finally, though, I found one who didn't look like Professor Plum. His name was Joe. He was thirty and worked in the music business. He was handsome, he was sexy and on our first date we clicked. An intense romance developed over the hot summer of 2006 until a weekend away to Brighton when the cloning of his bank card led to the uncovering of his big secret and the sudden end of our time together.

It all started whilst Joe was shopping in the gay shop *Prowler* for sexy underwear, a purchase I was more than happy to assist with, considering they were about to be put to good use back in our room at a local bed and breakfast. However, whilst paying at the till for the chosen pair of particularly skimpy undergarments that left zero to the imagination, Joe suddenly got paranoid when the shop assistant swiped his card as well as inserting it into the chip and pin machine. Panic on his part ensued as he was convinced that the contents of his bank account would be drained a lot quicker than the contents of his testicles. Trying to assuage his now mildly irksome anxiety, I suggested that we head back to our room so that he could call his bank and check that all was in order. Upon returning to the B and B, I should have sussed straightaway that something was odd, as whilst Joe was on the phone to his bank, I heard the woman at the other end of the line ask him to confirm his date of birth, a question which made Joe's face suddenly pale as he stuttered and hesitated. I threw him a strange look as to his apparent amnesia of his birth details whilst Joe, looking more than flustered now, quickly stepped out of the room and into the hallway, not taking into account the paper thin walls through which I heard him dictate the year of his birth as 1972. Now, no-one needed to be a maths genius to work out that someone born in April 1972 would be thirty-four years old in September 2006 and not thirty as Joe claimed to be. As Joe came back into the room, I asked him how old he was.

"*Thirty.*" he re-iterated, as if I was a clueless child asking if the Earth was still round. But I was undeterred.

"*But I just heard you say you were born in 1972. That makes you thirty-four.*"

"*No, I'm thirty,*" he stammered defiantly and petulantly.

Now, I was not some wayward time-traveller left confused as to what year it actually was.

"*I don't mind that you're thirty-four, Joe*" I said. "*It's hardly a huge difference, but there was no need to lie about it.*"

It was then that Joe suddenly started freaking out.

"*I'm thirty! I'm thirty! I'M THIRTY!*"

"*No, you're not, you're thirty-four.*"

"*Okay, I'm thirty-four! I'm thirty-four! I'm thirty-four!*"

For fuck's sake, was I trapped inside some histrionic game of Bingo here? The main prize being a boyfriend who was lying about his age and was now having what looked like to be an epileptic fit because of being found out? Alas, my discovery of Joe's true age ended in him packing his bags and driving back to London a day earlier than planned whilst I was left stunned as to what the hell just happened. I was dumped the next day.

I felt embarrassed. My enthusiasm at meeting Joe had been related to my Mum, who by now really wanted to see me settled down with a decent man. And now I had to tell her, that just like all the other men that I would naively wax lyrical to her about, he was now yet another one who had unceremoniously exited through the swinging saloon doors of my love life. And this was in the year when civil partnerships were coming into law. But I had no-one to get civil partnered with. I was concerned as Mum was about my lack of boyfriend. It wasn't for my lack of trying. And then, just before my membership of *My Single Friend* expired in spring 2007, I exchanged messages with an American guy called Brent. We seemed to have quite a bit in common. It was more than promising despite having sworn myself off American men after my stint in Los Angeles. I agreed to meet him.

An hour before my first date with Brent, I met with Sandra in a nearby pub, discussing with her my wish that maybe he would finally be the man that would be The One - and make Mum happy at my long-term commitment with a male partner.

Brent and I went on to have a four and a half year relationship. What I didn't know when I first met him, was that he would end up being the last man that Mum believed I was happy with.

22 – GOODBYE MUM

January 2009 (aged 34)

As long as I live, I will never forget - or be able to explain - that whispering voice that woke me up in the very early hours of 18th January 2009 to alert me to the fact that my Mum was about to die.

I've never been a stranger to spooky encounters, something that I shared with Mum herself, who would claim to be regularly visited by a black man in a red jumper who would appear sitting on the end of her bed, just watching her, the rest of the house alerted to his latest visit by Mum's bloodcurdling screams. I myself had met other similar unexplained visitors throughout my life, the most memorable being the young boy and girl who would stand by my bed in the dorm at the Travellers Rest hostel in Sydney, the same room that also bore witness to a grotesque disembodied head which woke me up by counting down from five to one in my ear, making me turn and see 'who' was whispering, as I screamed in terror, convincing myself that it must be a bad dream until a Dutch girl in another bed also started screaming, saying she could see exactly the same thing as me.

I am not remotely religious but am happy to sit on the fence when it comes to other, more ghostly stuff. The one thing I do find incredibly fascinating is the notion of consciousness, how we as humans, as well as other animals, developed consciousness and awareness when we are all made up of exactly the same atoms as a table, a cup, a bottle, water, soil, anything and everything, created from the cosmic dust that exploded out of the Big Bang as time began.

*

I was Christmas shopping in *Debenhams* on London's Oxford Street in late November 2008 when I first got the call that would bring on the event that would change my life completely. As I was struggling out of the revolving doors laden with bags, my Auntie Janet phoned to tell me not to worry but my Mum had been taken suddenly into hospital. Mum's diabetes had taken a turn for the worse and she had been sleeping far too much and on this occasion, Dad had struggled to rouse her from her sleep and insisted she be taken to hospital, in this case, Queens Hospital in Romford. I rushed home to dump my shopping then took the train to Romford to find out exactly what was going on. I was heeding my Auntie Janet's advice and trying not to worry too much, after all Mum was a bit of a hypochondriac but conversely was always too afraid to go to the doctors to deal with any ailment, preferring instead to let it *"get better by itself."*

I was horrified at what awaited me at the hospital. The woman lying on the gurney barely resembled my Mum. I hadn't seen her for about a month due to a holiday to Chicago to visit Brent's family but now here she was, looking unrecognisable as she squirmed and screamed and kept trying to rip out all of the various tubes and needles that had been inserted into her. I burst into tears just at the sight of her. It transpired that, unbeknownst to my Dad or anyone else, she had not been taking her diabetes medication for months. Within hours she had been placed into a medically induced coma to undergo emergency dialysis. I sat at her bedside, wondering how on earth it had suddenly come to this when only five months before we had celebrated her sixtieth birthday with a trip to Westcliff-on-Sea where we devoured a large dinner before letting Mum run riot with her gambling in the local casino. Only the irony now was that she had gambled with her life by secretly not taking her medication.

Mum stayed in a coma until just before Christmas, the doctors giving her slim odds of survival. I refused to believe such a fatalistic outlook. That had always been mine and my Mum's job, forever joking about making wills and funeral preparations whenever a milestone birthday was reached. *"Ooh, you're fifty now, we'd better reserve a coffin!"* *"Fifty five? Not long now!"* It was the dark humour that we had both shared over the years of my childhood, each taking it in turns to 'play dead', me lying on the floor when Mum came back from shopping or Mum in her armchair, head lolled to one side and mouth open, to frighten me as I came back from school. It was dark yet harmless fun, it was never supposed to be real. No-one had agreed that we were still playing the game and that it was Mum's turn to 'play dead' as I watched the machines help her breathe and filter her blood.

Things took an upward turn just before Christmas when Mum was woken from her coma and started to make a recovery. The whole family were overjoyed. Mum was awake and chatting, although her spark had clearly diminished and her thought processes sluggish. But still, she was on the road to full recovery. She wanted to be out of *"this bloody hospital!"* by Christmas but had to remain bedbound until just after the New Year when she was finally allowed to go home. Mum had given us a real scare, but she was now under the watchful eye of my Dad, her own Mum Nan Shirley and the rest of the family, making sure she was now taking her medication as strictly required. She was going to be fine.

But on the 12th January 2009, I got another call to tell me that a blood clot had developed in one of Mum's ankles and she was going back into hospital for its quick removal. I was assured that it was nothing to worry about at all and Mum was in and out of hospital again within a day. As she recovered at home, I went to visit her, jokingly noting that the benefit to this whole drama was that she had finally had her toenails cut for her. Mum could never bend to cut her own toenails due to her size and just let them grow wildly rather than let someone else cut them for her. I would always make her laugh by draping a tea towel over her feet to hide them from view on my visits to see her. As I left her to rest and for myself to return home, I had no idea that this would be the last time I would ever see my Mum alive. I called her the next day to check on her. We exchanged the usual chit chat and I promised I would come and see her again at the weekend.

"Alright, love, see you then" were her very last words to me.

*

On the night of Saturday 17th January, I had gone to bed around midnight, routinely putting my earplugs in to try and drown out the sound of Brent's snoring and turning my phone to silent. For once, I quickly fell fast asleep.

It was around 1.30am when I heard it.

An ethereal-sounding voice, hushed to just a whisper, saying *"She's going... she's going... she's going..."*

I sat bolt upright at the sound of it, which had somehow penetrated my earplugs. I popped out my earplugs, startled as the voice continued, now faster with a more urgent tone *"she's going, she's going, she's going"*.

I shook Brent awake, asking if he could hear it. Bleary-eyed, he told me to go back to sleep, shaking it off as a bad dream. Agreeing that it must have been my imagination, I lay my head back on the pillow, just in time to notice a glow from under my mobile phone that I had turned upside down on the bedside cabinet. I grabbed my phone and looked at the screen to see I had sixty-seven missed calls and texts, mostly from my sister-in-law. Immediately I knew something was terribly wrong. I called my sister-in-law back as she informed me that Mum had been taken back into hospital where she had suffered three heart attacks in quick succession. I had to get to the hospital asap as she wasn't expected to live beyond the hour. She *"was going"*.

A desperate panic consumed me as I woke Brent and tried to get dressed as fast as humanly possible. As Brent called a taxi, I pulled on a green jumper then decided to change it, suddenly remembering my Nan's superstition about green being an unlucky colour for the family after Auntie Janet and Uncle Roger had both been in car crashes in green cars.

The cab ride all the way from Kentish Town, North London to Romford in Essex was quicker than I expected, what with the lack of traffic on the road at 2am. I didn't say a word all the way there but sensed that I was too late. I could feel that Mum had already gone. I was destined to repeat history, to re-enact my Dad's own frantic journey to a hospital in 1990, only to arrive too late to say goodbye to his mother. Now it was my turn.

We arrived at the hospital and Brent and I got inside the lift, as I hoped beyond hope that when the lift doors opened, I would still have enough time left to say goodbye to the woman that brought me into this world.

I was too late. The sight that greeted me when the lift doors finally opened was that of my entire family crying. Auntie Carol spotted me, and came over to tell me that my Mum *"had gone."* My eyes fell on my Nan Shirley, as I saw an eighty-five year old frail woman who had just lost her daughter. It wasn't right. The natural order of her life had just been irreversibly messed up. Children were not to meant to die before their parents, no matter how old they were. And yet my Mum was only sixty years old. She was too young to die. I had assumed I would have her for at least another twenty-odd years. But she was gone. I was numb.

My Dad was sitting with Mum's body inside the curtained off cubicle where she lay. As I stepped inside to see her, I was shocked to see her head lolled to one side and her mouth open in exactly the same manner as when she used to play dead.

My Mum was a woman who been born into an era when homosexuality was illegal so had reacted badly to my coming out but had come around and still loved me for who I was and ultimately just wanted me to find happiness, laughing in later years at her reaction of calling me a rent boy transvestite with AIDS when I came out to her as gay.

But with her lifeless body now beside me, I was overcome with guilt. How I wished I that I had phoned more often, visited more often, had kissed her goodbye when I left the house each time, had told her that I loved her. I wished I possessed Trevor the camp hairdresser's supposed ability to time travel so that I could go back to that morning when I left for Australia and when Mum appears sobbing in her bedroom doorway begging me not to leave, I could go up and hug her and tell her that I loved her rather than saying she was being silly for creating such a fuss. I would go back to every visit I ever made to the family home and make sure I always remembered to give her a kiss goodbye. I couldn't even remember if I kissed her goodbye the last time that I saw her alive. I understood it all now, the unconditional love of a mother. Throughout whatever life throws at you or you throw at your mother, she never stops loving you.

*

About a week after Mum died, she came to visit me in a dream. It was one that felt so real - more like a visitation than a dream. It was like she had come back. I'm always in wonder at how when we close our eyes, all we see is darkness, but in this void during our dreams, we can still conjure up such colour, such vivid imagery. And the detail in this subconscious reunion with my Mum was incredible. I was on a hillside, being drawn towards a village in the distance and I as approached it and walked through it, I was amazed at all the fine details surrounding me - the engravings on the shop doorways, the chickens on display in the butcher's window, the cobbles on the village square. And that's when I saw her. Mum. She was coming towards me, laden with shopping bags as if she had just done one of her supermarket runs and bought too much food, a myriad of bags that it looked like she could hardly carry any further. As soon as I saw her I burst into tears.

"*Mum!*" I shouted. I knew she was dead, that she wasn't supposed to be here. But she was. She was standing in front of me, smiling at me. I just couldn't stop crying as she tottered towards me. She looked at me and said she didn't like my new haircut as it *"made my face look fat"*. I told her I had got it cut for her funeral. I just hugged her and wouldn't let go. We sat down on a bench and that's when she asked me if I had got to the hospital in time, whether I got a chance to say goodbye to her? I said no, I didn't. Cos I had my bloody earplugs in. I felt that I was such a bad son. I told her about the strange voice that woke me up. And then I heard my alarm clock buzzing and I realised it was all just a dream. I screamed no! I didn't want to wake up! Not now! I just needed a few more minutes, just the chance to say I'm sorry, to say how I wished I'd always kissed her goodbye after visiting her rather than just saying it. Just a few more precious minutes with my dead Mum. Please. But my alarm clock wouldn't stop buzzing. I woke up, shaken to the core. How could that be? How could I have had this dream at the exact moment my alarm was due to go off? What terrible, cruel timing. The dream rattled me so much that I couldn't stop crying whilst cycling to work that morning.

*

Eighteen months later my Nan Shirley also died, aged eighty-seven, having never recovered from the loss of her daughter. After Mum's death, Nan's health deteriorated gradually yet rapidly, as cancer came calling for her and consumed her until she finally gave up and passed away peacefully in the very same hospital that Mum had died. But with Nan, we knew her death was coming, which enabled everyone to be able to say goodbye to her. The last time I saw my Nan, many members of the family were crowded around her bedside, preparing for the loss of the matriarch who kept us all in check, the chain-smoking Essex version of Queen Victoria meets Peggy Mitchell meets the Catherine Tate Nan. As I left, I knew I wouldn't see my Nan again and so kissed her goodbye. The next day she died peacefully with Auntie Janet at her bedside holding her hand.

23 – A HAPPY ENDING

2010 - present (aged 35 - 40)

I had found the love of my life. Well, in actual fact I had been blessed with two. I've never been a greedy kind of guy but I was more than thankful to have two people who I loved most in this world - and who loved me back.

This final chapter is quite short, there's no need to go into the details of happiness. It is what it is. You are either happy or you're not. That is something I have learnt many times over the years. And when you finally find that happiness, you bloody hold onto it, gripping its handlebars tight on the final loop of the rollercoaster of finding love.

My life had changed forever with the loss of my Mum. It was like the light inside of me had suddenly dimmed. I lost my way, misplaced my focus on life - and my relationship with Brent suffered as a result. I just couldn't deal with the sad reality that the woman who brought me into this world, who had rebelled against but then unwaveringly accepted my sexuality - was gone forever. I was a mummy's boy without a mummy. It hurt like hell.

*

But then my life transformed forever again - but this time in a much happier way - when, in Summer 2010, I became a Dad to a beautiful baby girl, created into a family of two mummies and two daddies.

Brent was the biological father but had asked me to be 'Daddy D' to a child that was being conceived between him and his lesbian best friend. For me there was no difference between biological or non-biological parenting, safe in the knowledge that being a parent is more than just about a blood connection - it's about the unwavering love and support that you give to a child, the solid bond that you create and nurture as you help them shape their lives and watch them grow up.

And from the moment that I met the little girl who I was 'Daddy D' to, her just minutes old, being cradled by her two mummies in a birthing pool in Brighton Hospital, I fell in love with her in an instant. By becoming a parent myself, it all came clear to me as to the cause of my Mum's distress that morning I left for Australia seventeen years before. It was unconditional love.

Sadly Brent and I were not destined to stay together and we broke up in late 2011. But nothing changed the fact that I was Daddy D. My daughter had two mums and two dads, and even though her two dads were no longer together, she would still be loved by us all as she grew up by the sea in Brighton with her two mummies, with me spending regular weekends with her as much as I possibly could, grateful for every smile that she gives me, every hug and cuddle and every time that she tells her Daddy D that she loves him.

*

I stayed single for a while after the break-up with Brent, seriously considering whether I actually really wanted another relationship. Maybe being a Dad and having a family of friends was enough. That's not to say that I didn't once again dip my toes into the dating scene, now mostly facilitated by smartphone apps such as *GrindR* which made no bones about the fact that relationships would never be found on them, apps that made the adventures on *Gaydar* now seem like a *Downton Abbey* garden tea party. Needless to say, most of the men I encountered on these apps were given short shrift by me as I nonchalantly shrugged each one off, laughing at the ludicrousness of endless selfies, fake ages, getting blocked because I was considered ancient at thirty-seven and shallow conversation punctuated with lazy emoticons that did nothing to endear me to anyone, no matter if they were five or five hundred metres away. But then my flatmate Dave introduced me to another website called *Plenty of Fish* and it was on here that I ended up having my final disastrous date.

It was with Jeremy, a radio show host who wanted to meet in a cafe that only served tea as the idea of alcohol was abhorrent to him. So far, not so good - until I showed up to find that he resembled nothing like his profile photo, clearly having used a picture of his hotter, taller, less odd-looking brother who I assume was either missing or dead and was thus having his memory honoured with an impersonating sibling carrying on his pre-arranged dates. I was instantly regretting the lack of alcohol, something in my bloodstream that might have made me cope for longer with Jeremy's incredibly annoying penchant for punctuating every single statement or answer to a question with a shrill *"Good for you!!!"*.
"I think I'll have a cup of Earl Grey."
GOOD FOR YOU!!!*"*
"Yes, I cycled here."

"GOOD FOR YOU!!!"
"No, I've never had genital warts.
"GOOD FOR YOU!!!"
"I'd quite like to strangle you right now with your hideous polyester scarf which I'm sure actually WILL be good for me."
"GOOD FOR YOU!!!"

Sadly, his enthusiastic exclamations of approval strangely ceased as half an hour later, I unchained my bike, shook his hand and told him to *"take care,"* a two word farewell that always translated as *"I never ever want to see you again, let alone agree to a second date."*

It was my date with Jeremy that made me decide to finally give up the dating game and resign myself to spinsterhood, ready to order that rocking chair, stock the cupboards with *Pot Noodles* and adopt a dozen or so cats.

But it was on the morning that I logged on to *Plenty of Fish* to finally delete my profile, that I received a message from a handsome thirty-six year-old Italian TV producer who would turn out to be my ultimate partner-in-crime, my other half, the love of my life. We clicked in an instant on our first date on 3rd December 2012, spending hours laughing, chatting, kissing - and me making him take his socks off to check he had nice feet.

Our connection still goes stronger than ever three years later. Together we have travelled to the USA, Iceland, Japan and many other countries. I have met his family and spend time with them in their house in the Italian Alps. My daughter loves him and he has taught her how to make his amazing homemade pizza and macaroons. I am even learning Italian, picking up the skill of another language that won't this time be hindered by a teacher being bombarded with rubbers.

We want to spend the rest of our lives together and this time, for the first time with any boyfriend or partner, I really think that we will.

Sometimes I still marvel at the cause-and-effect chain of events in one's life that lead to meeting 'The One', not unlike the wondrous million-to-one chances of being alive in the first place. What if I hadn't had watched *Neighbours* and *Home and Away* and thus decided to go to Australia? What if my return home had not coincided with when Bluebird were recruiting, if that job there had not directed me to meeting Sam, if my escape from that awful relationship had never led me to *Gaydar* and meeting Will? And what if my unhappiness with him had not guided me towards a failed love for Patrick, which in turn drew me to the USA, if my experiences with flaky Angelenos had not seen me retreat back to London and to internet dating again and then meeting Brent, whom breaking up from led me to a house share where my flatmate would introduce me to *Plenty of Fish* at the time when the future love of my life was also on there looking for love. What if? The mind boggles. Is it destiny? Maybe every step and misstep in our lives has some meaning, just pavement slabs and their cracks to be hopped, skipped over and walked on, down a path that eventually leads us to where we want to be, to whom we are meant to be with and to love and be loved in return, no matter how long that journey might actually take to complete.

EPILOGUE

2015 (aged 40)

    I am on the train back from Brighton. I like to get to the station early, to bagsy a decent seat much in the same way that Mum used to do at the family parties that ceased to exist long ago. There's so much of her in me. I miss her terribly, think about her every day and most of all wish she had lived long enough to meet my daughter who I know she would have doted on - and the man that has made me truly happy. And that she could have seen the man that I have become, the Dad, the partner, the writer, the forty year old who has finally stopped dying his hair and let it go naturally grey.
    It was my daughter's fifth birthday today and I had arranged for a magician to come to her party and do a magic show. My Mum and Dad had hired a similar entertainer for my sixth birthday party, leaving me with fond memories of card tricks and pulling a white rabbit out of a hat, which were now being paid homage to thirty-five years later for my own child. Sometimes, I like things to come full circle.
    On my previous visit to see my daughter, I did the school run and as I waited outside her classroom for her to emerge, I thought of my Mum waiting for me at the gates to Leys Infants all those many years ago - and especially of the time that she surprised me with my very own copy of my favourite book *The Musicians of Bremen*. I love being a Dad, especially to a child who has grown so quickly into a confident little lady. It makes me swell with pride that I am a proud gay dad to a little girl who is growing up knowing it is not abnormal for her to have two mummies and two daddies, to have a Mum who loves another woman and Dads that love other men. Some of her friends are even envious. What's even better is that my daughter's two mums are getting married next month, to finally be able to legally solidify their love in an era when marriage equality and gay rights are sweeping the globe. I am glad that such a positive leap forward

has happened in my lifetime although I am well aware of the homophobia that still exists and of which we should never be complacent about. If there is a little boy in an infant school somewhere, maybe a classmate of my daughter, confused as to his feelings towards another boy who might or might not wear a green parka, I will tell him it will all be okay. He can love whoever he wants to. One day other people will stop obsessing over who can love who. He doesn't need to hide, to deny himself. Let him love and be loved. It will be the same message that I will pay forward to the teenager that my friend Jenny has asked me to mentor, a young lad who has just come out, met with disapproval from his mother and is so scared at what lies ahead for him. She has passed my contact details on to him but he hasn't contacted me yet. Whether or not he does, I hope he is brave enough to fight for who he is, to make himself heard.

*

The ghosts of the past lurk around every corner. When in Brighton, I often pass by the bed and breakfast where I sought refuge from Sam. When hiding there during that cold January week over sixteen years ago, I would never have imagined that years later I would be a regular visitor to this same town to spend time with my daughter, to bring my partner down so that he could meet her, to attend the gay wedding of people that mean so much to me.

Back in Dagenham when visiting my Dad, I sit in his living room and look at the spot where Mum freaked out as I told her I was gay or the view of the now much diminished Fords car factory from my childhood bedroom window. On the way home, I can stroll past Stuart Pincer's old house and glance up at the window to the bedroom where the infamous sleepover happened, or walk past Leys Infants where I can still see the fence through which I would gaze at the Boy in the Green Parka. Nearby is Fiona's old flat where The Postman Knock Kissing Debacle occurred.

Rush Green hospital where I was born and Dagenham Priory have both long been demolished. I'm glad I left Dagenham when I did, that my life's adventures took me to many other destinations far and wide. Sometimes I look up these places on Google Earth - my old flat in Bondi, the chemical factory in Perth, Lady Jane Bay, Nananu-i-Ra, the Abbey bar in West Hollywood and the crummy apartment a few streets away where anxious Charanna might be locked in a bathroom at this very minute. They are all places to be joined and dotted together in a criss-cross tapestry of one's life. So many memories, the good and the bad, the stuff of life itself.

*

I still sometimes wonder about the many people that have come and gone from my life over the years. Some disappeared from my life forever, some I crossed paths with again. A couple of weeks ago, I was bored and spent an afternoon on Facebook, looking up people from my past out of curiosity. I found so many on there. Fiona, the Cooper Twins, Phil Miller, Ant, Daz... I didn't request their friendship. For what I have come to learn over the years as friends and lovers have come and gone from my life, is that, whether you like it or not, some people belong in different eras. Someone once told me that people are in your life for a reason, a season or for life.

And there are those that just vanished, such as David Compton - and the likes of Sam that were banished. And of course there were the people that didn't leave my life through choice, those whose lives ended whilst mine carried on. My Mum, my grandparents, Uncle Jimmy and Billy - a gay couple whose sexuality was once defined by illegality and who sadly did not live long enough to see in an era when they could have legally got married. And the others, Barry and Dean from ASDA who both died so young - and of course, David Mills. Each and every one in some way helped me on my personal journey. I wish I could find David Compton, I hope Patrick is happy and that Jason doesn't moan any more about the lack of air-con in foreign countries. I wonder if Sam is still alive. Despite the horrible way he treated me, I forgive him. I wish I could find peace with Brent. And what is James the Boy in the Green Parka doing now? All our lives intertwined, for days, weeks, months or even a few years.

I have taken many risks in life, made many mistakes, royally fucked up on more than one occasion, hurt people that I really didn't mean to. I've wasted time and yet savoured precious moments, had incredible adventures, experienced love, both real and unrequited, heartbreak, fun and laughter. I'm human. We all are, gay, straight or otherwise. I'm forty years old, I'm gay and I'm happy and if anyone doesn't like that then they have no place in my life. We are who we are. We all love, lose, make the same mistakes and have the same dreams, insecurities and definition of joy as everyone else. We sometimes pin our hopes on the wrong people and achieve our dreams with the right ones. Sexuality is part of our DNA. We should never be judged for it, nor made to feel worthless. Every person has the right to find love and happiness. As Marilyn Monroe once said:

We are all of us stars and we deserve to twinkle.

THE END

***

ABOUT THE AUTHOR

Dylan Costello writes for stage and screen and his plays include *Fresh Meat, Secret Boulevard, Hello Norma Jeane* and *The Glass Protégé*. He is also Artistic Director of Giant Cherry Productions, a company created to produce a slate of LGBT-focused works. Dylan lives in West London with his partner.